THE NOAH PRINCIPLE

By

Steven Clark

Author Website: www.writerclark.com

Table of Contents

Dedication

For my beautiful Elaine.

Acknowledgments

Thank you, Elaine, Anne, Rachel, Sisca & Stephen.

It's been an adventure.

About the Author

Like many Scots before him, Clark was eager to see the world. He studied International Politics with a focus on East Asia before spending half his life working there as a Broadcast Journalist, Documentary maker, and International News Desk Editor. Media was the perfect sector for someone fascinated by the region's history and culture, allowing him to visit many countries, learn how people lived, and absorb useful fragments of languages.

Grateful to everyone he met in Asia for all the fascinating experiences and fond memories, Clark returned to his native Scotland, where he now lives with his wife Elaine in the beautiful county of Dumfries & Galloway.

1982, Dry Season

Prologue: Unspeakable

Ibu Santoso said Om Jacob was tired because of an illness people got when flying in airplanes over long distances. Then the old Ibu told her to go to bed and closed the bedroom door. But he was in her bed, so she stood and watched him sleep. Om Jacob came into her life three years ago when she was nine, and since then, she'd been his 'special girl.' He said she was clever like him because she watched people and quickly understood their character. Then he'd taken her little hands in his and promised to help her achieve all the success she deserved.

He enrolled her in a school with rich girls from all around the world, and even though he'd only visited her home four times, he always gave her presents when she told him how good her grades were, especially her English. Ibu Santoso, who was like a mother to her, always insisted that she pay special attention to her English studies because it would make her uncle Jacob very happy.

Looking down at him, she was confused and felt a flash of anger. He'd never hurt her before. Afterward, Ibu Santoso washed her and replaced the linen on her bed.

He'd always been so nice. He clapped when she danced for him and read her stories. During his last visit, she'd giggled when she awoke to find him snoring in her ear. But this was the first time he'd done that thing to her. He explained that she was a young woman, and it was what men and women did. Sobbing while Ibu Santoso bathed her, she quickly stifled her tears when he came in and watched. Through her discomfort, she forced a smile as Ibu Santoso agreed with him that her body was starting to look womanly.

He told her he'd be gentle. He said it might hurt, but he still did it? Why would he do that? She looked at his chest going up and down and tried to remember how she laughed when she first saw his hairy body. But she couldn't make herself feel better even if his sarong was now covering that thing that had hurt her. She felt different. Was it because she was a woman like Om Jacob said? She took no solace in his promise that it would feel better next time. Trembling with fear, she crawled into the bed as Ibu Santoso had instructed and waited for a sleep that would not easily come.

PART 1:

A Somnambulist's Awakening – 1997 August

1) Delusory Tales

Extremes thrive here. Ruled by a General, it's been a long time since this city of ten million souls has classified moderation as a virtue. Even its name, which can be translated as 'Complete Victory,' gives no quarter to half measures and embraces only the unconditional and the absolute.

Jakarta's people give it life, but the city remains supremely indifferent to the lives it confers on its inhabitants. Constrained by the limited options of its predilection for extremes, the rich have extraordinary wealth, and the poor are dealt their hand of poverty without constraint. The nature of the entire archipelago is no different. Living on such a seismically volatile fragment of the earth has long taught Indonesians to distrust the physical realm and instead put their faith in the shadowy forces that govern it. Small wonder, then, that when Chance does confer the status of wealth on a newborn, its family will go to any lengths to prevent that capricious force from ever influencing its life again. The child and the wealth into which it was born are guarded with a zeal that extends deep into the spiritual world.

In the centuries since traders brought Islam to these shores, the unchanging, gentle cadence of the faith has come to guide the majority of the archipelago's communities. Other imported religions have also sunk their roots into the fertile, volcanic soil, but the Orang Asli – or sons and daughters of the soil – still turn to the older beliefs that guided the lives of their more distant ancestors. And just as the all-too-common curse of poverty drives Indonesians to seek spiritual or supernatural help for a better life, those same acts of supplication are also offered to protect the much rarer blessing of wealth.

Amongst a myriad of other gifts or condemnations, birthright also designates whether a person commutes on the city's decrepit public transport; or is conveyed by a driver in an air-conditioned vehicle. Mindful of that stark reality, the sight of a Caucasian foreigner emerging from his car and taking to the city's uneven, baking hot sidewalks is guaranteed to provoke curious stares.

It wasn't Cain Shaw's usual habit to walk anywhere in Jakarta, and the idea clearly surprised the company's friendly driver, Pak Lubis.

"You have car. Why walk?" he questioned with an exaggerated expression of confusion.

"I just want to clear my head Pak," Cain explained.

The fatherly Batak, a Christian from the huge neighboring island of Sumatra, gave a shrug of grudging acquiescence and declared, "I do not understand you, Bulé, you Westerners."

Cain waved but waited to see the driver slip off his shoes before he closed the car door. He knew Lubis preferred to drive barefoot whenever he was alone.

And after the morning he'd had, that was where Cain wanted to be. Alone with his thoughts in the sea of humanity that crowded the city sidewalks, enveloped by the cloud of pollution created by thousands of inadequately maintained vehicles jamming the adjacent six-lane roadway. Cain watched Pak Lubis drive off and began walking to his nearby office.

Deftly negotiating the hawker food carts, cigarette vendors, cobblers, beggars, and frantically charged bus queues that populated the pavement, he simmered angrily; "How much longer can I keep on dealing with tossers like him?" Cain had barely moved his lips as he uttered the words, though, in truth, he hadn't meant to give voice to them at all. Impelled by the prickliness of his irritation, they'd just slipped out. The client with whom he'd just met had imparted a vexing tale that completely invalidated his admittedly scant preparation. Worse still, it had undermined his bottom line, an aspect of his work that had become all-too-familiar since the onset of what the media was already calling 'The Asian Financial Crisis.'

[ ]

The quarterly 'check-up' had taken place at the engineer's spacious bungalow. He lived in the Kemang enclave replete with decent bars, even better restaurants, and a supermarket called Kem Chik's that stocked the kind of imported titbits expats crave during their 'Asia experience.'

As a maid led Cain to her employer's study, he noticed that whilst the landlord's tasteful furnishings remained, there was a distinct lack of Grant's personality. Confronted by the olfactory assault of disinfectant, Cain recalled the now absent, sweet scent of fresh flowers. Bare nails and inverse white shadows on the walls bore silent testimony to the missing photos and artwork that had previously boasted the life and tastes of the happily married occupants. He was curious, but Grant was only a client, so he held fast and didn't ask why the house looked so different.

"Hello, Edward, good to see you. You're looking well," Cain lied easily to his unkempt client. "Oh, hello Cain, good to see you too. Hold on and I'll get us some grub."

Grant pushed past Cain toward the study doorway and shouted after the retreating maid: "Nur! Bring us Kopi and Kueh please." His voice echoed around the curiously empty house.

Cain found it difficult to be excited about his presentation, and his client seemed even less interested. Stocky, with red hair and sunburned skin from playing golf under a tropical sun, Grant was usually quite a character. This morning, however, he looked defeated, stripped of personality like the walls of his house. Weariness oozed from his face as he slumped further into his chair. Cain's body instinctively stiffened as Grant's eyes filled, and he began to sob.

There was a knock at the door, and thankfully the maid didn't wait to be invited in, relieving Cain of the need to comfort his client, who was obliged to stifle his tears and pretend there was something in his eye. As the maid put down the tray of coffee and snacks, he even faked a sneeze for good measure.

When she departed, Cain made an educated guess at what was coming and provoked by both scorn and an attempt to facilitate some kind of momentum for the meeting, he cheerfully urged: "Hey Edward, I've got some fund switch suggestions to get your portfolio back on track."

The implication of the need to get on with the meeting was, however, lost on Grant. "I've met a girl," he blurted.

"Not just any girl, you understand," he added, fixing Cain with an ingenuous stare. "It happened on a night out with some of the golfing gang when we found ourselves at Sting."

Cain knew it violated his professional propriety, but he guffawed at the 'found ourselves' excuse and its suggestion that blameless chance was responsible for a night of laddish misadventure at the notorious basement club of a local 5-star hotel. Grant simply watched. His sad, questioning eyes made him look even weaker as Cain thoughtlessly explained his laughter. "Come on, Edward, no one just finds themselves at Sting."

Cain tried to maintain a sense of congeniality by thinking about the naivety of his client and the other mid-life crisis casualties this country generated with startling regularity. Did any of these blokes ever really ask why they'd suddenly become so desirable since departing their native lands? Even if they did, the allure of the opportunity for personal reinvention in an exotic foreign land, fueled by unfamiliar levels of female attention, would overwhelm any impulse for self- examination, Cain surmised, answering his own question with dismaying ease.

Not unusually strict for a Staff Sergeant, Cain's father had always brought his son back to earth with the phrase, 'Catch on to yerself wee man.' Trying to maintain the appearance that he was listening to the deluded engineer, Cain began to wish that phrase wasn't quite so parochial.

"One thing quickly led to another with Devi," Grant prattled on, his verbal tempo quickening as he warmed to his topic. "Before I knew it, I'd rented an apartment for her. The sex was unbelievable! Devi had an insatiable appetite for…."

Cain held up both palms in front of his client. "Save it for your golfing pals, Edward. We need to keep this meeting professional."

Grant was one of Cain's rare older clients. His own youthfulness determined that the majority of clients steered to him by Temple-Speer's management were in their 20s or early 30s. But as Grant continued to spin his yarn, Cain started to feel older than his client.

Are Human Resource departments in Europe really so naïve? Cain wondered. He remembered a friend's comment; 'They're rarely resourceful and almost never fucking humane.' Based on their ignorance, this hapless case had been dispatched to a tropical island about which he'd hitherto derived all his knowledge from TV ads marketing a deodorant called 'Java.' Grant would neither recognize the need for nor ever want to be thrown the lifeline of critical self-awareness, and the ultimate result would be a very bitter, expatriated wife.

Oh yes, the wife, Cain mused, advancing his client's story.

All that was left now was the 'Santa Cruz Express.' The phrase had been coined by his colleagues to label the method by which the victim – typically an expat wife – disappeared, using the eponymous international moving company to pack and ship all her belongings whilst her husband was at work. It was all Cain could do to prevent his face from forming an 'I knew it' expression when the sun-burned philanderer declared, "And the wife said nothing! While I was at the office, she called our moving firm to come and box up our stuff and have it sent it back to Dudley. She left in such a hurry that the movers even packed up my CDs, including the disc Billy Joel had autographed! Gemma left me with nothing but an angry letter stapled to a photo of Devi, along with this; the bloody invoice from the moving company!"

Cain failed to stifle a chuckle as he saw the Santa Cruz bill and joked, "Santa's come really early this year."

Again, there was no reaction from Grant. His tired mind was clearly elsewhere, just like his very pissed-off wife. Cain wondered if Gemma had returned to the UK directly or was still enroute via the thousand-kilometer detour to Bali. Renowned as the 'Island of the Gods,' expat wives gossiped and giggled about the 'Island of the Gigolos.' The 'Bali Boys' or 'Kuta Cowboys' prey on tourists and expatriated females who, in the face of their husbands' real or imagined infidelity, establish retaliatory relationships with all the angry sexual energy their bitterness can muster.

Cain was known to have a talent for shifting smoothly from a friendly chat to the business of achieving client sign-off. But with the lather Grant had worked himself into, he was struggling to bridge the gulf that now lay between his unignorable personal crisis and the serious matter of getting him to lighten his Asia-heavy portfolio.

To his surprise, Grant anticipated him. "So, as you'll probably agree," he said to his financial adviser, who was about to become really quite disagreeable, "I'll need to stop my contributions until I see how this pans out."

As part of his client banter, Cain often used the reassuring phrase, "As a Financial Advisor, I don't like surprises." It was one of a carefully devised color palate of gems recommended by Temple-Speer's abstruse business sage, Ernest Cunningham. Trained by old Cunningham at the firm's Singapore HQ, Cain was unpleasantly surprised to learn that his client advice would be scripted by others and that he was even expected to use a pre-approved stencil of spontaneous chatter.

But right now, he was floundering, and he desperately needed to keep Grant on the books. Whilst old Cunningham was a sharp money manager, he was also a strait-laced, old-school bachelor. Cain started to think that Cunningham's unerring priggishness had probably led him to believe that grooming his young protégés to deal with such base client issues as infidelity was grubby and distasteful.

Annoyed at Cunningham, Grant, and the world in general, he decided to stall. "In light of your present circumstances Ed, it would be better to reevaluate your portfolio one more time before classifying it as temporarily 'paid up.' I'll schedule another meeting in a fortnight, just ahead of your next contribution. We can then avoid making a hasty and perhaps regrettable decision today."

Cain started to pack away his things. "Better that I see myself out," he suggested, as it would be prudent not to let Grant's household staff see their boss' reddened eyes.

He let himself out of the study and was startled by the presence of the maid who was pretending to wipe the skirting board. Had she been listening at the door? Cain smiled arrogantly, wondering how embellished the tale of the Grants' marital woes had already become. Gossip was, after all, a free form of entertainment and, therefore, freely spread from the staff of one household to another in the tree-lined enclaves that housed Jakarta's wealthier residents.

[ ]

"Meester! Meester! Hongrry!" Two wiry street kids begged Cain for money, snapping him from his thoughts. He felt in his pockets for a couple of the ragged 1,000 Rupiah notes he kept for things like tipping and begging. He offered one to the grateful boys, feeling pleased with himself that he almost automatically used his right hand as per the polite way to handle things like money in Indonesia. He remembered Cunningham's advice about life on foreign shores; "First, the new cultural conventions are strange. Thereafter, they become habitual and then natural. Well almost"

Though he'd adjusted to some of the idiosyncrasies of life in Indonesia's capital, Cain's walk was quickly reminding him of the one thing he'd never get used to; the city's oppressive heat and humidity. It had only been five minutes since he'd stepped out of the car, but his forehead was already beading, and his calves were dripping with sweat. He'd wanted to clear his head after Grant's meeting, but he must have been agitated beyond reason to have left the air-conditioned comfort of his car to seek any mind-cleansing air on the streets of Jakarta.

Despite the heat, Cain still relished this chance to take in the sights, sounds, and in particular, the smells of the city at street level. Ever since landing at Mallorca's Palma airport as a child and smelling Spanish tobacco smoke for the first time, he'd acknowledged that every country had an olfactory memory trigger. Indonesia had two. The first was the clove cigarettes called kreteks, smoked so ravenously by almost every Indonesian male. The second was the air freshener used in Silver Bird taxis. The black Nissan Cedrics were like unofficial limos. Sometimes necessary, and always amazingly convenient, with the understanding of a reasonable tip, the driver would wait while you went shopping, dining, or even to a nightclub!

Without fail, the aroma of that air freshener would bathe Cain in a feeling of satisfied well-being, especially after running the immigration queue gauntlet at Jakarta's airport on his way back from Temple-Speer's Singapore office. Oddly, he realized he'd never identified any distinguishing aroma from that clinically planned city. Although thinking about it now, during his last trip, Singapore's sky had been shrouded in a smoky haze created by huge forest fires raging in Borneo and Sumatra. Those fires were the increasingly difficult-to-deny result of corporate-sponsored slash-and-burn operations to clear vast swathes of Indonesian rainforest for the palm oil industry.

Reaching the entrance of the towering glass and steel office complex that housed Temple-Speer, Cain returned the friendly salutes of the security guards before he turned to look back outside again. His walk had done the trick; his bad mood was almost gone.

It had its problems, but he liked Jakarta and its friendly, resilient people. Their continued verve showed no sign of the shock that had triggered economic convulsions throughout the region.

Cain wasn't feeling quite so resilient. He hadn't signed a new client in three weeks, and his existing clients were getting jumpy. He'd never experienced a downturn before, and not wanting to jump off the mouse wheel of Asian market optimism, he recalled the pre-crisis mood when Indonesia was still tipped to be one of the world's Top 20 economies by 2005. Status quo maintenance was the only proviso, and after 30 years of Suharto, that status quo was practically assured.

Hoping the World Bank's crystal ball was correct, he tried to convince himself that better times still lay ahead. Better times to attract more foreign investment, which in turn, would bring more Edward Grants to these shores, allowing him to prosper again. Mediocrity had always unnerved him, and looking out at Jakarta's newly minted business district, Cain momentarily dared to believe that this might still be the place where he'd achieve some form of success. And therein lay the problem, he wanted to be successful but never thought to ask himself how that might look. Cain knew what he didn't want, and that was a major theme in his nascent adult life.

Growing up, he'd moved house so often that he'd never been able to develop any life-long friendships, never mind a steady girlfriend. After university, he'd stuck two fingers up at the Tory politician Norman Tebbit who told people to get on their bikes if they wanted work. He got on a plane bound for South-East Asia. He only had one suitcase and was still too young to be burdened with much of life's other baggage, making it easier for the delights of the region and his accelerated career to connive and mold him anew. No one could help him. He had to recognize the irrevocable creep of disaffection, and it wasn't as if the tell-tale signs didn't exist. He'd been described as a young man who would look better when he'd grown into his features, and those features were beginning to harden. Getting respect and admiration beyond his years gently chipped away his good-natured humility while nurturing a new-found sense of superiority. He looked down on his bottom feeder clients, as he called them, and longed for the day when he'd manage the fortunes of the high-rollers invested in the Temple-Speer Fund. He didn't want to wet-nurse the likes of Grant forever, and he was terrified of becoming like him.

As he turned to head up to his office, he smirked, recalling Edward Grant's unguarded admission that he was a Billy Joel fan, and wondered if Devi really would prove to be his 'Uptown Girl.'

"Jaysis, what a shite song."

2)   Exiles from a dis-United Kingdom

Approaching his desk, Cain was ambushed by his friend Charlie. He jumped out from behind a filing cabinet, standing to attention and performing a grandiose salute whilst assailing him with his Cockney stylings to the tune of the British national anthem:

Gawd save old Jiang Zemin

Gawd rest old Deng Xiao Ping

Gawd save Peking

Da da da da da…

Recovering from the shock, Cain reacted quietly but forcefully before his colleague really let loose. "Bloody hell Charlie, keep it down!"

Undaunted by the termination of his party piece, Charlie declared, "Just like I said on the day of the Hong Kong handover last month: China's on the rise. Indonesia's Chinese know it, and they've put on their elastic-waisted trousers for the big boys' investment banquet with all the trimmings."

Cain ignored the incidental boast about Charlie's Temple-Speer Fund clients and reprised his condemnation of the handover coverage. "The world really lost all perspective that day. One headline called it the biggest story of the bloody century!"

"Ooh, hark at her! Who's Shaw come as?!" Charlie retorted in his Frankie Howerd voice. Then he prodded Cain's chest, adding, "Though you definitely have a point hidden somewhere inside your twisted knickers."

Cain laughed and slapped Charlie's hand away as he speculated, "Do you reckon the Thais were trying to bury the devaluation story? Because they did it the day after the Hong Kong handover."

"Didn't bloody help," Charlie replied. "But it's not all bad. The volatility they created is probably the real reason why the Chinese down here are moving so much money. I tell you, once Andy helps me account for last week's trades, old Cunningham and the Major will be well impressed."

"Yeah, the bosses are much happier with your team than mine," said Cain. He saw pity in Charlie's eyes and quickly changed tack to ask about his Indonesian assistant, Andreas Prakowo. "How's Andy coping with the volume of work this lovely crisis is creating?"

Charlie's grin reconvened. "Yeah, Andy's doing alright, and so it seems, are you. When I saw you come in, I said to myself; Young master Shaw's a bit too chirpy for a Monday morning. He looks as happy as an escaped Chinatown pig that's taken refuge in a local mosque."

Cain stiffened and hissed, "Bloody hell, remember where you are! It's a bloody good thing Andy's not around." Then he freed up his constricted vocal cords to add, "By the way, it's gone twelve, so it's Monday afternoon. And as for me, I'm just feeling pretty good about things."

Over his shoulder, Cain heard another voice. "Very glad to hear it, Shaw." Cain gave Charlie a perplexed look and whispered, "When did he get back?" Charlie mouthed, 'Oops,' and they both spun round at the sound of Ernest Cunningham's soft Edinburgh drawl.

"Thirty minutes, then I want you both in the conference room with Terence Pyle, the Major, and myself. Something came to my attention when Terence and I were in Hong Kong. Got a proposition for you. Fair warning, thirty minutes. Tardiness will not be tolerated."

The two friends unwittingly harmonized their "Yes, boss!" reply, and Cunningham disappeared back into his office.

Cain crumpled and flopped onto his chair. "You could've warned me he was back already."

"I was getting to it," Charlie argued unconvincingly. "Cunningham and the Yank caught an earlier flight. Seems the old man's been invited to a powwow with the country's Finance Minister tomorrow evening."

"Shit, that's massive!" Cain declared, taking in the news and implying that he wanted to hear more. "And what does the old fellah want to see us for?"

But the thought of possibly missing lunch had already annexed Charlie's mind. "Right, I've got half an hour to load up at the noodle shop. And when I return, I'll hopefully be sporting the same beatific smile that adorned your fisog when you sauntered in." Then he winked before adding, "Tell me about Granty later. The born-again stud was mentioned in despatches."

Realizing he'd better reschedule his two o'clock client meeting, Cain sighed heavily into the vacuum created by Charlie's departure. He was such a contradiction. Cain knew that, like others, if he'd only ever spoken to Charlie on the phone, he'd never have guessed that he was Chinese.

Everyone at the office loved Charlie, but there was always a wisp of uncertainty. Whilst his politically incorrect jokes should have fitted right in with the typical office banter, his slightly older, polite home counties contemporaries often didn't know how they should react.

He'd experienced this 'semi-conscious distancing,' as he called it, for much of his life. He told Cain it made him feel like a misunderstood outsider no matter how hard he tried to fit in. And Charlie wasn't alone.

[ ]

A year ago, when Cain started work in the Jakarta office, he'd mentioned to a colleague that his father was Northern Irish and could scarcely believe what happened next. With the exaggerated sense of nationalism that expatriated life can engender, he was once more cast as the proverbial 'Paddy.' The playground taunt of his childhood had echoed into his present. But these days, he couldn't deal with it by employing his father's advice to 'hit the biggest one first and make sure he hit hard.' He tried to reason away his colleagues' behavior, but there was another more odious tributary of anger sluicing into his taunt-polluted mind. Personal reinvention seemed like a fundamental rite of expat passage, and whilst he wanted to believe he was above such triteness, he was annoyed that his own chance to do it might have been scuppered by his colleagues.

Whereas Cain's light-hearted ostracization was obvious, the converse was true for Charlie. He suffered far beyond the ken of his colleagues from the pain inflicted by a slow rain of embers falling through the grate that obscured Temple-Speer's racial insensitivities. Feeling unable to confront his colleagues, he decided instead to help Cain by detonating a pronounced sense of collective shame throughout the office. Charlie started referring to himself as 'the Chink', and whilst it almost immediately halted the 'Paddy' nonsense, it never did quite clear the air of uncertainty around his own presence.

Cain's gratitude was profuse, but it was Charlie's response that really forged their friendship. "It's nothing, mate. You have to understand that most of them lads are alright. They're still getting used to the world beyond the bosom of their expensive school gates. The likes of you and me can only do our best to wean them off the teat of their middle-England existence."

Ever since that small victory, they'd referred to themselves as a 'platoon of two,' and together, they became a real presence in the office. "I guess that seals it for you and me, mate; we're a platoon of two, the Gweilo and the Chink." Cain had never been called a Gweilo or 'ghost man' before, but after what Charlie had just done, he didn't let it bother him.

Not long after that, Charlie asked Cain if he wanted to play hooky with him. He was having four suits tailored at the Pasar Mayestic market and wanted a second opinion. Cain had never known anyone with a bespoke suit, so he went along to see how the process worked.

"Hey Charlie, all your suits are different shades of grey," Cain observed.

The Indian tailor interjected, "Mr. Charlie is a fashionable man. He told me that in London, grey is the new black."

"And thank God for that," quipped Charlie trying on one of his new jackets. "Can you imagine wearing black in this heat?" The slim-fitting three-button jacket fitted perfectly. But examining the sleeves, Charlie reminded the tailor that the cuff buttons should be 'operational, not decorational.'

"So you can roll up your sleeves and get to work, just like in the old days," said the tailor, beating Charlie to the line he used when he first chose the fabrics.

Checking himself in the mirror, Charlie boasted, "Jakarta has a bit of catching up to do with 'Cool Britannia' tailoring Mr. Gupta, but you've done a spectacular job. Get one of these in your window, and your clients will soon be ditching their double-breasted blazers."

And Charlie wasn't wrong. One of the first customers for that new style was Charlie's young Indonesian assistant Andreas. But it wasn't just Charlie's clothes that made him so attractively of-the-moment. The spirited cocktail produced by mixing the accent, the swagger, and the bespoke suits, was enjoying a real renaissance in the UK, and Charlie didn't care whether it was shaken or stirred. He just couldn't get enough of it.

Andreas couldn't tell, but Cain would occasionally notice slight wavers in Charlie's accent and or a wobble in his swagger. And whilst it piqued his curiosity, he respected his pal too much to question him about what he suspected was a personality crafted by a consummate survival mechanism.

As part of showing Cain the ropes in Jakarta, Charlie prepped Cain to meet Temple-Speer's co-founder, David Speer. The man they all respectfully called 'the Major.'

"During my time in London, I worked with a couple of ex-forces types. They were generally alright," Charlie explained. "And David Speer, erstwhile of Her Majesty's Army Air Corps, is cut from the same cloth. His military manner still very much defines him."

As a former 'military brat,' Cain intrinsically understood the life-long sense of belonging the forces bestow on their personnel. He corroborated Charlie's observation; "A military bearing is hard to extinguish even if, like my dad, they don't talk much about their time in the services."

Charlie nodded; "Yeah, that sounds about right. The Major doesn't say much either, but his radio silence only encourages the rumors. Apart from a vague story about him helicoptering our founder Sir James, out of Iran during the final days of the Shah's rule, very little is actually known about how they hooked up."

"In Singapore, I heard that Cunningham was on that chopper too," Cain added. "But he never speaks out of turn either, so I guess it's hard to distill the reality from the fiction."

"Reality or fiction," Charlie continued; "Whatever transpired, Sir James and the Major were acquaintances well before Speer left the army."

Cain asked, "Do you know why Sir James and the Major didn't set up shop in Hong Kong? It seems like the natural place for a company like ours."

"Good question, Shaw," intoned a confident, crisp voice. It was Speer leaning against the doorframe. "Hong Kong was part of our desiderata, but we concluded that the territory wasn't a good fit." With that, he stepped forward, stretching out a hand.

"Major Speer. Great to finally meet you."

"Same here, Shaw. I was too busy over here when you were at the Singapore HQ, but I've heard good things. Also learned your father was quite something in Ulster. Good man. Spent some time on the 'Murder Mile' myself, and it was no picnic."

"I was only a kid," Cain explained, "Mum and me stayed behind in Scotland. All I remember is her being worried sick about him."

Charlie chimed in, "Scotland, Ireland, England? And you went to Uni in Wales, right? That's a full house, mate! Never been as far north as Scotland. And to be honest, the Jocks kind of scare me."

Cain joked, "Yeah, my mum's terrifying."

Speer nudged Cain and teased: "And Ernest Cunningham is the stuff of nightmares."

Charlie shook his head. "He doesn't count though, coz I can understand him without subtitles." Eager to be seen as professional, Cain interjected, "You were telling us about Hong Kong Major."

"Thank you, Shaw. Well, Sir James, Ernest, and myself decided there was just too much uncertainty clouding the years after the handover. Singapore, by contrast, was attracting a significant cohort of young Westerners seeking opportunities in what looked like a recession-proof Asia. So just ahead of a cabal of competitors, we established Temple-Speer to provide those future pensioners with the tax-free means to build retirement nest eggs. And that's the potted history of Temple-Speer."

"I heard that you called it a real turkey shoot Major," Charlie added, recalling some office gossip. Cain noticed Speer flinch when Charlie made the 'turkey shoot' remark.

"That was a very common observation at the time," he said before excusing himself, saying he needed to place a call to London.

With Speer gone, Cain spoke up, happy to be able to add something to the session. "Well, from my own experience, it can still sometimes feel like a turkey shoot. For many of my clients, meeting a Temple-Speer consultant is the first time they've ever considered their mortality, never mind their financial future. Just show them a few graphs and mention the joys of compound, tax-free interest, and you've usually got them signed up and investing more than they'd initially planned."

"Yes, but what's the most important thing we do?" Charlie asked, testing the new boy.

"It's not what we do; it's what we don't do," Cain replied with the Singapore office mantra he'd eventually bought into. "We don't mention the downsides or fee structures. Expats are usually on a two-year posting, and most don't twig that when it ends, the payments they can afford on their expat packages will probably start to hurt. So basically, we sell new clients on selective information, and the whole deal needs to be concluded in meetings with as little written communication as possible."

3)   The Price of a Seat at the Grown-ups' Table

Cain had witnessed Cunningham's performance of unflustered control before. It was a well-practiced element of his 'indifference is strength' act. But when Charlie burst into the conference room five minutes late, the old man contrived a flawless absence of reaction.

Charlie threw his palms up in front of his heaving chest, "I know. Thirty minutes you said, Mr. Cunningham. I'm sorry. I wolfed... I wolfed down my noodles... Just not quite fast enough."

Cain smirked and turned to Cunningham, who looked up slowly from the documents spread before him. "Whilst you may have *wolfed down* your noodles, it appears that you were less successful with the sauce," he observed dourly, wafting a finger at the stain on Charlie's left lapel. "Now sit down, Charles. We have a proposal to make."

Cain cringed. He knew his pal wouldn't let go of an opportunity like that. "A proposal? Oh my, this is all so sudden," he flapped.

Cunningham had had enough and extinguished Charlie's good cheer. "Very drole, Lam, but humor has a time and place. This is not the place, and none of us has the time for one of your admittedly jovial disquisitions." Then he pressed his lips together and paused as he clearly considered how to proceed. "By the way, how is young Andreas progressing?"

"Spectacular, Mr. Cunningham. You know I had my doubts, but that boy is seriously connected!"

"And you, Shaw?" Cain could feel the strength of the company sage's penetrating scrutiny. "You look tired. Are you quite well?"

Unlike Charlie, whose Fund team did sometimes mix socially with the senior management at client events, Cain was all-too aware of his junior rank and his lack of personal familiarity with his bosses. Under Cunningham's unflinching gaze, he was once more the schoolboy grappling with how to talk to a father whose typical form of address was more suitable for army recruits. He couldn't, therefore, escape his almost Pavlovian instinct to obey and please his elders; "Very well, Mr. Cunningham," he barked.

Charlie nudged Cain with his elbow and jested, "Don't worry about us, Mr. Cunningham. We're just pleased to be sitting at the grown-ups' table for once."

Cunningham allowed the trace of a smile to lift one corner of his mouth. Still scrutinizing Cain, he addressed Charlie again. "I know you're busy at present, Charles." His gaze finally migrated to Charlie. "But do you think Andreas could hold the fort for you this Friday?"

Sensing Charlie's discomfort, Cain could see that Cunningham wasn't about to brook any naysaying. Thankfully, Charlie had seen it too. "Friday? Should be okay. There might be a bit of profit-taking, but Fridays are essentially admin. Mopping up after the party."

It seemed to be what Cunningham wanted to hear, but his tone was bereft of gratitude. "You can rest assured that David, Terence, and I will be ready to assist Andreas in any way necessary. The Major and Terence will apprise you of our plans. I hope we can rely on you both." Then he gathered his documents and rose from his seat. "Now, if you'll excuse me. Lena is tutoring me in Indonesian etiquette. Our dear receptionist has taken it upon herself to prepare me for the Finance Minister's meeting tomorrow."

Cunningham closed the door behind him, and the Major got the briefing underway. "Alright, Charlie, we've established that Andreas can cover for you this Friday. But in fairness, you need to hear why and decide for yourself whether that contingency will be necessary. The same goes for you, Shaw, because this particular sortie lies well beyond your typical duties."

Cain saw Charlie nod his readiness to hear what the Major had to say and did likewise. Still recovering from Cunningham's unsettling stare, that comment about the task being very different from his normal job excited and unnerved him in equal measure.

"You know that before he joined us last month, Terence was a very successful business news correspondent in Hong Kong. As such, he interviewed the top brass at Harrier Bank more than a few times."

He looked at Cain; "You're familiar with Harrier, Shaw?"

To Cain's great relief, he could reply in the affirmative. "Yes, Major. It's one of the biggest private banks in Asia. It was founded by Tsang Yung Ming and is now run by his son Henry Tsang."

The Major gave him a warm smile. "And while the father was widely praised as a gentlemanly patriarch of the banking industry, rumors about his son indicate that he is cut from a very different cloth. Terence explained to me that every time he filmed an interview at Harrier, he always came away with a sour taste in his mouth."

Pyle butted in; "The Major's being way too polite, guys. I actually called them a bunch of assholes. Ernest drew the line at calling them 'insufferable' after we met with them during our trip around the region. They were nicer than I remembered, but Ernest was far from impressed. The whole thing was so weird that it prompted us to catch an earlier flight back here this morning."

"And that's the point," Speer asserted, tapping his hand on the tabletop and restamping his authority on the briefing. "On the telephone from Hong Kong last night, Ernest told me the Harrier representatives looked ill at ease as they hung on his every word. They were desperate for insights about Indonesia. And to cut to the chase, the whole experience gave his keen business antennae more than a twitch. He suspects the bank is overburdened with bad Indonesian investments and wants to know more than Tsang would ever admit."

Cain was mesmerized. This was nothing like any office discussion he'd ever been privy to. He sat back in his chair as if an incrementally wider view might afford him a better sense of what was unfolding. He looked at Charlie and back to the Major, who was tapping his chin with his index finger as if weighing them both up. "And that's where you two come in. I'll let Terence explain his plan."

Not for the first time that day, Cain heard himself giving voice to a thought he'd meant to keep within the confines of his mind. "Us?"

Pyle reached forward and gave Cain a friendly smack on the shoulder. "Darn straight! You and Charlie are perfect for this."

There was a sea change in the meeting's tone. The Major delivered a briefing; Pyle was delivering a pitch. "Okay, boys, the good stuff first. An all-expenses-paid, three-day trip to my favorite city, Hong Kong. Yes, it's an assignment, but if you're successful, you get a 10,000-dollar bonus."

Charlie wisecracked, "Just as long as it's not in Rupiah coz it's been tanking recently."

The same witticism had occurred to Cain, but as Speer and Pyle hardly cracked a smile, he was relieved to have been beaten to the mark. Instead, Speer asked, "Charlie, are you able to drop your accent and speak in plain old, received pronunciation English?

"No problem at all, Major," Charlie replied quite naturally in a rather posh accent.

"Excellent," said Speer. "Now try to maintain it throughout this meeting if you can. Ernest was confident that you'd be able to. He's created what he calls 'legends' for the pair of you to familiarize yourself with during the course of this week."

"Legends?" Charlie queried in his new accent.

Cain jumped in, eager to impress. "A term used by military and intelligence services. A backstory for a false identity."

Speer beamed. "A military childhood does have its advantages, eh Shaw? But I wouldn't call them legends per se. We're hoping you'll only spend a few hours with some younger Harrier staff, so there's no need for the intricate, deep-cover life stories a proper legend would provide."

Cain tried to appear composed, but his heart was racing as he absorbed the first indication of what he and Charlie were being asked to do.

Pyle took over from the Major. "Ernest also mentioned that the best false identities are typically as close to a person's actual life story as possible. So, Charlie Lam. We need you to be Charlie Yeo, a rich Chinese-Indonesian. Your father made his money in mining and logistics. The reason why you speak with that impeccable English accent is because you were educated in the UK from your first year of high school. You'll be meeting investment bankers who will hopefully infer that you have wealth to invest outside the same Indonesian economy they seem so worried about. Now, as for you, Cain…"

His mouth was dry, but still Cain swallowed. He'd wanted a chance to prove himself but never believed he'd be asked to play James bloody Bond up in Hong Kong. And bonus aside, the real reward would be the career kudos if he and Charlie pulled it off. But that was a very big 'if.'

Pyle continued, "You're Charlie's wingman, as the Major would say. Charlie needs to be the main focus of the bankers' attentions, but...." His tone became defensive; "That's not to say your role isn't crucial."

Cain realized his face had fallen when he learned he was in a supporting role. He tried hard to rearrange and harden his features to prevent any further slips.

"You're Charlie's buddy. You studied economics together at university. You moved to Singapore, and you're working as a business editor for Television Corporation of Singapore news. Living in the region, you've rekindled your friendship with Charlie. You're taking a short holiday in Jakarta, meaning you won't be carrying any business cards. You were staying at the Yeo residence, but Charlie wanted a change of scene, and that's why he's paying for you to accompany him to see an old friend from your college days who lives in Hong Kong."

The Major took advantage of a slight pause in Pyle's energetic oration. "Granted, this is a lot to take in and probably not what you expected. Do you have any questions?"

Cain saw that Charlie was about to speak and made sure he beat him to it. "I get who we're supposed to be, Major, but I'd like to know what you want us to do in Hong Kong?"

The question did nothing to curb Pyle's zeal. "That's the best bit because I can't do that without introducing you to your partner, who I know you're going to love. We need access to investment bankers, and Ruby Miller is our key. She's the college friend you've come to see. I was Ruby's mentor when she first started work in television news. She's Chinese, but as she was raised by her natural mother and

English stepfather, she can switch between Cantonese and English better than anyone in that newsroom. She's been courting the bankers at Harrier for some time, getting them to do 'lives' from the street or in the studio."

Pyle must have seen the confused looks on their faces. "Lives. You know, live TV interviews," he explained. "Anyway, when I told Ruby what I needed, she was chomping at the bit to get involved, her newshound moxie seeing the potential for a scoop. She also assured me that hooking up with some Harrier boys socially would be seen as nothing more than her overdue acceptance of their many requests for her company."

Cain may have become jaded by the sales aspect of his own job, but Pyle's energy was seducing him. Charlie broke his attention along with Pyle's verbal flow. "Forgive me, Terence, but if you're sending us on some kind of commercial espionage caper, then why not hire professionals?"

A twinge of concern crossed Cain's face; he couldn't help it. There was something about the word 'espionage' that scared him, some kind of vague memory of his soldier dad with long hair comforting his crying mother. He and Charlie were being tasked with some really serious shit!

Pyle adapted his delivery for a quieter, more thoughtful tone. "Ernest initially insisted on a professional investigator, but I advised against it. Third-party investigators aren't secure. They could take your intel and threaten to inform the target entity. It's a calculated risk, but the blackmail can prove very effective because clients will always want to protect their reputations. The alternative would be like a 'John' admitting that he uses hookers. It just ain't going to happen."

Speer looked askance at Pyle; "Not the analogy I would have chosen, but Terence is as correct as he is colorful. If you can help by keeping this matter in-house, it will be a great relief to us. In fact…" he paused looking momentarily unsure. "Sir James will also appreciate the security of having this done in-house. In '95, Ernest saved him a fortune by tipping him off about the impending collapse of Barings bank. As it transpires, Sir James has wealth invested with Harrier, and we think the bank may be in trouble."

Cain could tell that the Major had struggled before sharing that sensitive information. He also noted that he was being asked to undertake some very real risks for what he hoped might lead to significant recognition within the company. He'd been paying attention and knew what to ask. "If Ruby manages to get us in front of these Bankers, what info do you want us to get from them?"

Cain's question got Pyle firing on all cylinders again. "That's the spirit, Cain! Don't worry about Ruby. She'll definitely get you in front of their bankers. When Ernest and I spoke to Harrier, their top guys put a brave face on it, but they were definitely worried. Why? Is a big Indonesian investment the root of their concerns? If the three of you find out, you all get the bonus."

Charlie joked, "The trip itself is a bonus for me. My mum's always nagging me to visit my cousin in Hong Kong. If I get the time, I'll put an end to her nagging whilst putting one over on a bunch of investment bankers. And I don't need to tell you what investment banker means in rhyming slang."

There was a nervous edge to Cain's laughter that he hoped no one noticed. Charlie had joked about being at the grown-ups' table, and as it turned out, they were both being asked to sing a dangerous song for their supper. They'd been given a choice, but these older men must have known he and Charlie couldn't really say no. It had all the hallmarks of a fait accompli from the moment Charlie burst into the room.

Lena knocked and put her head around the conference room's glass door. "Major Speer and Mr. Terence, Pak Cunningham would like to see you both in his room."

4)   Between a Hard Rock and a President

Monday was usually 'legs night' at the gym for Cain and Charlie. But after spending Monday night familiarizing themselves with their so-called legends, they decided to shift it to Tuesday. After all, they reasoned, that still left three days of recovery before their Hong Kong adventure.

Getting that recovery process underway, they were luxuriating in the steam room at the Crowne Plaza hotel's gym. The hushed atmosphere was lulling an Indonesian gentleman into a meditative state while Cain and Charlie spoke in hushed tones about Edward Grant's self-induced woes.

Charlie's attempt at sustaining those hushed tones was, however, short-lived; and in a tone, only he could ever believe was quiet, he declared; "Three days isn't gonna be enough. It's really only two more days to Friday, and after those Romanian deadlifts, I'll still be straining to put my socks on next week!"

Cain was used to Charlie's loudness, but the Indonesian man had recoiled at the sudden disturbance and knocked over the cup of water at his side.

"Ma'af Pak," said Charlie, by way of apology as the man tied his towel around his waist and left.

When the door closed behind him, Cain swung round; "In the name of God, there's a sign out there warning people with heart conditions not to use saunas and steam rooms, but it doesn't say anything about Charlie bloody Lam!"

There was a moment of silence before the pair of them burst out laughing.

As their laughter subsided, Charlie complained, "The Edward Grant saga is so typical, but you're also a much-prized single male Bulé. White guys can score walking around a bloody shopping mall! Singapore, Malaysia, Indonesia, Thailand; the smiling welcome wagon of South-East Asia's finest is rolled out for you."

"It's changing," argued Cain. "Though maybe not here yet. In Singapore, the phenomenon is more muted. There's a real Asian self-confidence there, and rightly so. Plus, for a few years now, they've been calling local girls who go out with Westerners 'Sarong Party Girls' or SPGs. You know how they love an acronym."

Charlie erupted; "Finally, there's hope for BBCs – Brit Born Chinese – like me. I have to keep up my immaculate appearance just to have any chance at all." Then he shook himself and added; "Okay, enough moaning, that's definitely enough steam for a 'Nancy Shave.'"

The 'Nancy shave' was part of a wider grooming practice Charlie had passed on to Cain. He'd picked it up at the gym in Singapore's Mandarin Hotel. Surprised to discover that the sauna and steam room were unisex, he bumped into the General Manager's gregarious wife, who turned out to be Fijian. Nancy explained that because a soap-less shave is healthier for the skin, her German husband always shaved in a steam room. Charlie gave it a try and never looked back. The steam opened up his follicles for a shave that was so close it still looked good at the end of the next day.

Cain ran his hand over his face and started shaving when he realized he hadn't heard what Charlie had just said. Totally dumbfounded, he first underlined the rarity of his upcoming request before asking Charlie to repeat what he'd said and to speak up. Grinning smugly, Charlie cleared his throat and reiterated his disbelief about the news of Ernest Cunningham's meeting that evening with the upper echelons of Indonesia's Finance Ministry.

Then he added, "Fresh from their trip, Old Cunningham and the new boy Terry 'call-me-Terence' Pyle were only back in the office for five minutes before the news began to lift everyone's spirits."

Cain smiled, recalling the mood; "Yeah, the old, pre-crisis office mood was back. And today was quite a laugh too. Did you see Cunningham's face when Lena told him not to tuck in the Batik shirt she bought for him? He was horrified."

Charlie laughed; "Clinton must have felt the same in Bogor when the Indonesians insisted all the APEC leaders wear a Batik shirt for the end of summit photo."

"I saw that on the telly, and some of the leaders looked really uncomfortable," Cain recalled.

"It's the only thing anyone remembers about an APEC summit. Mind you, this meeting with the Indonesians does seem to have gotten old Cunningham quite excited.

Cain laughed, "Well, for him, I guess you could call it excited. While he went off to get Speer and Pyle invited, he directed the pair of them to start a meeting with big Rob Watson. He wanted an outline for company-wide investment strategies to be drawn up based on the intel from their trip."

Charlie waved his razor in the steam for the attention of an unseeing Cain. "It seems like they really gathered some good information during their fortnight away. Lena told me they met with all sorts of think tanks and some very well-placed government officials."

"Did Cunningham and Pyle actually meet Tsang, the bank's owner?"

Charlie realized he couldn't be seen shaking his head; "Harry Tsang? Nah, they were supposed to, but that's the problem with playboys; they're not the most reliable sorts."

Cain absorbed that logic while Charlie's mind raced on.

"I need to get out of this steam," he said. "My hands look like double-boiled chicken skin!"

Getting dressed after a cool shower, Charlie revealed, "I was briefing Pyle about our Chinese Indonesian investors, and he mentioned trying to persuade the Major to have dinner and then go out on the town."

Cain snorted; "That trip with Cunningham must have clouded his mind. The Major doesn't do night's out." He paused before sharing his hypothesis about the insertion of Pyle into the company's management structure. "And thinking about it, the Major might have felt a bit put out recently. He was left to manage the office during some very difficult days while Cunningham and new boy Pyle went on a jaunt. Speer might have his name on the company door, but it's like he's been playing second fiddle to the Yank since he arrived."

Charlie was applying gel to his hair; "Very perceptive young Shaw. I never thought of that."

"Course you didn't, you insensitive beast," Cain jested. "Now, if you've finished poncifying yourself, we'd better go and eat."

"I'm done," Charlie replied while covering his arm with a towel like a waiter: "A big plate of protein overload at Hard Rock Café for you, sir? Andy said he'd meet us there and drive us home. Well, he says he'll drive, but he'll probably get one of the family drivers to bring him."

[ ]

© Steven Clark 2023
Lynnburn, Amisfield, Dumfries & Galloway, UK

Indonesia's Foreign Minister concluded his statement by announcing, "I have sought advice on reserving the right to defend the Rupiah by pegging it to the dollar at a fixed exchange rate."

Eric Hudson would later claim he'd mistakenly eaten a raw chili from a plate of snacks he thought were mange-tout. But to those who witnessed it, the IMF representative's coughing fit coincided perfectly with him putting a glass of red wine to his lips as the words 'fixed exchange rate' were uttered. It prompted those not directly in his line of fire to comfort him by patting him on the back; their kind action helping to restore his health but not his dignity.

A period of disruption followed, and Ernest Cunningham lit the latest in a series of kretek cigarettes. Inhaling, he listened as the fragrant cloves crackled. Held at President Suharto's private residence in Menteng, the audience of about 20 foreign and domestic guests had been treated to an event that was more theatrical than expected. The President was absent, but his well-rehearsed and well-respected Finance Minister fully deserved his star billing.

Mar'ie Muhammad's script left no one in any doubt that the IMF was suggesting politically dangerous austerity measures. He then made it clear that the Rupiah was only being allowed to float freely on the currency markets that coming Thursday because the IMF had left Indonesia with no other option.

Having laid out his charges, Mar'ie smiled kindly and introduced Eric Hudson, the woefully under-rehearsed IMF representative, to share what Cunningham concluded was a conscious misreading of the floatation's possible consequences. Not missing a trick, Mar'ie looked over his heavily-rimmed spectacles and rubbed salt into the IMF's skin before the self-harming statement was read. He introduced Hudson with a much higher rank than he actually held.

"I fear you overstate my position, Minister," he said rather shamefacedly. "I'm not a Director. I assist the Director at the Regional Office for Asia and the Pacific. Happily, however, I can bring you the conclusions of my Deputy Managing Director, Mr. Stanley Fischer."

He drew a piece of paper from his pocket and read, *"The IMF welcomes the timely decision of the Indonesian authorities. Floating the Rupiah, in combination with Indonesia's strong fundamentals, supported by prudent fiscal and monetary policies, will allow its economy to continue the impressive growth it has enjoyed over the last several years."*

Aghast at the blatantly disingenuous statement, Cunningham began to realize that Terence Pyle may have been correct after all. While traveling together, the consummate journalist had shared a revelation from a contact at the US Treasury, a man with whom he'd served in Vietnam.

Going all the way back to Nixon's visit to China in '72, which wrong-footed the Soviets and cleared the way for the US to pump money into the economy of its strangely 'Red' new friend, Pyle reckoned it was payback time. In need of a positive legacy, Clinton had reportedly become quite obsessed with creating a budget surplus before leaving office. A happy convergence of increased tax revenues and wider economic factors made that ambition look very possible. But Pyle's contact claimed that in order to help ensure that the books did indeed balance, the White House had quietly asked China to ramp up its growing investments in the US whilst also buying up more American debt. Pressing the inevitable quid-pro-quo button, Beijing asked that Clinton use the levers at his disposal to help stifle the economies of its Asian neighbors. China would then use that window of fragility to turbo-charge its economy and further commit its 'Century of Shame' to the annals of history.

Cunningham had withheld Pyle's revelation from Sir James, who was still uncomfortable with employing 'a whoring Yankee scribbler'. Even if he could understand China's motives, the US seeking to extend the economic pain of its Asian allies at the behest of Peking sounded a little far-fetched. But after hearing that dubious IMF statement, any lingering doubts about Pyle's story were quickly burning away. With the cloves still crackling in his kretek, he started planning how to share the news when he called London later that evening.

A wistful look came over Cunningham's face as he recalled a memory from his university days. A student union leader claimed that Mao was the only true Communist leader because he understood the necessity of societal tumult. She argued that Mao's belief in revolution was built upon the underlying meaning of the Chinese word for crisis – Wei-ji – which apparently combined the words for danger and opportunity. Cunningham had always thought that translation was a little callous, and probably too simplistic. But dismissing his linguistic doubts, he reasoned that if the Chinese were going to make the most of this crisis, then the Temple-Speer Fund should also be positioned to harvest its opportunities. That very positive line of reasoning should create the right kind of mood for him to broach the touchy subject of retirement. He knew Sir James didn't like to relinquish control over people with intimate knowledge of his business affairs. Cunningham himself had engaged private investigators to make sure former staff upheld Sir James' reputation within the British Establishment. And he wasn't so naïve as to believe his own retirement might be any different in Sir James' suspicious mind. That was why he'd lobbied to hire Pyle. If required, he could be persuaded to help document a useful bulwark against Sir James' mercurial paranoia.

The Finance Minister's voice stirred Cunningham from his thoughts; "My dear friends, thank you for your presence and for sharing your wisdom this evening."

Hudson had recovered, and the guests began to stand and say their farewells. Cunningham was about to join them when a young civil servant hurried over. "Permisi Pak Cunningham. Excuse me. My Minister has asked me to invite you for a short chat with Bapak," he whispered, using the term of endearment Indonesians used for President Suharto, a word that means 'father' but is also a term of respect for older men.

[ ]

A Silver Bird cab was a must when visiting the past-its-prime building that housed the city's massive Hard Rock Café. The drivers would usually wait for Cain and Charlie while they dined inside, allowing them to avoid a moment's indecision when they were leaving, and run to the cab before the car park beggars closed in.

'Love All Serve All' may have been the well-intentioned Hard Rock motto, but the reality wasn't quite as all-encompassing as the sentiment. The bouncers denied entry to the starving but welcomed those in possession of a good appetite.

Being seated by the friendly Maître D, Cain held onto his menu and said, "We'll just have our regular meals Ginung, but I'll keep this menu for Andy."

"No problem," said Ginung, deducing that a VIP's son was coming to visit. "So, one Haystack salad with the dressing on the side for Cain and Chicken Fajitas for you, Charlie. All washed down with a couple of Cecil Orange Iced Teas."

Ginung hurried off to prep their orders. He knew 'Andy' was actually Andreas Prakowo. His famous father was a renowned General who'd masterminded a vicious period of the ongoing conflict with independence-seeking rebels in Sumatra. In retirement, he still had the ear of the President and had been allowed to dip his fingers into several lucrative business pies as a reward for his services.

Charlie had been worried about taking Andy on because of the cultural and ethnic divide between them. But the young Indonesian was intelligent and witty and quickly became just another one of the lads. In fact, ever since Andy had bought a couple of suits like Charlie's, Cain watched as he began to take the idea of integration to a whole new level. Approaching their table, Andy looked and even carried himself just like Charlie.

A serving of beef fajitas was ordered, and Charlie spotted the subject of an earlier discussion at the gym. "Isn't that Jakarta's latest addition to the singles' club sidling up to the bar?"

A city of ten million people can sometimes seem very small. Of course, it wasn't the size of the city but the select number of venues where expats went out to play. Cain turned to see Edward Grant following the suggestion of a friend to zip up his fly.

"Pissed as a fart," Cain sniped. "Just another expat dickhead making life harder for those of us who prefer to mix and break down barriers. I might have known that sad bastard would start to hang out at the expat nest over there." He nodded his head toward the ground-floor bar. It was almost wholly inhabited by foreigners, whilst the rest of Hard Rock played host to young Indonesians. Segregation is too strong a word; it was little more than a practical demarcation based on proximity to a bar and the cultural reality of drinking. Budget and faith restricted the quantity and choice of drinking options for the Indonesian patrons, and due to their comparative youthfulness, they usually spent their evenings on the dancefloor.

Cain's less-than-subtle self-declared exemption from the white expat crowd was lost on Charlie. He nodded, but he was thirsty after the steam room and glugged a mouthful of his orange and clove iced tea. Wiping his mouth, he pointed at Grant. "He's really hammering the drink. Maybe he's using alcohol to exorcise the memory of his very pissed-off wife."

Ginung sent his new waitress to deliver their meals. She arrived just as Cain quipped, "Forgetting to do up his zip, I wonder what diabolical portal Grant's demons will escape from."

They all roared with laughter, interrupting the waitress who was trying to introduce herself; "Hi guys, I'm Nisa and…."

Totally unnerved, Nisa hurriedly dispatched the meals leaving all three diners to swap their plates. Cain watched her flee back to Ginung. He hadn't seen her before and felt a little embarrassed as he watched her being comforted by her boss.

Even though the client who'd ruined his morning was under the same roof, Cain was happy in the company of his friends. They'd just started to tuck into their meals when a voice boomed through the sound system. With a; "Hello Hard Rockers! Welcome to Ruby Tuesday!" the band kicked off their long night with the Rolling Stones classic.

[ ]

The other-worldly sound of a Gamelan ensemble always unsettled Cunningham. He thought it sounded eerie and made a conscious effort to resist being enchanted by its hypnotic melody as he was ushered through a door to meet Indonesia's long-serving President.

Entering the small and notably unornamental room, he could barely believe what he was seeing and suspected the Gamelan musicians had indeed bewitched him. President Suharto was standing in front of him, offering him a glass of Arak and, in broken English, declaring how happy he was to see him again after so many years.

Cunningham was difficult to impress, but here in the unexpectedly cozy presence of this seminal figure of Asian politics, he was quite awestruck. Finance Minister Mar'ie helped jolt Cunningham from his stupefaction by introducing the other westerner in the room. Still recovering, Cunningham heard that he was American but asked him if he would please repeat his name. The man tugged at the rear hem of his Batik shirt, as Cunningham had found himself doing all evening. He was Associate Professor Daniel Shore from the highly regarded US-based Taisan Institute.

Switching to his mother tongue of Javanese, Suharto asked, by way of his interpreter, what Cunningham thought of the currency peg idea.

He resisted the urge to speak to the interpreter and tried to muster some semblance of his usual self-confidence as he maintained eye contact with Suharto. "I feel that Minister Mar'ie's currency peg provision is prudent. But I sense from Mr. Hudson's unfortunate reaction that the IMF won't welcome it. Malaysia's Prime Minister Mahathir is already digging his political heels in by rejecting a traditional IMF aid for austerity covenant."

They all waited for the translator to finish. The President nodded in agreement.

Turning from his President, Mar'ie added, "Your observations are very astute, Ernest. But the currency board is not my idea."

The minister and his President turned to Shore, who stiffened under the gaze of the powerful men and didn't quite manage to clear his throat. Looking at Suharto, he stammered slightly, "Thank you, Mr. President. If I may."

Then clearing his throat more purposefully, he explained, "As you know, Ernest, the Taisan Institute doesn't take sides, so I offered my assistance in this matter pro-bono. Your point about Mahathir is well observed. He's an adept politician playing to the electorate, but what if his pronouncements encourage other leaders to follow their own path? Food for thought that I suspect will be difficult for the IMF to digest."

Shore waited for the translation. Cunningham could tell that Shore's confidence was given a boost when Suharto chortled after absorbing the translation of his 'food for thought' line.

Shore continued, "As for the currency board, it's probably the most orthodox defense of last resort, and my data indicates that here in Indonesia, it will likely prevent bankruptcies. It might even save the entire banking infrastructure and would almost certainly help stabilize the Rupiah. Quite honestly, I can't understand why the IMF leaders didn't suggest it themselves."

Cunningham was tense but was also enjoying the exclusivity of this rare access. Suharto clasped his hands together, looking at each of them in turn and compelling their absolute attention.

"Gentlemen, I have a recurring suspicion about the IMF's resistance to a currency peg. A person such as I, tends to accrue powerful enemies. Some of them are perhaps moving against me, frustrating my ability to guide the Republic through these trying times."

His words were few, but they exposed the old man behind the armor-plating of his reputation. His audience was enthralled, hanging on his silences as well as his every word. Smiling at Cunningham, he gave his interpreter a nod and continued…

"Since my days as a young officer, I have always maintained close relations with the Chinese business community here. Recently one of those old associates made me aware of how a book of changes called 'I Ching' described the winter solstice. The ancient Chinese understood the solstice as a turning point." He looked up to the ceiling as if recalling the words in English before fixing his gaze on Cunningham.

"After a time of decay comes the turning point. The powerful light that has been banished returns. There is movement, but it is not brought about by force. It is in harmony with the time."

The president paused for dramatic effect. Cunningham, who'd been taught this ancient wisdom by an old Mi5 friend many years earlier, could barely contain himself under the spell of Suharto's gaze and silently mouthed the remaining words as Suharto spoke.

"Everything comes of itself at the appointed time."

The old General saw Cunningham's lips move in time with his own. He shocked and delighted his guest when he grabbed and shook his knee, declaring him to be; "An uncommonly learned individual."

Cunningham preened as the President continued. "My government has worked closely with our western allies. But 30 years on, maybe my rule no longer accords with the time and…."

Suharto stopped. He smiled awkwardly, nodded, and inhaled slowly. He gave Cunningham the impression that in nodding his head and inhaling, he was trying to reel in his words like a fisherman jerking his rod to reel in his catch.

The president stood, and they all did the same.

He thanked them and bade them good night before excusing himself. The clumsiness of his exit led Cunningham to suspect that Suharto had caught himself straying into territory that was a little too personal.

'As if this evening hasn't already been interesting enough,' he thought.

After seeing his President out, Minister Mar'ie wound up proceedings. "We are very grateful for Professor Shore's advice. Pak Cunningham, Bapak has asked if you would be so kind as to contact Sir James Templar-Hawes this evening and convey his wish to speak with him at his earliest convenience."

[ ]

Bill paid, and standing up from the table, Charlie cried, "This old town's getting way too small. And the Septic's achieved the impossible."

Cain and Andy gazed at the entrance when they should have turned their eyes to the expats in the ground-floor bar. Cain asked, "The Septic? If that's rhyming slang, mate, you definitely made that one up."

Charlie enlightened his companions. "Septic tank. Rhymes with Yank. And yes, I may have used some artistic license." He pointed, "But look over there. Terence Pyle and the Major!"

"Wonders will never cease," Cain exclaimed as he caught sight of the two bosses standing amongst the expat barflies and young women who exchanged their company for drinks. Realizing that any chance of studying his legend that evening was now dead in the water, he was going to suggest they say 'hello,' but Charlie was already on his way and waving at them.

Following Charlie, Cain felt a little awkward as he entered the unfamiliar territory of socializing with his bosses. Under Charlie's mentorship, even Andreas was more relaxed around them.

Speer smiled as they approached. He lifted his glass but had a 'deer caught in the headlights' look on his face that he tried to shake off with a forced blink.

Pyle, on the other hand, was in his element. Condemned as being brash and crass even before he arrived at Temple-Speer, he'd quickly won over most of the staff, even if he was a little loud. And in keeping with his lack of reserve, the self-declared Asian 'Old Hand' who'd been in the region since the '60s was already on first-name terms with the barman and a couple of the girls.

Charlie shouted, "This is a respectable establishment. Who let you two in?"

"Charlie, you cheeky bastard!" Pyle bellowed. "Cain! Andy! What are you drinking?"

Two beers were ordered. With Cain and Charlie, Andreas usually ordered a whisky and soda, but around the bosses, he asked for a coke.

Drinks in hand, the group stood around a table away from the busy bar. "Any updates from Mr. Cunningham yet?" asked Charlie.

Pyle looked at Speer, who raised and moved an open palm from Pyle to the boys in a 'go ahead' gesture.

"Nothing yet, guys. But when Ernest got off the phone with Suharto's people after they rejected the presence of myself and the Major, he said the meeting had been called to discuss a plan to allow the Rupiah to float freely on the currency markets."

Speer added: "That revelation became one of the central thrusts for our meeting with Rob Watson, who's working on a platter of investment strategies for the company.

Cain nodded earnestly till he heard glass breaking and a thud from over at the bar. He looked and saw an embarrassingly inebriated Edward Grant writhing and failing to get up from the floor. From babysitting the likes of him to the grave matter of national economic policy, Cain's job suddenly looked much more appealing. He couldn't help but smile when he saw the Major looking so approvingly at him. The moment was almost intimate.

Speer squeezed him on the shoulder and leaned forward; "Actually, it's rather serendipitous to have bumped into you boys. Over dinner, Terence and I were discussing Hong Kong and how we could more fully utilize the talents of younger staff like you."

This was exactly what Cain wanted to hear. Economies were convulsing all over the region, and he wanted a chance to play a more meaningful role. Despite still feeling a little overawed by the Hong Kong assignment, he ached to know more about their dinner conversation and the opportunity for a greater and perhaps permanent change to his role at Temple-Speer.

Pyle waved a hand in a manner that cautioned Speer. "No doubt the next few days could prove very interesting at the office, but Ernest is out there for us at Suharto's place tonight. With him in our corner, we should certainly be able to steer the Fund to outperform the market again. In fact, I'm so confident that I suggest we celebrate." He stared at Cain, Charlie, and Andy, not trying to hide the conspiratorial nature of his expression. "Are you three up for Tanamur?"

[ ]

The driver indicated that they'd arrived, prompting Speer to instinctively scan the sporadically tarmacked area for a parking position that would allow the car to make a sharp exit. He didn't realize such efforts were futile, but then, few people descended into Tanamur without first undergoing a process of socialization to loosen them up. Especially if, like David Speer, you were going there for the very first time.

A group of skinny, young gangsters toiled in the heavy night air for their intimidating boss, commonly known as the 'Fat Man.' Sitting in a deckchair surrounded by mosquito coils on a vantage point in the center of his kingdom, he was typically clad in a white shirt and sarong, accessorized by sandals and chunky rings on several of his stubby fingers, two of which cradled an ever-present kretek cigarette. His sweaty brow was adorned by thick, black-rimmed glasses that did nothing to disarm his air of casual malevolence as he shuffled around on gout-ridden legs, barking orders at his parking attendants.

They parked where they were instructed, and Terence Pyle led the way. "David, do you want to warm up in JJ's? It's the club just over there. Or do we head straight for Tanamur?"

Speer checked his watch and chose Tanamur.

Pyle grinned wickedly; "Shit, David, this really is your first time here. And there was me thinking you were just playing it cool."

Following the thump of heavy bass, Pyle headed toward the legendary club and disappeared behind the heavy plastic flaps that helped prevent its air-conditioned air from escaping. Speer followed reluctantly and found himself heading toward a dimly lit, crowded bar in an atmosphere thick with smoke. Pyle passed a glass over his shoulder to Speer, who took a sip. He flinched as his taste buds mutinied against the sharpness of the whisky, which was of markedly lower quality than the 18-year-old single malt he'd been treated to over dinner.

Pyle sniggered; "A bit different from what you're used to, eh David?"

"Nothing escapes the keen eye of a journalist," Speer replied, trying to remain cheery. "Guess we should stay here in sight of the door, so we don't miss the boys when they arrive."

"They'll find us, no problem. Come on, let me show you around," Pyle shouted, walking toward the edge of a flight of three steps that led down to the dancefloor. It was a great vantage point to take in the atmosphere of Tanamur. Just ahead of them, three girls were laughing raucously while dancing with glasses of beer balanced on their heads. Above everyone, a neon-clad dancer slid down a pole from the ceiling and into a cage. To her right, across the busy dancefloor, there was a podium on which two girls writhed and twisted around one another, tempting the good-time girls, the working girls, the transexuals, the gays, and even the straight men who beheld them, to joyously lose themselves in sensual and sexual expression: all fueled by the pulsating lights and the intoxicating beat of the music.

Speer struggled to take it all in. He'd been taken to so-called 'Superclubs' with clients all around the world, but this was Jakarta? And this wasn't a contemporary scene. It was wilder than any story he'd heard about the 60s. No, what was playing out in front of him, he imagined, was more reminiscent of Weimer Berlin's mythical excesses in the 20s. It was a driving, decadent orgy of sensual pleasure. And like many before him, Speer wasn't yet wasn't ready to make the required mental leap over the club's towering hurdle of behavioral disorientation.

Led by Pyle to the back of the club, Speer stopped next to the cage the dancer had slid into. She had a silver circle painted onto her forehead. The neon bodysuit she wore had an inverted triangular hole cut just below her breasts and reaching down to an apex that stretched seductively below her belly button. And she paired it with what appeared to be the silver moon boots, which she somehow managed to make cool. Lost in the music, she danced with energetic passion, using the bars of the cage to great effect and pumping her body to a bass beat that Speer could feel pounding through his.

Pyle shouted that he was going to the toilet, forcing Speer to tear his gaze away. When he turned back around, however, the dancer was smiling directly at him. The sweetness of her smile contrasted sharply with her aggressive dancing. Speer understood this. He saw the paradox, noting the temptation, the peril. But he couldn't take his eyes off her.

Lost in space and time, Speer was shocked when Charlie tapped him on the shoulder, shouting, "Hello, boss! What do you think of Tanamur, then?

Cain helped jog Speer's mind into action. "I'm sure this is all rather different for you, Major."

"You're not wrong there, Shaw," he replied, gathering himself together. "I've been to some impressive clubs in London, Juliana's in Tokyo, and a really wild place in Hong Kong called DiscoDisco, which you two might enjoy while you're there. But this place? Even seeing it for myself, I'm having trouble believing such hedonism exists in Jakarta."

Cain looked impressed; "You've been around the block, Major."

Speer was shaking his head, about to downplay his previous boast, when an American accent roared, "Boys, you made it! Hey, where's Andy?"

Cain replied, "His father needs the driver tomorrow morning, so he went home."

"Ah, well then," shouted Pyle; "Let me introduce you all to Yati." A young woman appeared from behind him and smiled. "Yati's from Madura," he announced before leaning toward Speer and adding for his discomfort, "Where women are famed for their strong vaginal muscles and sexual prowess."

The Major tried to smile but was clearly uncomfortable.

Yati returned her attention to Pyle, who dragged her onto the dancefloor. Charlie followed, responding to the wave of a regular girl on the scene that he and Cain had befriended long before.

Speer and Cain were left to gaze at the dancefloor scene. The podium dancers still writhed around one another, and the moon-booted cage dancer still pulsated in her own transfixing way. They were totally surrounded by people engaged in some form of overt sexual expression.

The evening's chance encounter had allowed Cain to feel closer to the Major after witnessing this slightly more personal side of him.

The Major pointed toward Charlie and asked, "Is this a regular haunt for you lads?"

Cain laughed; "When we come to this part of town, we tend to go to JJs next door. It's more fun because it's more erm… innocent, though that's not quite the right word."

Speer was checking his watch when Cain saw Yati bite a pill and kiss half of it into Pyle's mouth before swallowing the other half. He'd just told the Major that he sometimes partied here and didn't want his boss thinking he hung out in drug dens. He, therefore, tried to prevent Speer from noticing what Pyle was up to by asking, "What time is it, Major?"

"Almost midnight Shaw." He shivered at the discovery of the hour. "I should leave. If I take the car, I can send it back for Terence. There and back should take no more than forty minutes at this time of night. Can you please relay that to him?"

Asking the question, he was already stepping away and glancing over Cain's shoulder toward the dancer's cage.

Cain was happy for the chance to assure the Major that he could be relied on, but he noticed a brief flash of disappointment on his face. After watching him make his way through the ultra-violet haze of tobacco smoke, Cain checked over his shoulder to where his boss had looked. He also saw that the dancer was gone and understood the disappointment.

"Yeah, boss," he muttered. "She was amazing."

Thrilled by the unexpected turn the evening had taken and more than satisfied with how he'd conducted himself, he determined that if he was ever to get any sleep that night, he should join Charlie and dance away some of his energy.

[ ]

Speer was about to push aside the heavy plastic refrigerator flaps at the exit when they parted, and two young women grabbed him. They begged him not to go with a level of false seriousness that made both of them laugh hysterically before skipping past him and into Tanamur.

Outside, he thought he saw the dancer from the cage. A strikingly beautiful woman was smoking a cigarette, standing against the wall at the end of the path that led to the club entrance. Dressed simply in what appeared to be a long grey zipper cardigan and training shoes, she said, "Hello."

Speer hadn't expected her to speak and didn't know what to do. Maintaining his reserve, he acknowledged her greeting with a nod but didn't break his stride until she stepped directly into his path. More words revealed a smoky voice. "You don't recognize me?" she asked, feigning a sad pout.

Speer remained silent, caught short by his indecision about how to handle this encounter.

"You were watching me dance in there," she added, using her cigarette to point at the club entrance.

"I thought that was you," Speer exclaimed unconvincingly. "But you look so very different!"

"Oh, so now you think I am ugly?" she teased.

"Not at all. You actually look even better now. You're so, well… different."

Thankfully she was polite enough to rescue him; "My name is Feronika. May I know yours?"

Not even thinking to give a false name, he replied, "I'm David. Nice to meet you."

"Would you like to come with me to JJs?" Feronika asked, once more using her cigarette as a pointer to indicate the club next door.

Speer was still grappling with what was happening, but he was so drawn to her beauty that he was impelled to do something he'd never done before. He handed her his business card, saying, "This really isn't a good time Feronika, but perhaps we can arrange to meet soon."

Feronika placed her cigarette on top of the wall to graciously receive the card with both hands. Thanking him, she smiled, took a step forward, and kissed him lightly on the cheek.

He hadn't expected that and struggled to say, "Good night Feronika."

Walking away from her, he had to make a conscious attempt not to look over his shoulder.

She picked up her cigarette and took a long, slow drag as she watched Speer walk through the parking area. He'd been unsure of his words, but he was sure-footed. She continued to watch as he got into the back of a silver Volvo.

Feronika extinguished her cigarette and slipped Speer's business card into the large duffle bag that contained her make-up and costumes. Happy with the outcome of her evening, she walked toward JJs in a self-satisfied manner and gave a nod to the Fat Man. He returned the gesture, fished a mobile phone from his pocket, and made a call.

5)   The Morning After

Lena Ngurawan placed her treasured Balenciaga handbag in a drawer as she sat down at the Temple-Speer reception desk and reached into that same drawer for a toiletries bag.

Her journey to work was markedly different from that of her Bulé colleagues. Every morning the petit, well-dressed young woman braved the morning macet by jostling with fellow commuters to squeeze into dilapidated, non-aircon buses. Macet was the local word for the rush-hour gridlock that broke Lena's journey into a jolting series of staccato accelerations and sharp braking. Acceleration caused the vehicle to belch black smoke, and when the driver stamped on the brakes, that same smoke drifted back onboard through holes where windows should have been. Touts hung from the side door shouting their route at potential passengers whilst frantically gesticulating to other drivers to give way as their bus lurched through the jammed traffic. The touts also helped pull commuters aboard as the bus slowed down. The practice was dangerous, but it was in nobody's interest for the bus to come to a complete halt because if it ever did, there was a very real fear that it wouldn't start again.

Two women had initially been hired for reception duties, but after a month, 'glamorous Anna' quit to join an advertising firm. Thankfully, Lena rose to the challenge of managing the desk alone and was promoted to Office Manager. Well, that's how it looked. In truth, Lena had always done the lion's share of the work, but nobody had noticed, and she hadn't complained because she enjoyed Anna's company.

Anna had resolutely believed that looking your best was more important than any actual work you performed, especially at a Bulé company. Recognizing that she was a fashion and deportment neophyte, Lena listened and diligently practiced Anna's politically incorrect advice from head to high heels. That's why her first task every morning was to brush her thick black hair and erase any make-up imperfections sustained during her hellish commute.

She also took immense pride in the upkeep of her workstation. The reception was, after all, the most attractively decorated area in Temple-Speer, as Cunningham and Speer had resisted the temptation to make the office appear prestigious in any way. Their rationale was clear; as high-wealth clients preferred to be seen at their homes or companies, the office décor should be simple so as not to scare off the burgeoning client base of young, first-time investors who actually came to Temple-Speer for their meetings.

But simplicity soon became plainness. Apart from Lena's reception desk, the only other notable design feature was a string of oversized clocks. Their function was to display the time in the world's major trading centers. The staff, however, called them 'Cunningham's clocks,' believing them to be nothing less than horological weapons with which their punctiliously punctual boss could destroy any excuse for tardiness.

Plain white walls filled the vertical space between dull Styrofoam ceiling tiles and hardwearing carpet tiles, all outlining an unfashionable, open-plan office as Temple-Speer boasted none of the cubicles that were so popular elsewhere. With the exception of black swivel chairs, everything else was white.

Before the crisis took hold, good cheer and friendly competition between teams had helped soften the austere ambiance of the décor. Since then, however, boisterous shouts of deals being struck and congratulations being shared had been replaced by quiet, doleful conversations about the shrinking client base, lost revenue, and the possibility of heading home to the UK.

Lena was about to go and set up the conference room for the daily 9:30 meeting when she saw Cain and Charlie almost fall out of the elevator door and into the lobby.

"Selamat soré kawan-kawan," she sang, using Indonesia's early evening greeting to say 'hello friends.'

She knew Charlie wasn't a morning person at the best of times and chuckled when he responded limply, "It's 8:30 am somewhere, Ms. Ngurawan."

Even Cain, who was normally quite formal with her, jokingly argued, "Yep, we were on bona fide company business till the wee small hours."

She smiled and tutted. "I don't care about your nocturnal activities. It is not 8:30 here, Charlie, and you are both late. The briefing starts in five minutes, and Pak Cunningham is all about the business this morning."

"He always is," Cain whined. "What about the Major and Pyle?"

"They were already in a meeting with Pak Cunningham when I arrived," Lena sniffed.

Cain raised a skeptical eyebrow and then rubbed the tired eye beneath it. "Well, I know the Major probably got to bed before us. But God knows when or even if Pyle saw his bed last night."

With a wan smile, Lena tutted again. "That older generation of men simply has more discipline and staying power than yours. Come on now. I need to get to the conference room."

Cain and Charlie followed her to their desks and slid into their seats to boot up their computers in a vain attempt to pretend they'd been there all along.

© Steven Clark 2023
Lynnburn, Amisfield, Dumfries & Galloway, UK

Sitting nearby, Andreas had clearly enjoyed the entertainment, and Lena patted him on the shoulder as she passed by.

[ ]

"Struth! Lena was right," Charlie whispered as Pyle and Speer ushered Cunningham - the man of the hour - into the conference room. "How do they look so…" he searched for an appropriate adjective; "…Unsullied? I needed a rocket up my arse to get going this morning."

Cain smirked. As expected, he'd not slept much, but that had more to do with his excitement at the promise of change than his very late bedtime.

Speer greeted the assembled staff in his customary business-like tone, replete with military and flying references. They'd all become familiar with his vernacular, but it irked Pyle, who'd acquainted himself with the lexicon of business journalism many years ago, despite secretly loathing it.

"Good morning, gentlemen. As you know only too well, it's tough out there; and I thank you for the extra effort you've given to cope with some very harsh economic downdrafts. If we can overfly this turbulence, you will be duly rewarded."

All present recognized the significance of those last words. The fact that Speer's mention of rewards had neither surprised nor upset Cunningham implied his collusion and support.

Speer continued, "During their trip, Mr. Cunningham and Terry … Sorry, Terence." The correction prompted several grins, and Cain was reminded of his newly enhanced relationship with the Major as he heard him hint at the 'call-me-Terence' joke they all shared.

Charlie whispered into Cain's ear, "I bet he doesn't mention Tanamur."

"During their trip, Mr. Cunningham and Terence paid courtesy and working visits to some of the more venerable financial institutions around the region. And after two thorough examinations of the remarkable intel they gathered, we can now share how we aim to use it for our collective advantage. But that's not all. While Terence and I were discussing the trip's more illuminating details, his travel companion," he pointed to Cunningham and let his tone become more animated, "That man there was helping Temple-Speer punch above its weight. With hardly a moment to draw breath from what sounds like a punishing trip itinerary, and while we were all enjoying our free time, he was meeting with the highest echelons of Indonesia's government. And what he learned has given us a 24-hour advantage to destroy our competitors. Ernest, would you care to explain?"

"Told you," Charlie whispered. Pleased that he'd been proved right about the Tanamur omission.

Cunningham began. "Thank you, Major." His quiet, considered delivery was clearly going to contrast with the tone Speer had adopted to lift the spirits of 'his troops' that morning.

"Good morning, gentlemen. I'll be brief because, as Major Speer has already indicated, time is literally precious today. Last night, I met with Finance Minister Mar'ie Muhammed and…" he paused; "President Suharto."

There was an audible gasp around the room as he confirmed the rumor.

Letting the reaction wax and sufficiently wane, Cunningham continued. "Thursday will herald a Finance Ministry announcement that the Rupiah is to float freely on the currency markets."

He looked out over his audience and witnessed his staff exchanging glances. Catching Robert Watson's eye, he invited him to speak. With the exception of Cunningham, everyone called the company's Senior Economist 'Big Rob.' Uncomfortable with public speaking, Rob shifted his considerable mass and crossed his arms. "You and I spoke at length last night, Ernest, but I still think that a free-floating Rupiah sounds like a controlled suicide, even with an IMF aid package in the offing."

"Yes," Cunningham agreed dryly. "Like Robert and I, many of you will be questioning the wisdom of what will, at best, become an amplified correction of an over-valued currency. The IMF has, of course, been doling out aid packages to Thailand and the Philippines in return for their acquiescence to politically poisonous financial conditions. But I was privately assured last night that Suharto's people might yet test the IMF's resolve with a dollar peg if they deem it necessary. For now, that information is ours and ours alone." He clicked his fingers. "The question is, what are we going to do with it."

Stepping over to the whiteboard, he wrote the words 'Workload' and 'Strategy.'

"Let's consider workload. There are real bargains in Asian stocks for true long-term investors, but as we know, most clients talk long-term while fretting about the here and now. So, if any of you still have expatriate clients with heavy Asian portfolios, act swiftly and position them in the more cautious Hanthorpe options highlighted by Robert's team. With respect to our fund clients, be prepared for a significant uptick in requests for local currency transfers to Sterling, Deutschmarks, and the Dollar."

"Now," he pointed to the whiteboard again. "Strategy. We alone know that the Indonesians may well reinstate the dollar peg for their currency, but we'll deal with that later. Right now, we need to act on some first-class intelligence Terence has gleaned. Intel that, when shared, must stay within these walls. Do I make myself clear?

The crisis might be killing off Cain's client base, but it was also regenerating his sense of wonder about the world of international finance. He looked around the room, taking in the air of anticipation. Everyone was nodding.

"Okay then. But dismissal will be immediate for anyone who leaks this information."

Cunningham let the warning sink in before continuing. "China is ramping up its US investments and buying large quantities of US debt so that Clinton can balance the budget before the end of his second term. In return, Beijing has asked Washington to ignore its first impulse to remedy the dire economic outlook here in Asia, allowing China to make the most of the market misery. The Fund is bullish on US markets already, so I've instructed Robert and his team to mine new China and China-related opportunities because we also need to make the most out of this crisis. Today will be the perfect opportunity to boost our Fund's performance this quarter."

He glanced briefly but pointedly at 'Big Rob,' "And with the Chinese opportunities Robert will doubtless discover, our medium and long-term outlook will prove very positive too."

Excited chatter immediately followed Cunningham's call to action, and David Speer used it to round off the meeting. "A Fund that beats the odds in a downturn will buy you and Temple-Speer some extremely valuable credibility." He clapped his hands and gave his battle orders. "Okay, troops, three trading days till the weekend. We have a 24-hour head-start, so let's make sure we devour the competition."

© Steven Clark 2023
Lynnburn, Amisfield, Dumfries & Galloway, UK

The re-energized staff banged their fists on the conference table enthusiastically. Charlie shouted, "Jia You!" The looks he received obliged him to explain, "It's how the Chinese cheer each other on."

Cunningham added, "Jia You. Literally to add oil." Then ignoring Charlie's look of bewilderment, he added, "By the way could you and Shaw remain behind for a short while? Terence would like to learn how you are getting on with your preparations. The next couple of days are going to be hectic but rest assured, I will look after Andreas on Friday."

After that statement, he finally lost his increasingly desperate battle to stifle a yawn.

[ ]

As well as the surprise encounter with a strangely anxious President Suharto last night, Cunningham had also dealt with a very tetchy Sir James and a sleepy Rob Watson.

Sir James made sure their telephone call got off to a bad start when he reminded Cunningham, 'I don't trust bloody journalists.' He'd been 'most perturbed' when Suharto's people telephoned to enquire if Pyle really was employed by Temple-Speer. Cunningham should have known his attempt to get Pyle invited to last night's soiree would prod Indonesia's secret service into action. He defended the American by belatedly sharing his revelation about Clinton and the Chinese. Sir James also doubted the US would actually allow its Asian allies to suffer unduly, but just like Cunningham, he changed his mind when he heard the IMF's reading of the Rupiah floatation. His belligerence vanished, and he told Cunningham to find new China investments. Cunningham capitalized on the change of mood by conveying the President's request that Sir James get in contact. Then he won approval for the Hong Kong plan he'd already launched before deftly leveraging the growing self-satisfaction at the other end of the line to mention his intention to retire. Sir James seemed to take the news in his stride, but Cunningham was still wary.

Feeling relaxed after skillfully navigating that mentally demanding conversation, Cunningham's joy proved as capricious as ever when he called and awakened Rob Watson. He was supposed to be pulling an all-nighter, devising investment strategies. Cunningham's late night drained into an equally early morning to receive a debrief from Big Rob, and now he just wanted to sleep.

[ ]

When everyone had left the conference room, Pyle looked at Cain and Charlie and came to a swift conclusion. "I reckon you two need a bolt of caffeine just as badly as me. I'd prefer a hit of local kopi if you know a good place. That stuff's so strong it'll get me through the entire friggin day."

Swapping the cool marble floors of their office tower for the baking-hot concrete outside, they discussed their 'legendary progress,' as Charlie called it, during their walk to the coffee shop. Their lack of questions should have been of greater concern to a man who'd spent his entire adult life asking them, but Pyle's sleep-deprived brain was still trying to recover from last night's revelry. He'd made it through the early briefing with Cunningham, Speer, and Rob, but he was fading fast.

A step up from sitting at a street cart, the coffee shop frequented by Temple-Speer staff was clean and simple, boasting an air-conditioning unit that actually worked, and most importantly, served fantastic coffee and local snacks.

Lena arrived just as a second round of cups brimming with thick, aromatic Indonesian kopi was being delivered to the table where her

© Steven Clark 2023
Lynnburn, Amisfield, Dumfries & Galloway. UK

colleagues were sitting. They persuaded her to join them, but glancing at her watch, she still asked for a takeaway cup of tea.

All three men were obviously starting to feel the benefits of their first shot of caffeine and were chatting quite animatedly.

Pyle had barely begun working at Temple-Speer before Cunningham sequestered him for the crisis-spawned fact-finding trip around the region. So having read the man's colorful bio while stuck in a traffic jam one day, Cain wanted to know more. Pyle obliged with lines Cain recognized from the bio suggesting that he'd recited his story many times before.

"Yeah, dropping into the aftermath of Tet in '68 was rough. But as a cameraman, the viewfinder distanced me. What should have been terrifying was actually exhilarating. I did multiple tours and eventually became a correspondent. The cold war cliches like 'Bamboo Curtain' and 'Domino Theory' served me well throughout the '70s transitioning from Vietnam's anguish into Polpot's reign of terror in Cambodia. But by the '80s, Asia was changing. War and dislocation gave way to economics and interdependence. I needed to change my script, so I turned to business journalism, charting the rise of Asia's Four little Tigers' and post-Mao China.

Despite Pyle's almost verbatim recital of his bio, Cain still shook his head in respectful disbelief. "Wow, what a life."

"Most definitely Pak Terence," Lena chipped in. "And you are quite famous too." She paused as a coy smile spread across her face. "Such an Asia expert. You have lived here *much* longer than I have."

Pyle feigned indignation at Lena's little dig and they all laughed.

After taking a sip of his coffee, Charlie tilted his head with a ponderous expression. "Yeah, such a successful career in journalism. Makes me wonder why you'd jack it all in to come work with us."

"I nearly didn't. Ernest treated me to a fantastic meal, but he strafed me all night with questions about possible outcomes from the Thai Baht meltdown. I mean, Jesus, this was barely 24 hours after it happened. But as grueling as he can be, Ernest is also very persuasive. He'd read my bio and pointed out that it was almost two decades since my last 'change of script,' as he put it. He suggested another script change, and here I am."

Cain looked at his watch. "Shit, we better get a move on. Today's the day we're supposed to be killing the competition. Cunningham's going to kill us if we stay here much longer."

6)   Meeting Ruby

Hong Kong's hotel rooms are notoriously compact, but that wasn't an issue for Cain and Charlie, who were happily ensconced in two huge, harbor-facing JW Suites at the Marriot. They'd been relaxing in Cain's suite, eating the complimentary fruit and cakes while watching CNBC Asia try to get to grips with its Rupiah floatation punditry.

Charlie yawned and announced, "Right, I've been up since before dawn, so I need a perk-me-up shower. If I'm gonna be a rich boy, I better be smelling a lot fresher than the Fragrant Harbor tonight. And Pyle said this Ruby would be worth the effort."

Hearing his door close, Cain stood up and walked over to the window. With a cup of Jasmine tea in one hand and a Lao Po Bing or 'Wife Cake' pastry in the other, the young man who stared across the harbor to Kowloon from his 33rd-story suite was both nervous and self-satisfied.

Not so very long ago, he'd been able to savor a moment of contentedness. But like an old television that's beginning to go on the blink, his inability to stabilize a picture of happiness in his mind's eye was becoming more pronounced. An unwelcome memory occluded the harbor view, obliging him to relive the time when his father advised him to pursue a Master's degree instead of 'running away to join a bunch of shady salesmen.' He, of course, ignored the advice and, for a good 18 months, had basically forgotten the whole episode. But ever since the financial crisis began to unhinge the deadbolt surety of his job, the memory began to haunt him. Gazing through the window where his intruded mind had created the image of his father, he used his present circumstances to answer back. "Just a salesman, eh?" he muttered. "Well, I must be doing something right. You got as far as County Fermanagh. If only you could see where I am."

He tried to ease away his anguish with a sip of tea and realized that, in this moment, he actually felt closer to the Major than his father. He shook his head but couldn't uproot the thought as he considered the delicate new shoots of an advantageous new relationship.

Not long after he'd returned from the coffeeshop with Pyle and Charlie, the Major called Cain into his office, where he showed such a degree of concern that Cain was forced to defend his decision to go to Hong Kong, a defense he blithely fashioned into an opportunity to demonstrate his appetite for advancement.

"To be honest, Major, I'd like a position with greater responsibility. I have a firm grasp of what's happening in his historic moment for Asia, and I hope this assignment will allow me to demonstrate my true worth."

The Major nodded slowly, but the concern in his eyes was undiminished. "As long as you're sure, son. But don't push too hard for information. On one level, trying to winkle intel from a company sounds like a bit of a caper; but be under no illusion, this caper comes with inherent risk."

That was the first time the Major hadn't addressed him by his surname. And of all the forms of address he could have used, he'd chosen the word 'son,' an intimacy that wasn't lost on Cain. It strengthened his waning conviction, and he answered, "Yes, Major," with renewed gumption.

They heard Cunningham's voice from beyond the Major's door. "Come on, everyone, make the most of this invaluable head start!" he barked. "Let's make some real money today."

Speer sniggered at Cunningham's unusual gusto and then reached over to his mobile as it beeped. "It's made that noise twice. I know how to make calls, and Lena showed me how to play 'Snake,' but beyond that, this phone's a bloody mystery. What does that sound mean?"

"It means you've got an SMS, Major." It was a return to surnames, but the formality had been breached, and Cain was just grateful for another opportunity to help. "Nice phone, the 8110, or 'banana phone' as it's known."

Speer nodded, but it was a nod that suggested Cain be more focused on his explanation. His employee pointed at the screen. "See that icon? It means you've got an SMS, a text message."

"Text message?" Speer looked confused. "How do I see it?"

Cain asked for the phone and showed Speer how to navigate through the menu. "You have two messages. Both from the same local number. Do you want me to open them?"

Speer got calls from work and less frequently from his wife, who more typically contacted him on his apartment telephone. "Go ahead, Shaw, every day's a school day, eh?" Cain opened the first message. *'Hi, David. Call me when u hv e time.'*

Speer looked confused, so Cain explained, "That's text-speak. It saves characters because you only get 160: 'hv' means 'have' and 'e' means 'the.'"

"Shorthand, understood," the Major asserted. "Kind of fun, really. But no one contacts me this way. What does the other message say?"

And there it was. Cain could feel himself blushing, and Speer looked equally embarrassed. *'BTW, this is Feronika e dancr frm Tanamur last nite. Remember? Call me xx.'*

Cain watched as Speer's face fell. He filled the ensuing silence with words that bought him time to assess his next step; "Right then, Shaw.

That was plain enough." He paused, arriving at a compass bearing for his future relationship with the lad in front of him. "Secrets are preferable to lies, Shaw. Don't want you second guessing."

Cain was squirming even before Speer had finished speaking. Feronika must be the dancer the Major was watching. He must have somehow spoken to her. Although he was wishing the ground would open up and swallow him, he smiled and could only imagine how hollow it looked.

Like a precious ornament that's been accidentally knocked, the Major's pride began to wobble. "Feronika was performing at that club last night. I bumped into her outside, and we chatted."

He sighed, the final wobble giving way to the inescapable fall. "Over the last few weeks, I've been almost at the end of my tether, especially when Ernest and Terence were away. It really wore me down. Talking to Feronika last night, I recognized that I needed to relax and possibly enjoy the company of someone who has nothing to do with work. So, I gave her my number." He paused again. Cain could feel the Major longing for his compassion. "As I said, secrets are better than lies, and I'm trusting you with my secret. I will probably call her. More than that, I can't say because I just don't know."

Cain knew he was blushing. He'd been absolutely right about the Major feeling left out by Cunningham and Pyle. He needed to say something and made a real effort to sound as mature as possible. "Major, as you said, secrets are preferable. You know you have my respect. You also have my word."

Speer nodded and crossed his arms. "Thank you, Shaw. I know I can rely on you."

[ ]

The doorbell rang, and Charlie shouted, "Allo meester Shaw, time por your sensual massage." Stirred from his thoughts and chuckling, Cain ran to open the door to make him stop.

Showered and wrapped in a hotel dressing gown, Charlie barged in and stood by the window. "What a bloody view, eh? We need to come back here on our own time for a platoon of two 'Jollyboys' on the Fragrant Harbor."

Cain was still emerging from the memory of the Major's revelation, prompting Charlie to ask, "Hey, Earth to Cain! You in there?"

"We should definitely come back," Cain stammered. "Charlie, just out of interest, why do you keep saying 'Fragrant Harbor?'"

Charlie stood closer to Cain and pointed, "That water down there is the arse-end of the Pearl River delta. You can only imagine how it used to stink in the old days. Hong Kong's Chinese name is Xiang Gang, which can be translated as Fragrant Harbor. Probably one of the world's greatest euphemisms."

The phone rang. It was the front desk asking if Ms. Ruby Miller could be sent up.

"Dear me, she's keen. I was hoping for a nap," Charlie complained after Cain told the front desk he was expecting her.

"It's already four o'clock," Cain pointed out. "And you should be well rested. You weren't even conscious for take-off! Mind you, those Cathay Pacific business class seats were really comfy."

"You're not wrong there," Charlie affirmed. "So nice to be spoiled rotten up the front of a plane."

Cain straightened the bed linen where he'd been lying earlier. "You know, Charlie, we've been stuck in the office with a bunch of hairy-arsed blokes for the last couple of days, so we need to watch our language around this, Ruby. And I reckon you need to switch on that well-to-do accent of yours again to make sure it sticks all night."

"I definitely will, mate. But I don't want this Ruby woman to think that I actually talk like that. Maybe just give her a few minutes of pure, unadulterated Lam before I become Charlie Cheung."

Cain did a double-take. "I thought you were going to be Charlie Yeo?"

Charlie shrugged his shoulders; "Cheung, Yeo, what's the difference? If Cunningham had bothered to do any proper research, he might have chosen Limanto. I believe that's a common switch for Chinese Indonesians who used to be called Lam."

"Well, use Limanto then!" Cain urged.

"I'm not squandering this opportunity on a bunch of investment bankers. While I'm performing here in Hong Kong, I want to borrow the family name of Jackie Cheung. In my opinion, the absolute God of Cantopop's 'Four Heavenly Kings.'"

Cain might have argued, but there was a knock at the door, so he warned Charlie, "I just hope you can remember who you are while keeping up that posh accent."

"Well, I'm guessing you're probably not Charlie," Ruby declared as Cain opened the door. Stepping forward with a beaming smile, she introduced herself, kissed him on both cheeks, and waltzed into the room. Without breaking stride, she proclaimed, "Charlie! Super pleased to meet you too!" and conferred the same cheek-kissing routine on him.

Despite her high-energy persona, Ruby's voice was wonderfully smooth, and her accent impeccably posh. Slim and athletic, her skin tone and sun-streaked hair suggested a woman who liked the outdoors. When she turned to him again, Cain saw the detail of her pretty face and her remarkable hazel-colored eyes.

"I hope my arrival hasn't interrupted anything," she intimated in a cheeky tone.

Cain and Charlie looked at each other vacantly. Seeing they were none-the-wiser, Ruby tugged at the fleecy lapels of Charlie's dressing gown.

"Jaysis!" shouted Cain as Charlie tried to protect his modesty. "I was just telling him that we'd better watch our Ps and Qs. I didn't even notice he wasn't bloody dressed!"

Charlie declared, "There's no need for the verities of fashion when one is in repose." Now his accent seemed to mirror Ruby's gently.

Recovering from her laughter, Ruby wasted no time. "So, are you ready for tonight? We're meeting three of Harrier's bankers: Richard Stokes-Leighton, Jeremy Lyons, and Jared Hing. I thought it was only going to be Lyons and Stokesy as they're good friends, but it seems Hing invited himself along. And as he's the nephew of the bank's owner, I guess the other two couldn't say no. I've interviewed Lyons several times about ASEAN and Indonesia because that's his area of specialization. Stokes-Leighton is decent enough and quite a funny, campy character. I've only met Hing briefly once. But people here tend to move between banks quite often, and I've heard rumors that he can be a bit schizo at times. He's easily identifiable from the other two. Says he's Eurasian even though he's only a quarter European. He's basically Chinese, as the surname suggests."

After hearing Ruby's thumbnail sketch of Tsang's nephew, a look of concern furrowed Cain's brow. "Tsang's nephew? Seems like we've attracted some top-level attention."

Ruby registered his concern, and he was reassured when she explained, "He's not at all top-level. His designation is probably lower than the other two guys we're meeting."

Charlie was hot on Ruby's heels, adding, "Maybe he's just gunning to impress his uncle then. He heard we were from Indonesia and thought he'd try to see if he could get any insights about the economy down there. I mean, that's what got Cunningham's so-called antennae twitching about Harrier and Indonesia in the first place."

Cain put his momentary discomfort down to a misunderstanding of Hing's position at Harrier. And if Charlie was right about him just trying to impress his boss, then maybe Hing wasn't so different from himself. He stole another look at Ruby's pretty face and, feeling quite dazzled, thought he should attempt to sound more confident with an offhand remark. "Jeremy Lyons, Jared Hing, and the inevitable double-barrel with Stokes-Leighton. How come these fellas are never called Jimmy MacLeish or Billy Flynn?

"Actually, there are loads of toffee-nosed, wanky bankers drinking, snorting, and bonking their way through Lan Kwai Fong. Or, if they're too old and fat, they're paying for it by taking their todgers to Lockhart Road in Wan Chai..."

Ruby paused, aware of the fixed stares she was receiving. "Did I say something wrong? "Nothing wrong at all," Cain replied. "Just relieved to hear your... frank way of speaking." "Oh, I can be all high-nosed when necessary, but this is more me," she confessed.

"That's a relief," admitted Charlie. "Now, what else should we know about Lyons, Stokes-Leighton, and was it, Hing?"

"By the way, both of you get a gold star for remembering the three names. As I said, Lyons is our man for Indonesia, and I suspect he has a crush on me. I'll try to ensnare him if you two can handle the others.

And if I'm not wrong about Stokes-Leighton, I think he might be rather taken with you, Charlie. Just a hunch."

"He's your man, Charlie," Cain teased.

Charlie ignored him. "No problem at all, Ruby, I'll manage young 'Stokesy.' You go for Lyons, and Shaw here will thrust his Celtic charms at young master Hing."

Cain didn't bite at Charlie's homo-erotic tease either. "You know, I don't think these banker types will believe that high-born sophisticates like you two would hang out with the likes of me."

Ruby responded with a giggle in her voice, "Nonsense Cain, 'high-born' types like a bit of rough once in a while. By the way, where's that lovely accent from? Is it Irish or Scots?"

Cain was pleased with Ruby's use of the word 'lovely' to describe his accent. He didn't even mind the slight hint of condescension, so long as the 'bit of rough' remark might prove true.

He made sure he gave her a charming smile and said, "Fair play to you, Ruby. It's actually a mix of both, thanks to my parents." Quite pleased, he told himself; Less is more, Shaw, leave it at that.

And Charlie's next quip was helpful too; "Yeah, a mix of Paddy and Jock, and yet I can understand him. Mind you, it could have been worse." He switched to a northern English accent; "Ee could've been wun of them incomprehensible whippet-hugging, clog wearers from up north."

Ruby laughed. "Goodness, Charlie, you're good at accents."

"Yeah, he's a real dark horse," Cain grumbled. "Mind you, this is Charlie Cheung. Charlie Lam is utterly talentless."

© Steven Clark 2023
Lynnburn, Amisfield, Dumfries & Galloway, UK

"Cheung?" Ruby intoned, her hands settling on her hips, "I thought we were calling you Yeo?"

"Long story," Cain advised, still a little annoyed with Charlie's devil-may-care attitude. "Needless to say, Mr. Lam is dedicating his performance tonight to his hero Jacky Cheung."

Ruby looked peeved. "Don't you think you maybe should have told me? What if I introduced you wrongly?"

Caught out and head hanging, Cain was mortified and could see that even Charlie's vim had been dented.

"Okay, you two," she chided, hands still on her hips, "Are there any more changes I need to know about, or are we good to go?"

Trying hard to convince Ruby he was equal to the task ahead of them, Cain rested his hand on Charlie's shoulder and assured her, "Everything else is just as you read. We're good to go."

Ruby's face broke into a smile; "Okay then. Cheung. I can live with that. Jacky's song 'Wen Bie' is one of my all-time favorites.

With that, she and Charlie started singing, "Wo he ni wen bie…" but Cain was still conscious that he needed to be taken seriously. He interrupted them to ask, "Ruby, where are we going tonight?"

"Japanese restaurant first. The Harrier boys", she readied her hands to make finger quotation marks, "Simply adore the food of the Samurai."

"Tossers!" snarled Charlie.

Ruby countered cheerfully, "So you'll need to put those urges for good Cantonese grub on hold. But don't worry, I'll treat you both to a slap-up meal tomorrow night after you undoubtedly, help me win the dosh 'Yankee Pyle' promised."

"I'll let you know tomorrow," said Charlie, "I might be slumming it at the Peninsula with my cousin."

Cain happily noted that he might get some alone time with Ruby. "Local food sounds great to me. But thinking about tonight, where will we go after the restaurant?"

Ruby replied excitedly, "From the Queen's Road restaurant, it's a short walk to Lan Kwai Fong and Club '97. It's a favorite with the Harrier boys when they can actually get passed the door bitch. But as I happen to be very good friends with said door bitch, we'll be 'walked.' That should buy us some real cred."

"Great stuff!" said Cain while recalling a chat with the Major. "By the way, is DiscoDisco still considered cool?"

Ruby laughed. "DiscoDisco? Wild in its day but so last decade, darling."

Charlie froze. From his expression, Cain could see that a problem had occurred to him. He snapped his fingers in front of Charlie and reanimated him. "Hey! We'll need to confirm whether and why Harrier is spooked by Indonesia before we leave the restaurant for a noisy club."

Cain flinched; "Shit, you're right. We'll need to work fast!"

Ruby gathered them close, motioning with outstretched arms for a pre-match huddle. "Okay, boys, we need to stay focused on the job at hand. There will be alcohol. Make sure it loosens their tongues, not yours."

She then pulled back and slapped them both lightly on their shoulders. "Now get your glad rags on. That Japanese restaurant gets super busy. We'll have reservations, but time waits for no one in Hong Kong… and neither do good tables."

That evening…

7) A Scent of Fear on the Fragrant Harbor

"Irasshaimase !!"

The traditional Japanese welcome was bellowed at every arriving group of diners by the exuberant staff and their one-eyed head chef, Kobayashi-san.

The popular restaurant called 'Ureshii,' or 'Happy,' was buzzing with a lively Friday night crowd who'd clearly arrived straight from work. Sky-high rents in Hong Kong dictated that apartments were generally places to spend as little time as possible if one wanted to avoid the onset of claustrophobia. So here they all were, out on the town and living it large because their domiciles were simply too small.

The focal point of Ureshii was a central cooking island that created a perfect theater-in-the-round stage for the flamboyant Kobayashi and his equally dramatic staff. Pyromaniacal Teppanyaki chefs whipped up the crowd by flipping, chopping, slicing, and dicing exquisite meats, seafood, and vegetables at lightning speed among the flames; while the Sushi chefs enchanted diners with their artistically crafted morsels.

Conjecture over Kobayashi-san's missing eye ranged from freak kitchen accident to gruesome Triad or Yakuza punishment. But he made sure he put the survivor to good use, monitoring his higher-spending regulars to predict their culinary desires. Such clients included the high-spirited Harrier bankers in one of his highly prized, arched booths, so he made sure they were well plied with sake on the house. As usual, they'd only made a couple of orders before leaving it up to him to keep bringing 'interesting' dishes to them.

Ruby introduced Cain and Charlie to the three bankers. Richard Stokes-Leighton was by far the friendliest. Short and slightly pudgy with dark brown curly hair, he cheerily advised them to call him 'Stokesy.' Tall and stiff-backed, Lyons was a master of the firm handshake. A rather serious-looking character, his floppy blonde locks served to soften his overall bearing. And as Ruby had described him, Jared Hing was indeed Chinese.

Cain paid particular attention to Hing, who was of a similar height with a facial structure that was tight and defined. He noted how slim Hing was and tried to bolster his spirits, thinking that if push came to shove, he could take him. He, of course, recognized the folly of such a thought but needed a confidence boost after the way he'd handled himself during the introductions. Even Ruby noticed how anxious he was and gave him a look that suggested he get a grip of himself.

Thankfully, Stokes-Leighton and Hing took themselves off to the toilets, and Cain got a moment to calm down while Charlie and Ruby anchored the friendly chatter with Lyons. Seeing how relaxed they all were, his breathing became a subconscious activity once more, and his hands stopped sweating.

Nothing was said, but when Hing returned from the toilet, he was rubbing the side of his index finger against his upper front teeth. And Stokesy might have regretted his choice of a purple tie as it contrasted beautifully with the trace of white powder that had obviously escaped his nose.

Cain watched them knocking back Kobayashi-san's sake and knowing his head was clearer than theirs, and his self-confidence was largely restored. As well as the sake and the fine Japanese food, he realized they were also being fed generous portions of ham-fisted, alcohol-muddled sales banter. Cain also watched with admiration as Charlie made noises about the Cheung family's wealth and the search for safe havens before Suharto's government took steps to prevent large-scale capital flight.

True to her word, Ruby Miller was taking merciless advantage of the arched booth's cramped space down at the far end of the table to isolate an obviously smitten Jeremy Lyons. In doing so, she was also preventing him from playing any meaningful role in the conversation being led by the uproarious Stokesy and his slightly quieter colleague Hing.

The chatter about Indonesia was only partially attributable to Charlie's presence because the currency flotation was being debated at several Ureshii tables that evening. Stokesy, however, had had enough, and his almost petulant declaration that 'it was now the weekend' helped facilitate a conversation shift from current affairs to current fashions, a topic with which Charlie was well-versed. All three bankers wore the same three-button style of suit that Charlie claimed he'd introduced to Jakarta. And just like Charlie, they paired those suits with colored shirts and closely matched ties. Of the three, Hing was the most committed to such color coding, pairing his red shirt and tie with the red-framed, rather feminine spectacles he was constantly adjusting. The only clash that undermined the ensemble were his curiously striking green eyes.

Cain wondered if they were just being polite to a prospective client, but Stokesy and Hing did appear to be genuinely fascinated as Charlie preached the grooming wisdom of 'Nancy's Post-Workout Overhaul.'

"Oh, my God!" Stokesy shrieked. "Shaving in a steam room! That makes so much sense, doesn't it, Jared?"

Hing tutted at Stokesy's over-the-top reaction and nodded uncommittedly. "Yeah, I guess I never thought about shaving so much before."

Cain, who'd heard Charlie's male-grooming sermon many times before, was very aware that time was slipping by. So too was Kobayashi-san. After delivering a steady supply of dishes to the Harrier table, he deduced that it was time for a dessert and served them with mochi balls filled with green tea and red bean ice cream.

Stokes-Leighton screamed, "These are an absolute triumph!"

Noise levels dipped considerably as satisfied diners left the restaurant to shake off their working weeks at a bar or club. And with fewer new diners, Ureshii staff members were no longer compelled to roar their "Irasshaimase" greeting every few minutes. The unruly noise coming from the Harrier bankers' table, therefore, drew some unhappy attention. Cain was used to being called 'Gweilo' by Charlie but heard another diner direct it at their table in a much colder manner. Thankfully the ever-watchful Kobayashi immediately attended the offended table, offering sake samples to the diners.

Charlie's face had become red, and he looked quite tipsy when he put his hands over his sake cup and beer glass to prevent Stokesy from refilling them. "Slow down, Stokesy, I need a piss."

But Charlie wasn't about to get any respite from his new best friend, who shouted, "Me too!"

As they waltzed off to the toilets, Hing had to prod Cain to get his attention. He pointed at Lyons and Ruby; "If I were a betting man, I'd say that Stokesy was about to steal a potential client from under Lyons' nose."

There was no reaction from Lyons, so Cain attempted to be both supportive and funny whilst keeping his voice down so as not to offend Ruby. "Yes, one colleague on the job while the other one is…" he nodded his head in Lyons' direction, "on the job."

Hing smiled at his comrade-in-mirth, but there was no warmth in it. He then turned to Lyons and shouted, "Trying to be funny over here, but Ruby is clearly the only one who can get a rise out of Lyons." He began laughing at his own joke in a horribly exaggerated fashion.

Ruby's admirer turned slowly to his colleague, smirked, and kissed her passionately. Cain's face fell, and Hing saw it. He observed with a sneer, "I agree. I also thought you were more her type."

Cain was taken aback by what he'd seen but hoped Hing was correct. Meantime, he needed to concentrate on the matter at hand. The Major had warned him of the assignment's potential dangers, but apart from Hing's inability to tell the difference between humor and crass insults, these guys all seemed pretty harmless, he reassured himself. Recognizing that this might be his best opportunity to chat with Hing and try to find out about Harrier and Indonesia, he said, "Actually, Jared, what you said about Charlie as a client was spot on. I've been staying at his family home for a while, and from what he says about Indonesia, I reckon his family will be looking for an institution like Harrier to park their wealth."

Hing downed the sake in his ornately pottered doll's house size of cup and settled it on the table noiselessly. "You two have known each other for quite a while, yes?"

"Since our university days," replied Cain.

Hing spent an absurdly long time contemplating Cain's brief answer. So long, in fact, that Cain had time to cross his arms, realize how defensive that looked, and uncross them again, only to find he no longer knew what to do with them. In his discomfort, he started to re-evaluate his view that these guys were indeed harmless, and feeling obliged by the silence to say more, he started, "We met at fresher's week and that…."

"So, what does Charlie do with his time these days?" Hing asked, smiling almost contritely at the effects of his own rudeness.

Cain assumed the banker meant work and was just about to respond when Hing spoke again: "In terms of work, I mean. Did he venture straight into the family businesses after he graduated, or does he do his own thing?"

Cain had endured this destabilizing kind of questioning from his father, and fear gripped him as he realized he might be out of his depth. Hing was already in control, and he seemed to know it too. Cain looked for Charlie. What the hell was he doing in those toilets? Shit! He was all alone. He smiled under Hing's gaze. He needed to deal with this posh boy and told himself he was more than capable.

He needed to take a risk and venture well into the margins of Cunningham's so-called legend. Speer would surely want him to improvise. So long as he was confident and consistent, Cain could steer the conversation back toward Harrier. He remembered a phrase he'd never heard before meeting Charlie, a phrase the Chinese-looking self-declared Eurasian would also know.

"Charlie's a good guy," Cain began. "Like yourself probably, he understands the importance of family and…" he paused for effect, "Oh, what's that phrase Charlie uses? Ah yes, he understands the importance of Asian familial piety, so he went straight into helping manage the various strands of the family business."

A lopsided smile settled on Hing's face, and this time, it contained a little warmth. Cain felt that he'd connected somehow as Hing adjusted his spectacles once more and wriggled forward in his seat, casting a faintly exasperated look at Lyons. "I only found out that Westerners had no idea what familial piety meant when I was schooling in the UK." It was as if Hing couldn't help himself, he had to provoke ill-feeling with an insult. "Of course, having spent so many years in the

UK, I quickly realized that Westerners had lost all respect for so many things. I suppose that's why familial piety is a forgotten term for you people and evidently a forgotten concept."

"You're probably right," Cain conceded. "I mean, now that I'm living in Singapore, I hear their politicians talking about the importance of Asian family values almost every other day." He rubbed his hands, which were sweating again. "Charlie's very westernized but still wants to uphold those values. It's family and, therefore, the family business that must come first. That's why he's looking to protect the family's wealth. And it's not a good time to have money in Indonesia right now."

Hing glanced at Lyons, and Cain thought he detected a flash of anger. He started to think that maybe the two bankers had a grudge because there was definitely more fueling Hing's intensity than the lines he snorted in the toilets. Cain couldn't help but swallow when Hing's eyes settled on him again, but he'd covered his neckline by letting his chin rest on his hand.

Hing's expression had thankfully softened. "You're right about Indonesia." He looked at Lyons again. "Any Asian analyst worth his salt would tell you there's nothing worthwhile down there. Unfortunately, my uncle Harry trusted a Gweilo to manage our South-East Asia business, and despite all the omens, our love-struck friend at the end of the table stubbornly maintains his bullishness. I mean, you've just visited the place; have you ever been on a bus in Jakarta?"

"I guess I'm lucky. I've been driven around in Charlie's cars," Cain lied. "But from what I've seen, Jakarta's buses are terrible. The city's crying out for the kind of metro system you have here and in Singapore."

"But until that unlikely day arrives…." Lyons' voice interrupted Cain. He was standing right over the pair of them, and his eyes were burning into Hing while he tried to maintain a ghoulish smile. "…Our Indonesia investments will remain safe and sound, my friend. Isn't that right Jared?"

"Safe and sound," Hing echoed, glowering at his sake cup.

Lyons' tone changed completely. "Right then, I was just about to charge Ruby's cup. How about you two?"

Cain was about to take a drink but thought better of it. 'What the hell is Harrier invested in?' He held out his cup for Lyons, who could only add a small drop before the cup was full. Given that Charlie's face had already turned red, as it did whenever he drank too much, Cain knew he had to carefully restrict his own alcohol intake.

At that moment, a notably less gleeful Stokes-Leighton returned with Charlie. They forced Cain and Hing to make space by sliding down the benches on their respective sides of the booth's table. Their return destroyed Cain's ability to focus on what Lyons had said during his angry intervention in the conversation with Hing. He searched his memory, but Lyon's words meant nothing really.

Charlie and Stokesy were regaling the group with their adventures. After the toilet, the pair of them had sneaked up the staff stairwell and managed to get onto a third-story balcony. Cain was quite relieved. He thought he'd seen a whole new side of Charlie emerging.

"The night air was so good," Stokesy bragged.

"I can't believe we got away with it," Charlie admitted in a quieter tone.

Cain tried to ignore them and use their return as cover for his thoughts. Jaysis, what did I say that made Lyons defend Harrier's Indonesia investments? I'd just spoken about the mass transit networks in

Singapore and Hong Kong. Lyons said their investments would be fine until the day Jakarta ever builds its own metro system.

Stokesy shouted, "Come on you lot, let's get off to Club 97."

As Cain hadn't responded, Charlie repeated the instruction loudly into his ear.

"Fuck!" Cain hissed, annoyed that his thoughts were disturbed. He glared at Charlie.

"Come on, the night's not getting any younger," Stokesy claimed. And after having forced his way onto the bench, he slid back down it again and stood up. Placing one hand on the table and reaching across to Charlie with the other, he declared, "Come on, Charlie, these slow coaches will need to catch us. Lyons, as you've been so bloody anti-social, you can pay the bill."

"I wouldn't call him 'antisocial' at all," retorted Ruby. Gazing into Lyons' eyes, she purred, "Club '97? Oh yes, I'm well up for it."

"Lyons is well up for it too, by the look of things, but you need to ask yourself what 'it' actually is," said Hing, pointing his index finger at his smitten colleague's crotch and reprising his quite disturbing laugh.

They took themselves out into the humid air that enveloped Queens Road Central. Charlie was chatting to Stokesy and Hing, the latter sporting a venal smile that occasionally broke into a leer.

"Don't worry, Charlie, I'll make certain Stokesy here gets started on your relationship with Harrier first thing on Monday. And as our newest client, I hope you can provide us with some referrals to reach out to some of your friends and family."

Cain was disappointed at failing to get to the bottom of Harrier's apparently contentious Indonesia investment. But watching Charlie, he perked up, knowing he could probably take the piss out of his friend for weeks about that toilet break. He sighed and then inhaled the warm night air, comparing Hong Kong's humidity to that of Jakarta and Singapore.

He looked up to see the balcony Charlie and Stokesy had mentioned. It was nothing special, so he let his gaze drift higher. At night, Hong Kong's streets glisten with neon advertisements, uber-chic building facades, and alluring shop windows; but as Cain's eye-line rose beyond the fourth and fifth floors, he realized his vision had strayed into taboo territory. No structural facelifts had ever been conducted up there. Naked, apart from the decades of city dirt that veiled their unappealing concrete skins, these buildings were grotesquely obliged to reveal their true age to anyone who happened to look above the street-level retail smokescreen. Mercifully, their modesty was rarely breached as their sheer drabness proved to be a most effective ally in the struggle for invisibility. Like a child losing the battle to stifle a sneeze during a game of hide and seek, the only attention these upper floors ever received was when a drip from an overworked air conditioning unit splashed on the head of an unpleasantly surprised pedestrian.

Charlie startled Cain from his after-hours daydream. "You alright there, mate?" It took a moment, but Cain identified the problem. "Charlie! Your accent."

Charlie's eyes were wide, and his stare was frantically intense, but he still recognized the urgency in Cain's tone. "I wouldn't worry, mate. I'll watch it, but I honestly think we're okay from here on in."

Cain was confused; "I thought you were pissed. Your face is red."

Charlie checked the bankers over his shoulder. "Nah, I'm just like loads of Asians. My face goes red after a single drink. I've quietly spilled loads of sake.

Cain took a chance. "I think Harrier does have a problem. Something to do with Jakarta not having a mass transit system."

Charlie commented, "So long as Jakarta doesn't have one, dilapidated buses are the only option for people like Lena."

Cain hissed, "Buses! Hing asked me if I'd ever been on a bus in Jakarta."

Charlie cautioned, "We've been talking too long already. I only came over here to pass you this card for a tailor. Stokesy gave it to me. I got nothing out of him. Nice guy, but useless. Try to remember exactly what was said between you, Hing, and Lyons, okay?"

With that, Charlie swung around and was once more the tipsy, fun-loving scion of a Jakarta multi-millionaire.

Ruby and Lyons poured themselves out of Ureshii. Kobayashi followed them, bowing deeply and wishing them all good night; "Oyasuminasai!"

"Omsumyamenai Kobayashi-san!" Stokesy shouted, engaging in his very own version of the Japanese language.

With Hing cackling and teasing his colleague about his dreadful Japanese, the group made their way along Queen's Road, following the crowds and increasing noise up D'Aquilar Street into Lan Kwai Fong. While trying to remain sociable, Cain wracked his brain to recall the exact words of the tantalizing chat with Hing that provoked Lyon's simmering reaction. He also tried but failed to ignore the remora-like presence of Lyons walking hand in hand with Ruby. Catching up with them, he asked, "How are you doing, Ruby? Seems like ages since we chatted."

Lyons looked a little put-out, but she laughed; "And hello to you, my dear Celtic pal. I was telling Jeremy that your multifaceted lineage is a lot like his name in that it encapsulates the British Lions. But in answer to your question, I am doing absolutely fine, darling."

Her rather personal response made him happy, and he was genuinely pleased to note that she seemed to be in control of what was happening between her and Lyons. He also hoped he'd manage to demonstrate that he'd regained his composure after the nerves Ruby had spotted at the start of the evening.

Chinese rule or not, people still needed to let off steam in the overcrowded territory. Post-handover, Club 97 was still the place to be seen, and getting on the water-tight guest list was notoriously difficult. It was, therefore, astonishing to behold Ruby breaking from the clutches of Lyons and shouting, "Hey bitch, Let me in! I'm here to play," as she strode past a long queue.

Hearing the declaration of intent, a tall, strikingly tattooed, platinum-blonde Chinese girl placed her guestlist clipboard on a podium and shouted back, "Come to Freda bitch," before embracing Ruby and sharing a full-blown, open-mouthed kiss with her.

Ruby wasn't the only one recovering from the kiss when Freda asked, "Who are your handsome boys? They can't all be yours."

A rather flustered Ruby introduced Cain, Charlie, and the bankers to "Freda, the meanest door bitch in Asia." Then, much to the displeasure of the queue, Freda gestured to the doormen to let her friends through. Ruby thanked Freda and was grabbed for another kiss that silenced the brief disquiet of those still waiting to get in.

Cain was gobsmacked by what he'd witnessed. He looked over to a clearly stunned Lyons until Stokes-Leighton slapped him on the shoulder to knock him out of his stupor. Then the happy banker skipped around Lyons and through the club's entrance shouting, "Wow! Ruby Miller strikes, and boom, we're in!" Then he yelled above the thumping bass sound emanating from 'Club,' as it was known by its regulars, "Jared, get our bottle of Chivas, and you better buy some champers too."

The purchase of two bottles of champagne prompted the staff to remove a reserved sign from a table near the dancefloor. It was a prime spot, and the bankers reveled in their VIP exposure. Cain had already learned that Ruby was doing fine, so he dragged Charlie, who was still ably performing the role of drunken rich boy, onto the dancefloor.

'Club' was packed, limiting any dance aspirations to little more than shuffling from one foot to the other and sticking one's hands in the air when the crowd's collective brain appreciated a particular tune.

Ruby and Lyons also took to the floor. Cain watched her with indiscreet admiration. "Jaysis, but that girl knows how to make the most of a tiny plot of dancefloor," he told Charlie.

"Can't say that I disagree, Shaw, but have you had any more thoughts about what Hing and Lyons said to you?"

Cain shook his head, still looking at Ruby. 'I wonder if she's managed to get anything out of Lyons yet." His voice took a sarcastic turn; "Christ knows she's putting in enough effort."

Charlie grabbed Cain's forearm. "Okay, I get it," he said in a weary tone. "You like the girl. Just remember why she's putting up with that arsehole. It's not an easy thing to do. I thought I could handle Stokesy, but I ended up telling him in no uncertain terms to back off. Of course, I immediately felt awful and tried to rectify the situation with kinder words. He said he was okay, but I definitely closed off an avenue of opportunity there."

Cain sighed; "Sorry you had to go through all that, pal. I'm also sorry to learn that I can't take the piss out of your mysterious toilet adventure anymore. And fair play to Ruby. She's trying her best."

Charlie added, "But from the look she gave me on the way here, I don't reckon she's made much headway."

Two and a half hours later, their much-coveted table was surrounded by a crowd that had somehow become even denser. Using the lure of champagne, Hing successfully landed a couple of girls who joined the table.

The initial happy and very excitable spirit of the group was shifting. Charlie leaned over to Cain and said; Well, we haven't worked out what's spooking Harrier, but at least we've survived the night. We'll soon be tucked up, safe and sound in our suites, ready to head home tomorrow."

Disappointed and tired, Cain had almost nodded off half an hour ago, but Charlie's comment instantaneously revived him. "Safe and sound. That's what Lyons said."

Charlie looked perplexed, so Cain explained. "I said Jakarta needs its own mass transit rail network, and he said, "Until that day comes, Harrier's investments will be 'safe and sound.' He raised his eyebrows when he said that, but I thought he was just doing it to make a point."

Charlie was suddenly reenergized too. "Safe and Sound. Those are the buses Lena takes to work every morning. Same red and white coloring as President taxis, and just as lethal."

Cain looked over at the bankers, who were absorbed with Ruby and the two champagne girls. Stokesy was dancing with a German banker friend. "I knew I'd heard 'safe and sound' somewhere in Jakarta. Hing even asked me if I'd ever ridden on a bus there."

Charlie gestured for Cain to come closer again. "Well, it won't take long for Big Rob to work out if our hunch is correct. Let's wait for Stokesy and his chum to sit down, and then we'll announce our intention to leave. We can call Lena later to let her know we think we've cracked it."

No sooner had they turned round to re-engage with the bankers when Ruby stood up to announce that she was leaving. Lyons said something about sharing a taxi, but Ruby advised that he'd be better making sure Hing and Stokes-Leighton got home safely. She then shouted over to Cain and Charlie, "Guys, if there are no cabs outside, head to the Foreign Correspondents' Club and grab one."

Turning to look at Lyons with wicked intent, she decreed, "Come here you."

Cain girded himself to witness another passionate kiss, but to his private joy, Ruby dispatched a passion-killing peck and disappeared into the crowd, terminally altering the group dynamic. Lyons masked his irritation by immediately joining Hing and his ladies. Stokes-Leighton, who'd seen Ruby leave, also returned to the table with Felix, who he'd introduced to them earlier with a wink, as 'my old chum.'

"Thank God for that," Cain murmured. And remembering that he was supposed to be Charlie's wingman, he nudged his friend to announce their departure.

Charlie shouted, "Gentlemen, tonight has been a blast. And thank you very much for a delicious dinner. It's been a pleasure hanging out with you, but it's also been a very long day, so Cain and I are heading off."

The bankers looked surprised, but Charlie pre-empted their resistance to the departure of a very rich potential client by adding, "Remember to try Nancy's overhaul Stokesy."

"Certainly will, Charlie," he replied before turning to Felix. "Darling, remind me to teach you Charlie's wonderful grooming technique." He then kissed Felix on the cheek and pulled a face; "You must, must do 'Nancy's overhaul' with me tomorrow. Your stubble is like sandpaper."

Hing grabbed his spectacles from one of the girls who was trying them on and giggling. He stood up and shouted over the music, "Charlie does Stokesy have your contact details?"

Cain interjected, "Ruby has our contacts. Pointless doing it here." Then he laughed before adding: "Writing telephone numbers on napkins is the best way to guarantee losing contact."

"Don't worry," assured Charlie; "I have your business cards, and I'll be in touch with Stokesy."

Hands were shaken, and final goodnights were said. Cain and Charlie believed they might have achieved their goal. They were excited, but exhaustion really hit them hard as they clambered up Lan Kwai Fong's steep streets to get a cab.

"This place is like an Asian San Francisco!" Cain exclaimed. "It's all up and down. I'm just glad the Correspondents' Club is up here on Lower and not Upper Albert Road. I'd get a nosebleed if it was on Upper."

Charlie agreed, adding, "With the possible exception of Stokesy, who was alright, I thought I'd get a nosebleed in the company of those other two tossers this evening. Do you think they act like that all the time? Or is it all for show?"

Cain pondered his answer: "You know what, Charlie? At the office, you and I are treated as outsiders. We're also a couple of British lads living in Jakarta, but I feel more at home with the Indonesians I meet than I do with our colleagues! And as for them Harrier boys, they weren't just foreign. They were friggin alien to me."

Charlie nodded, "I totally agree, especially with what you said about the friendliness of Indonesians."

"Hey, you're still talking like Charlie Cheung," Cain chuckled, bumping his friend with his shoulder. "Charlie laughed; "Dear me. I was talking like that for so long, I forgot I was doing it."

"You still are!" Cain pointed out.

Charlie shook himself as if a wasp had landed on him and commanded, "Charlie Cheung, get out of me!" Charlie Cheung be gone! He rested his hand on Cain's shoulder and looked him in the face. "How about now, guvnor?"

Cain couldn't help but chuckle as he wondered who the real Charlie Lam was.

8)   R-&-R in the SAR

Hong Kong Island

"Oh my god Ruby, I love this Siu Yuk! Don't tell my mum, but it's way better than hers."

Charlie's outburst was delivered while tucking into a large platter of mixed roast meats consisting of Siu Yuk, which is crispy roast pork; the barbecue pork called Char Siu; Roasted Chicken, Duck, and Goose. After last night's Japanese food extravaganza, Ruby had kept her promise to treat them to some typical Hong Kong cuisine.

There was nothing flashy about this Hennessy Road hole-in-the-wall restaurant. It would barely take five paces to walk past, and yet, behind the frontage, festooned with slabs of pork and whole, cooked species of poultry on hooks, the proprietors had managed to squeeze every centimeter of seating capacity from their compact space. All but one of the shiny laminate tables were filled with local diners, taking the lack of elbow room in their stride and heartily tucking into their meals.

Ruby was over the moon that Cain and Charlie liked her favorite restaurant. "Look at that guy over there making a bit of a meal out of his meal. See the waitress hovering? Any second now… And there she goes."

The waitress swooped in to clear the customer's noodle bowl as soon as he put down his chopsticks. "Now that's how to generate high customer turnaround. Finished or even just nearly finished, he has to leave or order more. And that's Hong Kong in a nutshell…. or noodle bowl."

Cain gazed across the busy restaurant to the crowded doorway. Ruby had already introduced them to Mrs. Yip, the sharp-faced, middle-aged owner, who seated diners, tabulated and handed out bills, collected payment, and shouted orders in raspy Cantonese at the kitchen. Ruby followed his gaze; "And busy though this place is, they also do Ngoi Mai."

Charlie nodded with a mouthful of Char Siu and rice, but Cain looked vacant. Ruby noticed his expression and explained, "Ngoi Mai is Cantonese for Takeaway."

"That Mrs. Yip never stops," Cain observed with real admiration as she demonstrated incredible mental dexterity and nimble footedness, constantly darting through groups of diners waiting for a table as well as those who'd popped in to collect their Ngoi Mai.

"I knew you'd like it here," Ruby gushed. "I reckon Mrs. Yip and her husband, who you sometimes hear yelling in the kitchen, feed everyone in this neighborhood at least once a week. You'd never guess, but the Yip's are rolling in it, and ever since Tiananmen eight years ago, they've been 'planting pearls' in the West."

Cain looked confused again, so she added, "Their plan is to sell up and join their kids. Mrs. Yip wants to escape what she calls 'Beijing's tightening grip of totalitarian rule.'"

Cain stopped eating. "Reading reports about the atmosphere after the handover, I thought the nerves had settled."

"Not quite," replied Ruby, "Hong Kongers are smart; they keep face and avoid trouble by saying nothing. But just like in any other country, if one could only listen to the chatter around the dinner table, you'd hear the unfiltered truth. After Tiananmen, the Kowloon immigration office was totally mobbed. It's calmed down since then, but people like the Yips are quietly ferreting away small fortunes to build lives overseas."

"It was kind of the same for my parents," Charlie remarked, wiping his glistening lips with a tissue. "They weren't sure which way Singapore was headed in the final years before Kuala Lumpur kicked it out of the federation in '65. The so-called race riots in the year before independence were the last straw. Looters ransacked my dad's watch shop in Geylang. It might have been a Chinese business in a Malay neighborhood, but they'd never had any real bother. I don't know where they got the money, but my parents moved to London a few months later. When your world's been turned on its head, you have to do something. 'Fight or flight,' I think they call it."

They all nodded in agreement before Cain broke the temporary silence caused by Charlie's very personal story. "Why did you say the 'so-called race riots?'"

"Something my dad explained when I was young," said Charlie. "He pointed out that we Chinese often use the term 'race.' When you think about it, Chinese isn't even an ethnicity! It's a word to describe a nationality. Following my dad's argument, they couldn't have been race riots. After all, there are only three racial categories."

"Not according to Singapore," Cain noted. "They've got four; Chinese, Malay, Indian, and Eurasian. They're all classified as a 'race' on those identity cards they carry."

"Charlie pointed his chopsticks till he'd swallowed his food. "And after what my old man lived through, he always said they should remove race from those cards to dilute any residual tensions."

Cain added, "My dad says the same kind of thing about Britain, Ireland, and the EU. Calling ourselves Europeans could help dilute the language of sectarianism in Northern Ireland.

"Interesting," Ruby exclaimed. "You have to wonder where transnationalism and globalization might take us."

Charlie swallowed a mouthful of duck and added, "I'd like to take the optimistic view, but there's also a chance that if times get tough, the promise of globalization will come crashing down and lead to further fragmentation."

Ruby laughed; "Hmm, I sense you two have had this conversation before."

"Yeah, once or twice," Cain admitted. "Our job makes us talk like that. But I guess it's the same for your job. Hey, maybe there's a report in there for you somewhere."

Ruby nodded thoughtfully. "Yeah maybe. The future; globalization or fragmentation?"

Then she clasped her hands together. "Hey Charlie, speaking of fragmentation and the earlier topic of your parent's world being turned upside down just before Singapore's independence. I was watching old footage of Lee Kuan Yew on TV when Singapore was booted out of Malaya. He actually cried! It's amazing footage."

"I think you mean Malaysia, not Malaya." Charlie corrected her. "And don't forget he also had the whole patriarchal Chinese thing going on," he added, pointing his chopsticks for emphasis with yet another mouthful of Char Siu. "It takes a hell of a lot for blokes like that to cry."

Cain had studied Singapore's modern history at university and now felt confident enough to pass comment. "I'd imagine Charlie's right, but Lee's world really had been turned upside down. He'd always known Singapore within Malaya or Malaysia, and yet all of a sudden, he found himself in charge of a couple of million people on an island with no resources. That kind of pressure would break anyone."

He'd wanted to talk about a paradigm shift, but Mrs. Yip arrived to refill their Jasmine tea. As she poured, Ruby asked how her children were doing. Mrs. Yip thanked her for asking and said they were all doing fine.

"Your friends. Where they from?" she asked.

"They're visiting from Jakarta, aunty, but they're both British."

Mrs. Yip's smile disappeared, and her face morphed into an expression of angry sadness. "Your bloody Thatcher! Abandon us to Peking. No more Hong Kong. Now we only Special Administrative Region of China. Nothing but a bloody SAR. My family, we all had very good life. Now we scatter to the four winds. Soon I must go to iceberg Canada to live with my kids. UK don't care, but we Hong Kong people, we don't forget."

No one at the table had expected that outburst, maybe not even Mrs. Yip. Cain watched as she strained her facial muscles to smile again. To his relief, she tried to save the situation. "But you just kids. Not politicians. Tell aunty when you have eat enough, and I bring you warming dessert called Tofu Fa. Free for you. Okay?"

"Very kind of you, aunty," said Cain, grateful that her anger had passed but also seeing through the desolate fragility of the poor woman's fixed smile.

As she turned to go, Ruby jumped up and followed her to the counter.

Cain motioned for Charlie to come closer and said, "Jaysis Charlie, fragmentation or union, it seems you can't please everybody at any bloody time."

Ruby returned, saying, "I know you like Indonesian Teh Tarik Cain, so you must try the Hong Kong version called Nai Cha. It's made with Carnation milk instead of condensed, so it's not so sweet."

Charlie chuckled wryly; "Yeah, you keep drinking that Teh Tarik, mate, and you'll be a prime candidate for diabetes."

Ruby tutted and scolded, "Aiyoh Charlie, don't say things like that! Instead, you can tell me how your boss reacted when you told him about Harrier and that bus company?"

"All I'll say is, if the boys at Harrier really are invested in that company, they're in deep shit. We only worked it out because those are the buses our receptionist Lena takes to work. She tells some terrifying tales.

"Yeah, if Safe & Sound has taken a load of money from Harrier, they certainly haven't spent it on their bus fleet," Cain added.

"But," Charlie intervened, "The Harrier news seemed to have made old Cunningham's decade worthwhile. He was taking notes of who we'd met and how we got the info. It might be Saturday, but he's got Rob Watson and his entire team collating data and trying to verify what we think we found out. Fingers crossed, if and when Rob comes through with that verification, Cunningham's going to tell Sir James immediately. As for us three, we're golden. Cunningham's not usually the most emotionally demonstrative of characters Ruby, but he was so happy he even waxed lyrical about a Peninsula Hotel barman called Jimmy Li. Told me to pass on his warmest regards to his dear old friend when I mentioned meeting my cousin there for drinks."

Cain shared a look with Charlie, "Hmm, a 'dear old friend.' How intriguing. Well, the old man's reaction sounds good for us; and I would imagine, for Temple-Speer." Then he turned to Ruby to share more news. "Of course, there's the bonuses if we're right about 'Safe & Sound,' but Cunningham also told Charlie he reckoned Sir James might move some of his Harrier money into Temple-Speer. An emergency fund to get us through this 'challenging time,' as he put it."

Cain halted his chatter abruptly when Charlie glared at him. Ruby noticed too, but chose to look to one side whilst blowing on her refilled jasmine tea. Charlie slapped the table and grinned. "Right, kids, I'm off to meet my cousin at the Peninsula. I'll love and leave you to enjoy yourselves, but not too much, Cain. We've got a flight tomorrow. Thanks for the grub, Ruby. You've no idea how much I miss proper Char Siu."

Charlie was smiling as he departed, but Cain knew the smile also contained a warning. He would need to watch himself around this attractive woman who also happened to be a very ambitious TV news producer. They didn't know her. Not really.

Mrs. Yip arrived with two cups of Nai Cha. A third cup had been made, but witnessing Charlie's departure, she left one behind.

"Mh goi aunty," Ruby just about managed to say before Mrs. Yip scurried off to help a waitress unload a trayful of bowls, plates, and cups of Nai Cha at another table.

"Let me cut to the chase here," said Ruby, bestowing her full attention on Cain. "I was working last night. No, that sounds awful. What I mean is … You saw me with Lyons, and it's been bothering me all day that you and Charlie might think badly of me."

Cain watched her search frustratedly for more words. She stammered, "What I mean is, it shouldn't bother me what you think. But it does. I went home feeling … there's no other way to put it, … dirty. It was awful pretending to have feelings and being touched like that. And I can't even blame Lyons because I wasn't doing anything to discourage him. And that's not like me at all."

"Hey, hey, Charlie and I had a similar conversation last night at Club. Don't worry, because we knew what you were doing. We both said that it couldn't have been easy for you." He touched her forearm briefly. Charlie was the same. He admitted that he'd also tried to put up with Stokesy's affections but couldn't hack it. Did you see them go off to the toilets together at Ureshii?"

Ruby nodded and smiled crookedly: "They were gone for bloody ages!"

Cain's smirk almost caused him to dribble his Nai Cha. "I started to panic! There was no one I could turn to for help when that bloody Hing was clearly trying to throw me off guard."

Ruby was fascinated; "Yeah, that guy really was a piece of work. Quite different from the other two. Made me wonder what his job really is."

"I was thinking that too. He really gave me a hard time trying to find out more about our friend Charlie Cheung." Cain recognized that he'd created a good opportunity to boost his standing with Ruby and added, "But thankfully, I managed to handle him and direct the conversation to Indonesia's economy."

Ruby pointed at him excitedly; "And that's when Lyons got so pissed off! One minute his hands were all over me, and the next, he's in a Mexican standoff with Hing."

"Yeah, that was a revealing moment, wasn't it?" Cain acknowledged.

They both nodded, and then, with a strong note of sarcasm, Cain added, "You know, I reckon those two aren't really the best of pals." He saw her smile and finished his point, "But between them, they gave me the safe and sound clue, and we could all get the hell out of that restaurant and get you away from the clutches of Lyons."

Chuckling, Ruby clapped. "Very drole, Cain. But yes, I was glad to get out of there."

Then Cain brought up something that had crossed his mind; "To be honest, Ruby, when we were all outside Club '97, and you kissed Freda. You had me wondering if you preferred girls.

Ruby gasped, "Oh my God, I never thought of that! Freda's really cool, but I do sometimes fear she may want more than I can give her." She grinned a little nervously.

"So, there's still a chance for the likes of me?" Cain gambled.

"Put it this way, you've got more chance than Freda," she assured, bumping her knee against Cain's beneath the table.

Before Cain could say anything more, she asked, "What do you think of that Nai Cha?"

Sipping the thick tea again, he admitted, "Well, it took me some time to acquire a taste for the condensed milk version in Jakarta, and I think it might be the same for Nai Cha." He looked at Ruby. "Guess I'll need to visit Hong Kong more often."

Her smile was a little coy. "If you do, you'll need to keep your distance from Harrier. But at least I'll be here."

After what Ruby had put herself through last night, Cain surmised that the last thing she needed was another chancer coming on to her. She'd intimated that she'd see him again if he visited Hong Kong, and that was enough for now.

"Tell you what," Ruby began. "I know you have that great harbor view of Kowloon from your posh suite, but the view of Hong Kong Island from Kowloon is better. We'll take the MTR under the harbor so you can actually ride on the metro that helped you work out what Lyons' bad investment might be. And then we can come back on the Star Ferry if you like."

Cain pondered the wisdom of taking public transport after carrying out an act of commercial espionage but reasoned that, to his knowledge, there were about six or seven million crammed onto this patch of the earth's surface, and the person he found most attractive among them at this moment was inviting him on something like a date. He sighed, but it was a positive reaction. It was as if he was finally relaxing for the first time. He wasn't trying to impress anyone for professional ambition or personal wishes or any reason for that matter. His tone was happy and relaxed; "That sounds grand, Ruby. I'd love to do that."

"Aunty! Mai dan!" Ruby yelled across the busy restaurant, asking Mrs. Yip for the bill, and shocking Cain with the difference in her voice and its volume so much that he almost knocked his cup over.

Kowloon

Charlie was sitting with his cousin Chi Wei in the Peninsula Hotel's unimaginatively named 'The Bar.' By contrast, Chi Wei's nickname was much more creative. Chi is how the number seven is pronounced in Mandarin, so Charlie and his cousins called him 'Seven.'

Jimmy Li just happened to be on duty that evening, so Charlie passed on Ernest Cunningham's regards, obliging the cousins to listen to the elderly barman's oft-told tale about his encounter with Hollywood legend Clark Gable. The star was desperate for a Screwdriver, and according to Jimmy, he was the only barman in Hong Kong who'd heard of the cocktail. They ordered one each and sat down at a table to await their drinks.

"I thought our place over at the Marriot was nice till I came here," said a very contented Charlie. Buoyed by the possibility of the assignment's success and pleased to see his cousin again, he was ignoring the hushed voices of the other bar patrons and speaking at the volume for which he was infamous. "If Temple-Speer ever wants me to come back to Hong Kong, I'm gonna insist they billet me in here."

A voice that was even louder than Charlie's cried out, "Charlie Cheung! Is that you?"

To the speaker, the question was rhetorical, so more literal questions quickly followed whilst a visibly shocked Charlie tried to process the fact that Richard Stokes-Leighton and his German friend Felix were sitting right behind him and must have heard his conversation.

"Fancy seeing you here. Where's your sidekick Cain? I thought you were showing him around. Poor chap will be lost without you."

Charlie's cousin was taken aback, too, and couldn't help but ask Charlie why this stranger had called him Cheung.

With palms open and fingers splayed, Charlie looked at Seven, his expression imploring him to just go with it. But his cousin just looked even more confused.

Still on the back foot, Charlie turned to face Stokes-Leighton and Felix. Then discovering the discomfort involved in maintaining his 180-degree body twist, he stood up and walked toward the two characters he thought he'd never see again. Stokes-Leighton also stood up and kissed Charlie on each cheek, further bewildering his cousin. Charlie had been caught. He didn't know what to say. He didn't even know which accent he should use. His mind was on fire. Delirious, he imagined a maze. But this maze had doors. Every time he ran to one of them, it slammed shut, preventing him from finding a way out.

Finely polished manners and the simple fact that he was a genuinely nice guy determined that Stokes-Leighton fill the deafening silence and try to move them all past its accompanying unease. "Charlie, you must introduce us to your friend."

Seven approached and reached out his hand to parry any possible invitation for kisses. "I'm Charlie's cousin Chi Wei. But everyone just calls me 'Seven.'"

"Oh, another member of the Cheung clan!" Stokes-Leighton remarked with an arched eyebrow and a smile. "Come sit with us."

Sitting down as directed, Seven couldn't help but ask, "Cheung? Our family name is Lam."

Stokes-Leighton's eyebrow arched again, but there was no accompanying smile this time. He didn't react when Seven first questioned the name Cheung, but this second iteration couldn't be ignored. "Nice to meet you Seven. My dear Charlie. Cat got your tongue?"

Praying that Seven would somehow catch on, Charlie went with a toned-down Cockney accent. After all, he'd swayed between accents last night and got away with it. "Not at all, Stokesy. "Good to see you again, Felix. Did you two try 'Nancy's overhaul?'"

"We certainly did, as you can see," Felix responded, reaching out to stroke his 'chum's' smooth face, which now bore a tetchy expression. The smile that Stokes-Leighton then tried to form wasn't too dissimilar to Mrs. Yip's attempt earlier on. "So, are you called Cheung or Lam?"

Wishing he'd taken Cain's advice about using Limanto, Charlie had escaped his bizarre door-filled maze by adding another layer to the story of his family name. "Stokesy. Not sure you know, but we Chinese Indonesians usually adopt a name that sounds Indonesian. Back in the '60s, unlike Seven and the rest of the Hong Kong Lams, we went by Limanto. But when my father became successful, he took his mother's name Cheung."

He told himself that even though the banker was a nice guy, he was probably just another lazy, Gweilo expat who never bothered to learn anything about the culture he'd been dropped into. But it was clear that his initial shock at seeing Stokesy was undermining any attempt to explain himself. Stokesy may have been attracted to him last night, but his current expression was ice-cold. He glared at Charlie after he'd finished babbling.

Jimmy arrived with the drinks for Seven and Charlie. Setting them down on the table, he told Charlie, "I really enjoyed seeing your boss Ernest Cunningham when he was staying here last week. Please tell him everyone at the Peninsula misses him, and we'll be here to welcome him when he returns."

The barman's awkward expression indicated that even he sensed the tension. When he bowed his head slightly and turned away, he very deliberately avoided making eye contact with anyone.

Stokes-Leighton bristled, and Charlie saw him silently mouth the name, Ernest Cunningham. "Charlie, Cheung, or Lam or whatever. You know, I might have been willing to believe you if you hadn't been suddenly so frigid in Ureshii last night, but right now, nothing about you makes sense."

Then he resurrected his smile once more and turned to Seven. "Very nice to have met you, Seven. Love that name. It's so fucking cool! Felix, let's take our drinks on the lobby veranda." He conferred a mordant look upon Charlie and huffed, "It's less claustrophobic out there."

With that, Stokes-Leighton took Felix's arm and marched him outside. Charlie slumped back down into his plush leather armchair.

Seven downed his Screwdriver and said, "Thanks for an excruciating evening, cuz. You can pick up the tab. I'm off before tonight gets any weirder."

Charlie exhaled loudly and muttered, "And thanks for helping nail my fuckin coffin shut, cuz."

Sitting alone, he fished his mobile phone from his pocket. He checked the time and SMS-ed Speer, asking if it was okay to call him.

Jakarta

The warm night air was thick with aromatic smoke from the Satay stalls that arrived to attract a clientele of Saturday night revelers when they emerged from the clubs. The 'Fat Man' wiped his brow with a damp handkerchief and stood up to survey his kingdom. A couple of expats were jumping out of their Silver Bird taxi and heading through the ordered chaos of vehicles toward Tanamur, one of them shouting, "We'll do three hours here and then head to Stadium." Their driver had parked where he was instructed and was readying himself for a few hours of R&R. He wound down his window, reclined his chair, and stuck his bare feet out and over the wing mirror.

Refocusing his gaze, the Fat Man noticed a couple emerging from JJs. The male had been here before but was hardly a regular. He had, however, clearly developed a liking for the new dancer at Tanamur, who seemed to work only when she wanted. Based on his limited but lucrative understanding of their relationship, her new man was very taken with her.

He saw the Bulé stop, take out his mobile phone and look at it with an expression of surprise on his face. He pressed a button and put it back in his pocket before returning his attention to the woman while they trotted happily toward their unmarked Golden Bird, Mercedes. The Fat Man took note of the 1-2-3-5 number plate, but he was interrupted by the breathless arrival of one of his 'parking attendants' with a Styrofoam bowl of Mie Bakso soup and some satay.

They'd had just one date at the Borobudur hotel. As she'd expected, it was rather stilted at first, so Feronika took control and dealt with the clear and present issue of marital status. After examining the photos in his wallet, she said she'd guessed that he'd been in the military and that a man like Speer should have a wife. The latter part of her statement surprised him, but it also allowed him to relax. Feronika was surprised too, at how much she actually liked the rather stiff Englishman. He paid for the meal, but she told him that 'Jakarta is my city' and insisted on taking him home and paying the cab fare. If he'd expected more, then she'd disappointed him; but she suspected that he was actually relieved when she drove away after just one slow and tantalizing kiss on the mouth.

Tonight, however, was going to be different. She was dressed to kill, wearing a short skirt with a white blouse. The buttons were left undone, and it was tied at the front, revealing a tight, white, spaghetti-strap top. Her long legs were encased in knee-high boots.

Earlier that day, she'd been to a salon for a facial and the Indonesian ritual of a krim bath for her hair. Whilst there, she'd also been intimately waxed, leaving her feeling great about herself and determined to share that with David. He was older, but he was handsome, and thanks to his obvious physical discipline, he also had a very fit body.

Speer often used this driver, and Feronika was quite amused by his awkward attempts to deflect her advances in the cab. It was, however, patently obvious that he wanted her, and when Speer opened his apartment door, Feronika asked where the bedroom was. She followed his pointed finger and took a few steps forward, undoing the clasp of her skirt. She let it fall to the floor before coaxing the blouse to slip from her shoulders. She paused for a moment to let Speer take in the sight of her wearing the boots, a bejeweled G-string, and the little white top. Giving him just enough time to catch a first, lingering look at her from behind, she turned and strutted back toward him, peeling off her little white top as she did so. She had not bothered with a bra that evening.

Feronika took his hand and guided him to the center of the living room, where she undressed him. Dragging a dining chair slowly toward him, she sat Speer down and slipped her thong off, over the boots, before straddling him. He was trembling. She eased herself slowly down and onto him, groaning as she felt him enter her. They moved together. Speer couldn't help himself as sexual excitement prompted him to move faster. Feronika stopped and placed her hands on each side of his face. Looking deep into his eyes, she quietly implored him to slow down; "Pulan David, pulan."

Hong Kong Island

"Kuai. Kuai. Kuai! Faster boss, please go faster."

Charlie was desperate to get back to the Marriot, but the cab driver could only go as fast as the traffic would allow. "What were the bloody chances?" he seethed.

He knew he'd blown his cover and had to presume that Stokes-Leighton would be calling Lyons and Hing to tell them that there was something very wrong with the so-called Jakarta millionaire they met last night. He hit the cushion of the back seat and shouted, "Shite!" earning him a stern admonishment from the driver.

He ran down the hotel corridor from the elevator, banged on Cain's door, and then in desperation, did it again, even harder. Cain opened the door, and Charlie just barged straight in.

Ruby shouted, "Hello, Charlie. We weren't expecting you quite so soon." But her presence didn't seem to surprise him at all. "Is everything ok?" she asked in a quieter tone

"Hello, Ruby. Hi Cain. I've got terrible news. But I'm gasping. Any chance of a cuppa?"

Whilst skipping from 'terrible news' to asking for a cuppa was quite normal for Charlie, Cain could see just how distressed his friend was, and how that had prevented him from acknowledging any surprise that Ruby was there.

They'd had a lovely evening together. They chatted about their lives and found they couldn't stop, so Ruby came up to Cain's suite to carry on their conversation over some room service.

With the kettle on, Cain joined Ruby and Charlie around the coffee table, listening with apprehension as his colleague described his encounter with the dark side of chance. It was as if Charlie was reading his mind when he confessed, "I know, mate. I know I should've used Limanto."

Cain held up his hands; "Hey, I'm not saying anything."

Charlie put his head in his hands; "I just can't catch a break. What are the chances? Bloody Stokesy? I SMS-ed the Major, asking if it was okay to call him. But so far, no response!"

© Steven Clark 2023
Lynnburn, Amisfield, Dumfries & Galloway, UK

Ruby teased, "From what Pyle said, he probably switches off his phone before his 8 pm bedtime."

Cain blushed. He'd taught the Major how to view and send texts, so he knew that wasn't an issue, but he didn't want to reveal his suspicions to his friend. Ignoring Ruby's comment, he tried to be reassuring; "Yeah, who could have believed anything like that would happen in such a densely populated city?"

Ruby wasn't quite so understanding. She slapped both hands on her thighs and exclaimed, "Coincidence can happen any-bloody-where. What counts is how you react to what life throws at you. Did you tell him you're staying at this hotel?"

Charlie shook his head.

She spoke at a more conversational volume; "And Stokesy just walked off to have a drink with Felix as far as you know, so you probably weren't followed."

Cain couldn't help himself, "Followed! Why would anyone go to the bother of following us?" He'd asked the question but was starting to realize how badly he'd underestimated the danger of the work he'd been sent here to do.

Charlie's mind was clearly elsewhere as he didn't appear to even register Cain's comment. But Ruby wasn't letting go. "I'm not completely getting this. You bumped into Stokesy, and yet somehow this became a disaster? What exactly was said between you? Exactly!"

Cain watched his wounded friend as he slowly lifted his head from his hands and said, "It wasn't really my cover name. Not even my accent either. I'm sure they didn't help the situation, but I saw

Stokesy's face when the barman came over and said that he'd enjoyed seeing my boss Ernest Cunningham again."

Cain looked at Ruby, who was looking back with an exasperated expression. She turned to Charlie again and harangued him. "Excuse me, but how in the hell did the barman know Cunningham was your boss?"

Because Cunningham asked me to pass on his regards if I saw his barman friend Jimmy at the hotel," Charlie revealed.

"Christ almighty! Amateurs!" Ruby shouted before crossing and then uncrossing her arms in an apparent effort to put a lid on her simmering fury.

Cain had to defend his friend. "That's right, Ruby. Amateurs. That's what we are. But we still got the info we came here for. And, in actual fact, we've all been a bit cavalier. You and I were wandering around, hanging out like tourists this evening. Imagine if we'd bumped into Hing when we were hanging out this evening, wandering around like tourists?"

To his frustration, he noticed Ruby and Charlie exchange glances and tried to stifle laughter. It took him a moment, but then he got it. "Hing, hang, hung. Oh, come off it, you two, this is serious!"

It was serious and had threatened to become heated, but his unwitting choice of words smoothed the jagged edges of Ruby's infuriation.

Charlie coughed. "Well, it's happened, and Cunningham will need to be contacted right away. Then, he'll need to call Sir James in London. If he does have money in Harrier, he'll need to withdraw it pronto."

"But it's his money! Why worry?" Ruby enquired.

Charlie explained, "I guess Harrier could make it tougher for him to retrieve his funds. His money will be well-hidden, wrapped up in shell companies and the like. Accounts that would never appear to have anything to do with Sir James. Remember Nick Leeson and Barings Bank? Well, if Harrier fell it could be a whole lot worse, and Sir James might never see his money again."

Still disturbed by the thought of being followed, Cain tried again to be heard on the subject. "Charlie didn't say where we're staying, but what if he was followed? We could be in real danger?"

"Think about it, Cain," said Ruby with the faintest trace of condescension. "Charlie did piss Stokesy off a bit, but he's just a campy little banker and quite a nice guy. If Charlie had met Hing, I might wonder if there was more to it. But it was Stokesy. They met by accident, and what transpired was just bloody unfortunate."

What if Cain's right, though?" said Charlie in a strange accent that sounded like neither of his personas.

"Come on, you two, get a grip," snapped Ruby, almost devolving into giggles. She fished a mobile phone from her handbag. "Look, I'm going to call Pyle. He'll have a better idea of how to tell this Cunningham guy what's happened."

They agreed, and after listening to Ruby retell Charlie's story, minus the detail about his name choice, Pyle advised that Cunningham had endured a very busy Friday. More than that, he told them Cunningham was in the office with Big Rob and his team all day. "I suggest we let Ernest enjoy a sound night's sleep before I confront him with this. And it'll give me time to think about the best way to phrase it all. It's a shame, really, because Big Rob reckons you guys nailed it. Harrier seems to have been taken in by the promises of some venture capitalists working on behalf of that bus company. And that's just one of a number of investments that have gone bad. There's possibly a couple of hundred million at stake."

Pyle's news would have been fantastic if Charlie hadn't bumped into Stokes-Leighton. But given what had happened, Pyle advised Cain and Charlie to; "Call the airline and get on an earlier flight tomorrow. Your presence may be required at the office."

Not totally convinced by Ruby's rationalization, which had so horribly belittled his concerns about being followed, Cain didn't have to be told twice to book an earlier flight.

It was late, and they insisted on escorting Ruby down to the lobby to get a cab. There weren't many people around, but Cain read danger in every face they came across.

Charlie went to bed looking absolutely desolate.

Sitting in his own bed, Cain looked at his luxurious suite and imagined sitting in the jacuzzi bath with Ruby and then making love to her on that huge bed.

He switched off the bedside lamp and shook his head in despair. This trip had come along totally out of the blue, and fixating on the positive effect its success would have on his career, he'd totally neglected the danger. He might still get his bonus for finding out about 'Safe & Sound,' but that wasn't what he'd wanted. The opportunity he'd sought had passed, and right now, staring into the darkness, all he could see was the danger.

9)   Black Monday

"You'd have liked her," Speer insisted while telling Cain about his date.

Cain didn't see any reason to dissent from that judgment. But he still found it hard to believe that a man like the Major would fall for someone like Feronika. Speer was his boss, a married man with a distinguished military career who'd also enjoyed remarkable success working in finance. But right now, he was no different from Edward Grant and all the other middle-aged expats running around with girlfriends half their age.

Speer continued to list her qualities as if they somehow justified his infidelity. "She's a classically trained dancer. Studied in London and Paris. She even went on to study International Relations like you... although she's deferred the course for now."

The topic of the Major's new girlfriend was intriguing for the way it had humanized him, and Cain was happy to have stumbled into a new level of mutual understanding with his boss. That, in turn, had created a closeness that was evident in the measured way they discussed the weekend's highs along with its tragic nadir.

The Major concluded his point, "And given the very mixed outcome of your trip, Ernest has decided that neither you, Charlie, nor Ruby Miller are to be paid your task completion bonuses."

The bonus wasn't a real concern for Cain, and he appreciated the Major's straightforward delivery of the shitty message that had been delegated to him. But hearing the words 'task completion' set him on edge. Despite the fact that he'd gleaned the correct clues and worked out what Harrier had gotten involved with, the assignment had been deemed a failure. He tried very hard not to fixate on the fact that this unfairly diagnosed failure was simply due to Charlie's bad luck and was ultimately, Cunningham's fault for sending them in the first place and telling Charlie to say hello to a bloody barman!

But Cain was too conflicted to protest. He hated the thought of failure, but his eye was still on career advancement, and he found himself protesting when the Major offered to pay half of his agreed bonus out of his own pocket.

"You're better than that, I suppose, Shaw. I wouldn't take the money in such a fashion either. And perhaps you'll get another chance to prove yourself soon enough, as I do accept that you had nothing to do with the assignment's secrecy being compromised."

His words were just enough to keep the embers of Cain's desire for promotion alive. But they also returned his thoughts to Charlie calling himself Cheung and the Peninsula screw-up that he started to suspect had yet to be fully explained.

Speer, however, changed the topic entirely, asking if Charlie's suits were the latest fashion because he remembered similar suits from the early '70s. "A time of desperate fashion," he winced.

[ ]

Charlie paused with the barbell across his shoulders, "Just don't make me do them Romanian deadlifts. It's been a couple of shite days, and my anger at the world has drained me."

He'd never admit it, but he did wonder if his friend deserved to suffer a bit after the Peninsula cock up. "Right. Use that anger," Cain asserted, cloaking his feelings in the guise of helping Charlie. "Come on. One, two…"

Charlie gave up and clattered the weights down on the rack. "Sorry, Cain. I haven't slept for two nights, and after the day we've had, I just can't get into this."

Cain held his hands up. "No worries. I was only doing it because it's one of the few activities that can take my mind off things. The truth is, I feel shite too. Let's just detox and do a 'Nancy.'"

Razors dipped in plastic cups of water, they began to sweat out the debilitating toxins of their Monday.

Charlie spoke as the empty steam room heat got to work. "Pyle took me aside and told me he couldn't understand the blackness of old Cunningham's mood. He was so happy when I told him about 'Safe & Sound.' And yet, just because of a terrible coincidence – coz that's all it was – he went ballistic and refused to pay our bonus. I tell you, there are definite cracks appearing in that precious fucking indifference he's always harping on about. I wonder what Sir James said to him."

Cain flinched at the reiteration of 'coincidence' but didn't react, preferring instead to follow Charlie's line of thought to recall how Cunningham often paraphrased a line from '1984'. "He loves that 'indifference is strength' phrase of his. Told me it's what gets him through most negotiations. I wish I could somehow channel it right now and put Hong Kong behind me."

"Me too, mate, me too," Charlie agreed, a little too eager to please. He shifted his buttocks to get comfortable. "But I don't think the old man's handling things as coolly as he usually does. He's obviously finding it harder to contrive that so-called indifference."

"You know," said Cain, rubbing his fingers over his perspiring face to test whether he was ready to start shaving, "There was a moment in Ureshii when Hing was grilling me about you. I suddenly thought of Cunningham and how uncharacteristic it was for him to send the likes of us on a job like that. And just think about it, to send us off so ill-equipped. Recently Speer and Cunningham have been switching places in my head as to who is the most balanced and reliable. But after this weekend, to say I'm having doubts about both of them is putting it fucking lightly."

"You were in Speer's office for quite a while this afternoon," Charlie said with a tone suggesting Cain divulge their topics of conversation.

Cain began to despise and question Speer's remark about a secret being better than a lie. After all, he pondered, closed secrets were underhanded and grubby when compared to the dignity of open truths. For just a moment, Cain considered telling Charlie about the Major and Feronika, but he couldn't do it. He'd given his word.

Instead, Cain admitted to having been relieved that Speer had told him about the bonus. He'd conveyed it in a much nicer manner than that chosen by Cunningham who'd torn a strip off poor Charlie. "And the Major still comes across as more laid back than he used to be. He even asked me where you buy your suits. Seems he's taken a liking to that style of yours."

Despite all that had happened to Charlie, the Major asking about his suits lifted his battered spirits. "Mid-life crisis," he speculated. "But if our dear Major wants to bring his wardrobe into the 90s, then I'm his man. Glad you noticed the difference in him. Last week, Pyle commented on his 'unnaturally Zen-like disposition' when the shit was hitting the fan after the Rupiah flotation."

"Yeah, I think the entire office noticed that," Cain agreed, knowing Speer's personal situation but trying not to appear evasive. "Hey, what was Pyle saying to you about Hong Kong and Cunningham refusing to pay our 10,000-dollar bonuses."

Charlie leaned forward, glancing nervously in the direction of the door to make sure Cain was right. "He called me into his office to tell me about a Taiwanese firm planning to get a massive factory up and running in Mainland China to produce parts for Apple. Apparently, China mines more than 90 percent of the world's available rare earth elements. Computers and mobile phones need those elements, so producing hi-tech parts in China should be very lucrative for everyone concerned."

Cain snorted. "Lucrative? Who the hell uses Macs these days? Microsoft is killing Apple!"

"Maybe that's the point," Charlie shrugged. "Right now, the stock can only go up, I guess. Pyle said the tip was from a well-placed inside source and reckons the Temple-Speer Fund should start buying into the stock now."

"Sounds like a very long-term gamble," Cain said glibly before he properly thought it through and conceded; "Mind you, Pyle's been quite impressive since he arrived. I mean, it was him that tipped Cunningham off about the US and China working in cahoots to drag out this chaos down here."

Charlie agreed, "Turns out he's a pretty decent bloke too. We all heard him and Cunningham shouting at one another. Well, the trigger for that was Cunningham pulling a volte-face about the wisdom of sending us to Hong Kong instead of a professional investigator."

"Cain was indignant; "No way? We know he was the one who gave the green light for us to go to Hong Kong. And more than that, it was him who devised those crap false identities."

"Yeah, that really wasn't like the Ernest we know and…" Charlie had trouble finishing the line. Cain reminded Charlie, "You were telling me what Pyle said to you."

Charlie continued, "Well, despite Pyle getting the third degree from Cunningham, he still tried to make sure Ruby got paid. Cunningham was dead set against it but eventually agreed to pay half. Pyle said he felt obligated to pay the other half out of his own pocket. But she apparently argued against it, especially after learning that we weren't getting paid at all. She only gave in when Pyle pointed out that while he didn't agree with our non-payment, at least we could leave Hong Kong and any possible shit that we stirred up. She, on the other hand, can't go anywhere."

They silently considered Ruby's unenviable position before Charlie added, "By the way, did you call her? I know you had doubts on about the plane coming back here, but she was really quite lovely to the pair of us. You especially."

Cain looked sheepish. "I haven't. Well, you know what it's been like since we got back here. I'd rather call her when I'm in a good mood."

Charlie raised an eyebrow and said, "Pyle also told me that he thought Ruby needed to be paid to make sure Temple-Speer was protected."

"How does that work?" asked Cain, happy that the conversation had moved past him.

"Pyle explained that he was topping up Ruby's missing fee because Harrier was bound to become a big story sooner or later. She, therefore, needs to be kept sweet so that Temple-Speer doesn't get dragged into the spotlight."

"Makes sense," said Cain. Then after a slight pause, he acknowledged, "She was lovely, but she's also incredibly ambitious." The rejoinder was an attempt at deflection from the guilt that both he and Ruby had been offered money whilst Charlie had apparently received no such charity.

"Yeah, but that's where it gets a bit weird, mate," Charlie continued. "When Pyle mentioned his good deed to Cunningham, it didn't go down too well. Cunningham said that Ruby should still be happy with half her fee because, as we all heard him shout, 'Journalists are parasitic by nature; happy to be riding on the coat-tails of the newsmakers they pursue.'"

"Oh, so that's what that comment was all about," said Cain, recalling the argument that seemed to blow up out of nowhere. "That really pissed Pyle off. I heard Cunningham say something about junkets too?"

Charlie nodded; "That's right. He claimed, 'Junkets only exist to give journos a taste of the lives led by people who actually make a difference.' Hearing that, I even suspected the old bugger was trying to bait Pyle into doing a story on Harrier, with Temple-Speer sitting front and center."

"Surely not!" Cain appealed. "Look, you know, I think there's something off about the half-arsed way we were sent to Hong Kong, but Cunningham built this company. It's his baby. We also know it's his swansong. He wouldn't want to go out on a sour note." Then he paused. "But it's strange. Cunningham and Pyle were pretty tight before we went to Hong Kong. And now it seems like they've rapidly come unstuck."

Charlie slapped the tiled seat he was sitting on. "It's got me thinking about Cunningham and Suharto. What kind of connections get you into a private meeting with the President? And what kind of a relationship do you have when you walk away with the kind of insider market information Cunningham got that night at the Finance Ministry parlay? Something has spooked Pyle, I just know it. He told me he was wondering how much longer he could cope with Cunningham's behavior, but I reckon he's tougher than that, and maybe he's thinking the same as me about the links with the regime here."

Wafting his razor through the steam, Cain pointed out, "And remember, it was Cunningham who said he tried but failed to get Pyle and Speer invited that night. I wonder how hard he really tried. Whatever's happening to him, it's a bloody good job he's heading back to the UK for a week. Hopefully, he'll cool off because if he keeps this up, Pyle's the one he'll have to worry about, not Ruby."

Charlie stood up. "Hmm, maybe not. I'll tell you in a minute. But speaking of cooling off, I need to get out of here before I melt."

Sitting in the locker room with steam rising from their bodies, Cain wiped his dripping brow. Taking a shower right away would be a total waste of time.

Head in his hands, Charlie looked up at his friend, who asked, "Well?"

"Well," Charlie picked up, "Cunningham made Pyle sign a non-disclosure agreement when he joined? All the intel Pyle could ever gather about Temple-Speer is locked up in a legal vault, so to speak. If a story ever got written about Temple-Speer, it couldn't be penned by him."

"Wow, the old fellah really is a shrewd operator," Cain exclaimed.

"I used to think that too," Charlie countered. "But I really got both barrels today from his spittle-laden mouth. I reckoned he was just passing on the bollocking he'd got from Sir James, so I finally challenged him. I told him that Stokes-Leighton had heard his barman friend mention Cunningham by name as my boss, and it was completely beyond my control. I only said hello to the barman because Cunningham had told me to pass on his regards."

Hearing it all again, sitting there together covered in sweat, Cain couldn't help but feel a twinge of pity for Charlie. "I'd love to hear what kind of defense he tried to mount against that."

Charlie shrugged, "I think that's when the old bugger's indifference kicked in again. He maintained that we'd had enough warning during the briefing from the Major and Pyle and that we should therefore have been more careful up there." He looked pained. "And you know there's a little bit of me that can't deny he had a point."

"I know what you mean," Cain agreed. "My problem was that the Major had been so civil to me. It gave me a false sense of security. Which seems totally stupid now."

"And that brings me back to my first question. Why not send professionals?" Charlie griped.

Cain wiped the browbeaten expression from his face; "I tell you what, mate. I've had enough of this. I was hoping Hong Kong would get me promoted to your team, but I guess that's not going to happen. You know how I respected Cunningham, but he's really out of order." Considering that last statement for a second, he reached out and slapped Charlie's knee. "And despite the crapness of our bosses, we managed to get out of Hong Kong in one piece. So, let's celebrate that with a long weekend in Bali. Domestic flights are dirt cheap right now because nobody's going anywhere."

"Nah, not Bali," Charlie countered. "A client told me that if you really want to get away from it all, Lombok's the place. There are three small islands just off the coast called the Gilis. Pony and trap is the only way to get around, and there's little, if any, mobile phone coverage."

"Sounds brilliant," Cain acknowledged. "No phone signal equals freedom."

Charlie gave him a smug smile. "Maybe you could invite a certain journalist in Hong Kong, and we could all go together."

The same thought had occurred to Cain, but he'd kept quiet. He held up his hands in surrender. "Sheez! Okay, I'll call Ruby. I should caution you though, the chances of her taking time off her precious work are very slim."

Charlie ignored Cain's negativity; "Excellent, my good man. It'll give us something to look forward to instead of just brooding over the past."

Something had been bothering Cain since they'd left Hong Kong, and now that the mood between him and Charlie had finally lifted, he thought he'd ask. "Hey, Charlie. I really need to ask. Your accent has changed. To me, it still sounds London-ish, but it's not so erm… Michael Cain-esque."

Charlie looked a little uncomfortable, and he sniffed and rolled his shoulders as if getting rid of a crick in his neck. "I was wondering when you'd ask," he confessed. "I'm not going to make a big thing out of it, and I hope you won't either. Let's just say I grew up a bit after Hong Kong, and the accent just didn't fit anymore."

Cain pressed his lips together before observing, "I like the new style, Mr. Lam. Good on you."

And with that, Charlie stood up and seemed to summon all his will to rid himself of the melancholia that had weighed down his spirits. "Right then, on a day that reeked like a baby's arse, my face is now as smooth as one. Let's shower, get some dinner, and try to put it all behind us."

28-31/08/97, A Long Weekend

10)   Gili Trawangan

Cain looked at his watch. The drive to the harbor to catch a skiff bound for the Gili Isles was a lot longer than the driver had said. But despite his issues with timing, he definitely knew the best viewpoints on the coastal road and where to buy the sweetest fruit from the women who sat along the roadside every day, hoping to sell their produce.

Taking in the stunning clifftop view with mouth-watering freshly-cut pineapple slices on sticks, Charlie and Cain were stumped when Ruby rejected 'turquoise' as too obvious. But when Charlie muttered: "It's the same blue they use on Tiffany jewelry boxes," she jumped for joy.

"Darling, you're a genius!" she shrieked at a non-plussed Charlie. "A Tiffany box blue ocean laps onto the white sand beaches of this island jewel. If I ever get back here with a crew, that's going to be in my script."

Cain feared he'd been a little too quiet on the journey along the coast. He'd actually felt rather side-lined sitting in the front passenger seat while Charlie and Ruby chatted in the back. Seeking distraction, he gazed at the passing vistas but couldn't still the festering resentment in his head. August had promised and put him through so much. Now he simply longed for its end. Looking out the window at Lombok's never-ending series of steep cliff promontories dropping off into sweeping sandy beaches, he insisted to himself that the water was definitely turquoise.

Ruby hadn't waited for an apology during his unforgivably delayed call to her, but she said she forgave him anyway. Enduring that awkward moment, Cain laid out the plans for the Lombok trip only to be told that it would be hard for her to justify taking a holiday at the

© Steven Clark 2023
Lynnburn, Amisfield, Dumfries & Galloway, UK

124

moment. And even though Cain made noises about being sorry to hear that, he actually thought the trip might be better as a 'Platoon of Two' expedition with no accompanying memories of Hong Kong. Within a day, however, Ruby sent an email to Cain and Charlie to accept their 'lovely invitation.' She'd thought about it and was planning to combine work and play with a recce trip to Indonesia. Her aim was to position herself as the newsroom's first-choice reporter if Harrier Bank really got into trouble and the Indonesian side of the story needed coverage. To do that, she was prepared to spend her own time and money to reach out to Indonesian newsmakers and set up a meeting with a 'cool fixer' who could help her with the logistics of such an assignment. A day in Jakarta would be followed by two days in Bali gauging the tourism impact of the economic upheaval, after which she suggested they could all meet at Denpasar airport for the short flight to Lombok.

Most tourists take the ferry across the Bali Strait to Lombok, but the client who recommended Lombok to Charlie just so happened to own a company that flew small planes between the islands. And when he said they were small, he wasn't kidding. The inflight service for the 30-minute hop amounted to the pilot cheerfully shouting over his shoulder, "help yourselves to a Coke!" The bumpy ride in the aging Cessna Conquest did, however, set the tone for a weekend of fun on Gili Trawangan, a world away from the frenetic energy of Jakarta and Hong Kong.

At the harbor, they realized they were almost the only tourists. Their boat called at Gili Air and Gili Meno before finally mooring at Trawangan's small jetty, where Cain, Charlie, and Ruby were met by a quite desperate posse, shouting the names of their guesthouses. Cain was distracted with insincere concern by Ruby's discovery that her mobile had no network connection, but Charlie heard one of the touts shouting 'Karma Guesthouse,' which his client had recommended.

The tout threw their bags onto a cidomo, or pony and trap. Led by Ruby, however, the threesome retrieved their bags and walked as she was clearly upset by the sight of the small, flagrantly overworked Lombok Pony. Ruby tutted at two portly European guys, hopelessly overloading another poor animal by squeezing into the small carriage with their diving gear. "Tossers!" she hissed. "I had a pony when I was young, and you don't treat them like that."

'Of course, you did,' Cain griped silently.

Set back from the beachside cobble path, the guesthouse featured a swimming pool surrounded by ten thatched roof, traditional Sasak-inspired chalets with a daybed and semi-open-air bathroom on the ground floor, and a rustic bedroom upstairs. Ruby insisted they take a chalet each and that she paid. She felt guilty because Cain and Charlie weren't paid their Hong Kong bonuses.

"Thank you for inviting me on this trip. You're right, Charlie, I didn't see much of Bali at all, but this place is how one imagines Bali to be… until you actually get there. Come on, let's get our cozzies on and make the most of the next couple of days."

Not quite getting the smile she expected from Cain, she shook him by his shoulders: "Leave the office behind, Shaw. Come on, last one in the pool buys the drinks."

They spent the rest of the day sunbathing and swimming. Cain cursed his jittery clients for all but destroying his gym regimen when he saw how good Ruby looked in her bikini. But as time passed, he was slowly stirred from his disgruntlement by the fun the three of them started having in what appeared to be an otherwise empty guesthouse. The happy chatter, the laughs, and the moments when Ruby's body brushed up against his while larking around in the pool melted the ice Cain had unfairly packed around her. Hair dripping wet, and with no make-up or preciousness about her appearance, Ruby seemed even more beautiful. She was an excellent swimmer too, so it wasn't much of a surprise when she revealed that she'd like to put her PADI license to good use with at least one dive during her stay.

A young woman called Santi ran the guest house. She brought them drinks all afternoon, and when asked for things to do, she suggested a stroll to the western side of the island to watch the sunset. "It's just a 10-minute walk, but on your way to Sunset Point, be sure to reserve a cabana at 'Sonny's' on the beach opposite here. It's the best spot to enjoy a delicious seafood dinner."

The next morning, shortly after their banana porridge breakfast with toast and kopi, Cain and Charlie saw Ruby off at the dive boat. Santi had told them that a walk around the island would take about an hour and a half, so they decided to walk off their breakfast as well as the previous night's feast of barbecued barracuda and rice.

They headed east, past the jetty and along a quieter series of beaches. There was less accommodation here, but the few voices they heard spoke a mix of European languages.

"Not many Yanks," Charlie observed.

"Yeah, Europe and the Antipodes certainly lead the world in terms of backpacking," agreed Cain. "But do you remember the Japanese girl at the restaurant last night? Santi said she'd been on the island for two months, and I've noticed a couple more Japanese tourists this morning. Seems like they're ditching the guided tours for more independent travel these days."

Trawangan's northern shore was more exposed to the frequent but short-lived storms that blow through the Bali Strait, and sandy beaches were replaced by hardy rock. Noting the change in the landscape, Cain and Charlie came upon a strange site. It was as if a developer had tried to lure tourists away from the south side of the island with a large resort, complete with pools and even a full-scale pirate ship that, on closer inspection, was meant to be a restaurant. The place was totally deserted.

They climbed up the hull of the ship and sat on the rail that ran around the deck. From there, they had an elevated view of the ghost resort that was already being reclaimed by the Island's flora.

"This should be on the south shore," Cain reflected with a quiet solemnity. "Built at the wrong time and in the wrong place,"

"Very true," agreed Charlie. "Like my dad when he started his Singapore shop. Wrong neighborhood and bad timing. But he'd never have believed it would end up being ransacked by his bloody neighbors. Seems like this place was built by people who hoped the island would attract families, not backpackers."

Cain nodded, "Yeah like it was built on the old package holiday model. It's like…" He stopped because he could see that Charlie was itching to say something.

"I hear you, Cain," he said, "It's like someone mistakenly tried to transplant the Costa Brava model down here. My parents used to joke that you can always tell where white people go on holiday because the place is covered in sun loungers. But Asia also needs to cater to its home-grown tourists as more of them can afford and even appreciate the idea of taking holidays. For plenty of families, even just a generation ago, holidays weren't a thing."

Cain waved his hands, recognizing that Charlie was on a roll and would need a clear signal to indicate that he wanted to say something. "But that's definitely changing. I heard Mandarin, but I couldn't tell where those couples were from when we walked past the jetty earlier on."

Charlie winked, "Young Taiwanese. Their economy is nudging them toward valuing experiences over branded goods. I reckon it won't be long before more young Asians arrive at the same point and start spreading their backpacker wings too."

Cain's imagination obliged him to interrupt. "Wow, imagine the numbers when mainland Chinese start to join the crowd as well?"

Charlie put a hand up with splayed fingers. "Slow down there, boy," he said, mimicking Clint Eastwood. "I was just getting to that."

He scratched his head. "A couple of qualifiers first. Asians wouldn't accept a Westerner making predictions about their future, and with my upbringing in the UK, even my Asian-ness will be questioned." He looked confused for a moment. "And right now, I'm questioning it myself because I can't even remember the bloody name of the ancient Chinese book I was going to tell you about. But what I do know is that there's something in there about the winter solstice and turning points that can't be stopped because they… what was it… they accord with the time. Second qualifier: There are countries that hate one another and a lot that can go wrong, but it does look like the much-vaunted Asian Century might be upon us."

Charlie looked around at the overgrown resort. "Remember when we were talking about Lee Kuan Yew crying on the telly?

It took Cain a second to recall the conversation. "Oh yeah," he said before adding what he'd actually wanted to say that day. "Yeah, he was upset because the paradigm his entire life had been lived in came to an end when Singapore was booted out of Malaysia."

Charlie pointed at the resort. "Exactly. I mean, I don't know the background of this place, but it clearly failed. Think about it, Lee wanted progress, but was trapped in the crumbling model of old Singapore within Malaysia. The place didn't have much to offer the world except the port. It took the almost accidental independence from Malaysia to force his mind to see past the island's lack of natural resources. He took on consultants from around the world to reshape the place, but it was Lee who drafted a new style of reliable, corruption-free, business-friendly governance. He stuck to his guns, and Singapore prospered, probably beyond his dreams. Most of the world, to different degrees, is enclosed in the Western Democratic model, but Lee tweaked the system just enough for it to work in Singapore. And if we Asians are going to make the most of this unstoppable turning point, then we'll need to find our own political models that fit the coming century. Think about it, with China's economy finally waking up, before long, as you also suggested, there might be loads of Chinese backpackers inter-railing all over Europe. But unlike before, they'll have something attractive to return to. The grass won't be greener elsewhere, even if their parents aren't loaded like our dear colleague, Andy."

Cain could see that Charlie's stream of consciousness was gathering pace, and he was becoming more animated.

"Take the inter-railing to the next level. More and more Asian students are studying in the West. To a certain extent, that dilutes them the way that Asians will say my Asian-ness is incomplete. At the moment, those international students get all the good jobs. But eventually, locally educated Asians will get an education that's considered on par, or even better, and they'll be in charge. It truly will be our Century, and it makes me feel a bit giddy if I'm honest."

Cain was impressed. "You know Charlie, I don't think I've ever heard you sound so impassioned. I noticed something when you were talking that I don't think you were aware of. In the beginning, you spoke about Asia and Asians. But toward the end there, you started to say 'we Asians' and 'us.' You included yourself because you want to play your part.

Charlie smiled warmly. "I hope I can. But even as the Gweilo epoch fades away, there will be roles for open-minded types like yourself. There will be risks too, and you'll have to get used to being the minority with all the crap that brings along. Believe me, I know." He stopped to weigh up his friend. "Mind you, without risk, you may never get what you truly desire."

It worked. He drew Cain into an approving nod. "Definitely, Charlie. Like my dad used to say, 'Qui audit adipiscutur.'"

"I don't know Latin, but I know that one," Charlie boasted. "The Major has it on a paperweight. It's the SAS motto, 'Who Dares Wins.'"

"Very observant of you. All the times I've been in his office, I never noticed that," Cain confessed. Charlie grinned; "I've been observing you too."

Cain didn't raise an eyebrow, but his face instinctively did it for him; "Oh yeah. Do tell, oh wise one."

"I reckon you need to put yourself on the line with Ruby. You were a moody pain in the arse on the way here. Of course, this place has helped, but admit it, you love being around her. And despite herself, she still came here with us! Shit, she even paid for our digs! Put that all together, and there's a lot to like. You've been given a rare chance to spend time with a woman you described as having little time for anything but work."

"Yeah, but I meant…" Cain tried unsuccessfully to interrupt, sensing where Charlie was going.

"Hey, my time is precious too, darling. Let me finish. If she's as driven as you claim, then it's even more important that you act before we leave this island. If that's what you want, of course."

"I hear you, Charlie," Cain acknowledged looking around at the moss-covered deck and picking at flakes of rust. "Time waits for no man, I guess," he mumbled."

Charlie bumped Cain with his elbow; "Only your imminent decrepitude awaits."

Cain jumped down from the ship, and into the long grass, it appeared to be sinking beneath. "You cheeky old Chinese bastard! Need I remind you that you're three years closer to decrepitude than me. Come on; it's our last night. On the way, we can reserve another cabana at Sonny's."

[ ]

That evening, the Japanese girl they'd both noticed was eating alone in the next cabana. Ruby said she was a dive guide and asked her to join them. Sitting on their large cushions, each of them leaning against one of the four posts that held up the cabana's thatched roof, the mood was relaxed, and the conversation was lively.

"Sachiko's training to be a dive master," Ruby gushed. "She's amazing because she barely uses half the air that a typical diver needs.

"Ie ie chigaimasu!" Sachiko charmingly begged to differ about her 'amazingness' and told a story about how she recently let down one of her clients.

She explained, "Underwater, we rely on hand signals. I was a dive buddy for a very experienced Japanese tourist. Twenty minutes into the dive, he kept pointing at the glass on his mask, but I couldn't see anything wrong. The glass was clear. No fogging. But he kept waving his hands in front of his eyes like he couldn't see. I couldn't understand. Such an advanced diver would surely know how to clear his mask underwater. Finally, he grabbed my arm and made me look at him. He slowly moved two fingers toward his mask and then rubbed his eyes with them. My God, the poor man had been trying to tell me he couldn't see because the glass had fallen out of his mask!"

They all fell about laughing, after which the group discussion was slowly replaced by quieter chats between couples. Charlie asked Sachiko how he could come back to the Gilis and train for his diving license, sparking a very cozy conversation. Ruby and Cain also cozied up together, swapping observations about the fantastic time they'd had.

Charlie confessed that he didn't have a clue about dive equipment, so Sachiko took him to the dive center to show him what she was talking about.

Cain was happy to be alone with Ruby again, and it wasn't long before they were leaning against each other on the cushions and talking quietly as the surf lapped up on the shore.

Ruby scolded him lightly. "You know, mister; you were a real grouch that first day,"

He couldn't deny it, so an apology seemed apt. "Yeah, I'm sorry about that, Ruby. I just can't shake Hong Kong out of my head. I really screwed everything up for myself. Bonuses, promotions, you name it." He could tell he probably sounded a bit pathetic, so he picked himself up. "But hanging out with you in this place has been a real tonic."

Cain was going to continue, but Ruby cut him off. "So, you do like my company then?" she teased. "It took you long enough to call me. I was starting to believe that you didn't care because I didn't use you to have my wicked way in that swanky suite."

She wasn't entirely wrong. He'd been surprised when she said she'd come up to his suite, and the thought of sex in that place had been tempting.

"As a matter of fact, I had a brilliant time with you that night and wouldn't have changed a thing. It was lovely just talking." He ran his hand along the table edge and thought for a moment before raising his head to meet her eyes again. "Of course, I was... well, I am attracted to you, but after what you'd been through that weekend, I didn't want to be yet another guy seeking your attention. As I said, I just loved being in your company."

Ruby looked at him. It was as if she could see right through him. But far from being concerned, he actually wished she could see through to the feelings he was having for her at that moment.

She touched his hand. "That weekend was so screwed up in so many ways." Cain let his fingers caress her hand and wrapped his fingers in hers.

"Look at this place," she continued. "We're in paradise." Her tone mellowed, and she looked at Cain in a manner he'd never seen before from her. "Let's act like we have everything we could possibly want right here."

They kissed tenderly at first, then more passionately. Cain drew away from Ruby, saying, "I need to see your face."

She whispered, "I think we might be outraging the modesty of the staff. Take me back to my chalet, would you? I've never showered with someone in the open air before, and I desperately want to do that with you."

PART 2:

Asian 'Tiger' Cull – 1998 January

11)   The Writing on the Wall

The President had invited Sir James to Indonesia several times since Temple-Speer set up shop in Jakarta. But the most recent invitation was unusual. It mentioned his predecessor's downfall and concerns about the future, which aggravated Sir James' paranoia about his own well-managed and closely guarded reputation. He, therefore, accepted Suharto's invitation believing it might prove mutually beneficial, as both men could vent about the joys and burdens of success, be that in business or politics.

Even when one accounts for Jakarta's all-or-nothing disposition, to describe its Grand Hyatt hotel as extravagant would be a disservice. It housed two magnificent presidential suites, one of which was given to Sir James.

The old businessman could feel the old General scrutinizing him as he settled into his armchair. He followed Suharto's eyes down to his own feet. Sir James was a little jetlagged, but he still managed to diagnose the problem. Trying to draw no attention to what he was doing, he adjusted his sitting position to stop his left foot from committing the sin of pointing directly at the President. The compulsive social climber had long since overcome his fear of silverware etiquette, but he was keenly aware that he'd barely scratched the surface when it came to understanding the intricacies of Javanese manners.

Sir James enjoyed their conversations, and when they spoke, they tended to debate what they called 'their century.' Suharto had even confided that he appreciated such rare opportunities to converse with a man he'd known for decades. A man with whom he could be himself.

And Sir James wasn't about to disappoint his old sparring partner. Picking up from where they'd left off when they reached the hotel Sir James spoke plainly. "But if one talks of a post-war boom in South-East Asia, '75 is the start date, not 1945."

"But there was no Marshall Plan over here," Suharto reminded him. "US benevolence, such as it may be, is predicated on US victory."

He was right, of course. The Communist rout of the US-backed South Vietnamese bequeathed little more than a battle-scarred petri-dish of a region. And as the khaki-clad military advisers went home, they were replaced by sweaty business advisers dressed in polyester safari suits. Pre-empting them all was Jim Hawes. He arrived in Indonesia while Suharto was still quietly consolidating his authority in the slipstream of a brutal anti-Communist purge.

"Well, quid-pro-quo is the way of the world," Sir James responded. "Ho Chi Minh gave the Yanks a bloody nose, and in return, they took their bat home." He smiled cheekily and added, "Officially, they wanted out of South-East Asia. So unofficially, you got me."

Suharto pointed at Sir James, politely using his thumb; "And as you noted all those years ago, despite so famously losing to Indochina's Communists, the Americans preferred to keep quiet about helping my administration successfully eradicate the world's biggest non-ruling Communist Party right here in Indonesia. And back then, the Americans were almost as exasperating as they are now. At least I had more energy to cope with them back then."

Sir James listened to the translation from Javanese to English and took out his pipe. Then he set it down on the coffee table, hoping to distract the wily old ruler's attention while he thought of a way to direct the conversation toward his concerns about the future. Did Suharto have any clue that Washington and Peking were working against him? This man had long been party to the ever-changing 'logic' of geopolitics.

In 1965, the Yanks had backed his systematic destruction of Indonesian Communism, making them complicit in the deaths of up to one million people. Then, just a few years later, Nixon was cuddling up to Mao.

The translator stopped, and the President continued. "Your knowledge of Asian history is very good for an Orang Barat," he flattered, qualifying his praise and using the more literal term for 'Westerner' than the word 'Bulé.' "The Americans helped me because my predecessor Sukarno burned his bridges. And recent events have made me wonder if a torchlight has already been lit under my connection with the Americans."

Suharto was fishing, but it was almost second nature for Sir James to see the value of information and to trade it only when the right bargain was struck, be it financial or in kind. He deflected and adopted an expression of concern. "You've had a very good innings as President, my friend. Must be 32 years now."

"Almost 30 years," Suharto corrected him. "I officially became President in March '68."

"Thirty years is still amazing," Sir James flattered. "And my main point was going to be that no government agency could ever try to undermine you in the way they tried to unseat Sukarno. Didn't the CIA make a pornographic film with a lookalike to discredit him?"

During the translation to Javanese, he scrutinized Suharto's face looking for a reaction that might indicate what he might say next. He saw nothing.

"That's true, James. They did try that. And no, I don't think they would try that on me. But let's be frank, there are plenty of other ways the West could take aim at me, and I believe that certain actors already are."

The smile Suharto was famous for disappeared. It was a minor change in expression, and yet when this man did it, Sir James felt a tremble in his hand and had to put down his whisky tumbler.

The President raised his voice. "I'd actually have more respect for my undeclared enemies if they openly tried to assassinate me. They say poison is the coward's weapon, but it seems I am to be ousted by the poisonous odor of a currency war. A weapon so banal that it speaks volumes about the cowardly time in which we live."

The translator took the pause as a cue, but Suharto slapped the arm of his chair and spoke over her. "Where is the substance that used to govern human actions?"

Unnerved, Sir James had to swallow before he spoke. "I completely agree with the point about substance," he avowed before lying, "But I doubt your Presidency is under threat."

The President waved the fingers on his right hand, asking his old confidante to lean closer. "I disagree. My people are telling me that foreign agents are already activating cells on university campuses to kindle unrest. It's a vertical pincer movement, the economy striking from above and the students from below. Shortly before you arrived, I heard a piece of news that supported my suspicions. Whilst the IMF is forcing its austerity medicine down Indonesia's throat, just today," he repeated the words for emphasis, "*Just today,* the World Bank's Chief Economist, Joseph Stiglitz, is in Helsinki questioning the efficacy of that so-called 'Washington Consensus' medicine."

"Well then, Bapak," said Sir James, lifting his glass and standing up with a little groan of effort. His use of the common term of endearment given to the arch patriarch produced a smile. "They can prescribe and analyze all they like, but I do believe Stiglitz has strengthened your hand if you choose to ignore the bitter medicine that accompanies every dose of economic aid."

Sir James was going to carry on but felt obliged to pause as Suharto also stood up and walked past him into the glass-enclosed balcony high above the Selamat Datang roundabout. Sir James followed him.

Staring out at the massive city, Suharto switched to English; "Yes, my fellow Bapak. Leadership is a lonely place." He continued in Javanese, "I can never freely roam this city. And I fear that those streets you can see down there may soon be awash with blood if the IMF gets its way." He turned to Sir James; "Ordinary people can't help us, Jim; they can only be polite. So, if I am finished, I hope you can put nice words aside and tell me hard truths."

Ignoring the bloody prediction of trouble, Sir James was disappointed to realize that his own fear of a public shaming was perhaps his most important qualification for offering advice to the old General. "Men like us have led very full lives," he began. "With respect, you said it yourself: 'Leadership is a lonely place.' Friendships no longer belong to us; they belong to our success."

Uncharacteristically nervous, Sir James drained his whisky glass before continuing. It wasn't Suharto's absolute power that unnerved him; it was the profound gulf between that power and the apparent harmlessness of the grandfatherly figure gazing out of the window.

Sir James girded himself and began. "My friend, you need to engage what I call the Noah Principle. You know the rain is coming, and like Noah, you don't just sit and hope for the best. Noah said he heard the voice of God, but I believe we all have that little voice inside us. It frightens normal men, and they try to ignore it. Leaders like Noah, and ourselves, we take action."

He waited for the translator and then tried to lighten the mood. "I'm not saying you now need to round up all the animals two by two. Your task will be more complicated than that."

Suharto sniggered, and Sir James was relieved to see an expression that suggested he carry on. But mindful that the President might have already taken his words for the polite platitudes he'd cautioned against, Sir James followed through with some strategic detail.

"Let go of what's beyond your control and manipulate all the levers you can to survive, even if that means stepping down. I suggest you line up a malleable deputy. More manager than leader. If his presidency stumbles, he will assume more blame than he'll likely deserve, and you will escape some of the blame that would otherwise have been apportioned to you. And like Nixon, make sure you'll be pardoned by that successor if such a measure is ever required."

Suharto nodded and smiled when the interpreter finished the translation, giving Sir James the confidence he needed to wrap up his Presidential prescription.

"Have your bankers in Switzerland, Hong Kong, and Singapore shift your assets. I know a helpful Panamanian legal firm that will ensure your investments in my Glenrovia Fund remain virtually untraceable. Start now, Bapak, if you really think the rains are coming."

Both men walked back to their armchairs. Sir James poured himself another tumbler of Scotch as Suharto reminded him about the time he'd met with Ernest Cunningham. "I must say, I was surprised when my people told me that the journalist Terence Pyle was working for you. After reading the dossier they compiled, I declined Ernest's request to have him invited to the soft announcement of the Rupiah floatation. As you know, Ernest stayed back for a chat with myself and Mar'ie Mohammad, where he expressed his approval of our currency board idea."

Sir James replied, "I'm sure he did. The IMF austerity demands aren't fit for purpose. Or, as Ernest elucidates, their 'declared' purpose."

Suharto continued, "Pak Ernest makes a very wise distinction. Meeting him again, I was happy to see that he still possesses the sharp intellect he exhibited when you introduced him to me all those years ago. Consequently, I took the opportunity to test his logical mind and began to outline my concerns about the future."

"Is that so?" asked Sir James, intrigued that he may learn something about that night which Cunningham may have omitted. "Did you get anything out of him?"

"Unfortunately not," Suharto replied. "I knew I had made a mistake. Ernest is clever, but his very British awareness of rank would not allow him to offer anything but diplomatic niceties. That is why I am so grateful for your... unpolished advice."

Sir James knew he shouldn't say too much about his staff, but after Suharto's admission about Pyle, he wondered if Cunningham had also been monitored and what such surveillance may reveal about his notoriously private advisor. With his mood lifted by the extraordinarily good Scotch, he found a conveniently breezy segue to advance the conversation. "Bapak, I do like the sound of that word. I must get my people to call me that too." He paused to allow the President to enjoy this rare moment of levity before edging closer to broaching the status of their Harrier Bank portfolios.

"I'm trying to be fair," Sir James asserted. "When Ernest first mentioned his hunch about Harrier's troubles, I thought he was merely doing his job and protecting my assets. But there was something in his tone. For some time now, he's spoken about leaving my service. Having gained my attention and gratitude for the Harrier warning, I sensed he was also implicitly reminding me of the reward I gave him for helping me escape the Barings collapse. Sometimes Cunningham's manner can lead him to press an advantage he doesn't possess. I said nothing, believing it was best to keep him onside. I even suggested a bonus, contingent upon my recovery of funds from Harrier."

Suharto leaned forward; "And ever since you have been dangling that reward in front of him whilst delaying the withdrawal of your funds. I called you a 'puppet master' a very long time ago when you were just plain old Jim Hawes, and it seems your skills are just as deft these days."

Sir James made full use of the backhand compliment; "You took me to a shadow play many years ago. I never forgot the spectacle, and right now, I may need to engineer my own shadow play if we're both to prevail."

Making his point, Sir James crossed his legs again, but this time he made a conscious effort to avoid pointing his feet in the wrong direction. In doing so, he hoped that small act would help demonstrate that he could be trusted with the President's more serious concerns. That trust would place him in a better position to detail the Hong Kong enterprise that had led to their misgivings about Harry Tsang and his troubled bank.

Suharto was left with a perturbed expression on his face. "I also believe your man was simply a victim of unfortunate chance, but I think you have enraged a tiger. We both know that Triad connections are behind Harry Tsang's success."

Sir James put his whisky tumbler down. "We do indeed, Mr. President. I've always kept my distance from the man. After all, he was only one of a number of bankers I worked with. But this Tsang had the temerity to lambast me during a heated telephone call after his people worked out that Temple-Speer had been fishing for insider secrets. Of course, I denied all knowledge of the enterprise, but he claimed his most trusted chap – a relative apparently – had proof that it was my chaps who'd tricked information out of his people. So typical of a Triad to use a family connection. They're no better or worse than the bloody Mafia."

Hearing the translation, the President snorted, "Except that the Italians dress better." Then he motioned for James to carry on.

"Well, following that rather abusive phone call, I upbraided Cunningham. Couldn't help it. They say familiarity breeds contempt, and over the years, Cunningham's aloof detachment has often driven me to despair. But I detected that he certainly wasn't detached from his emotions this time around. Major David Speer, my other senior chap in Jakarta, informed me that Cunningham lost some of his famous control and became quite the office tyrant. He even picked a vicious spat with the American in front of junior staff members!"

"Pak Cunningham is very proud, but pride is only one aspect of his current obstinacy or perhaps truculence," Suharto discerned, once more reminding Sir James that he'd purposefully delayed withdrawing his money from Harrier to make Cunningham fret.

Sir James saw an opportunity to explain his actions. "On the plus side, delaying the withdrawal of my funds helped me convince Tsang that I was trying to appease him by preventing market sentiment from going against Harrier. His partially restored faith in my motives could make him useful to us. I reminded him of some of the contacts we shared from our previous lives and suggested they could be useful ingredients for his future. That's when I played to Cunningham's pride by telling him that I'd use a portion of my recovered funds to ensure Temple-Speer survives. Dispassionate as he tries to be, he'd take it as a great personal failure if the company folded and the fund investors have grown to trust him. My strategy may be finely balanced, but I've managed to placate Tsang and keep Cunningham at the wheel of Temple-Speer. The firm will need to close eventually when it appears that I was too late to get my money out of Harrier. By that time, however, your money will be elsewhere, and so will mine.

Then I will have to deal with Cunningham to make sure he maintains my reputation in the retirement he is so desperate to enjoy."

The President had just taken a drink from his cup of green tea as the interpreter finished, obliging him to nod until he managed to swallow the liquid. "Cunningham's service is one thing, but do you still have his loyalty?"

The initial point of this meeting was for Sir James to give counsel to the President, but he was getting the impression that the favor was already being returned. "I have less doubts about Cunningham's commitment after speaking with him when he was back in London for Christmas. He told me that after our meeting, he was going to the Glenrovia Fund office to search for helpful strategies in the old files. That was Boxing Day!"

Sir James couldn't think of anything more to add. Suharto's expression was disconcertingly empty and intense. In a commanding tone that was more than a match for his mien, he used English. "You must discover what files Cunningham looked at if you want to protect yourself."

Sir James swallowed involuntarily. "My P.A. should be able to determine that."

"I hope so," Suharto added gravely. Then he looked away, freeing Sir James from his halting discomfort. "Tsang may have been a playboy sailor, but he was quite good at it. As a banker, however, he lacks the foresight of that other old sailor you mentioned."

Sir James' looked confused, prompting Suharto to remind him of his own 'Noah Principle' axiom. "Oh yes, quite," he replied, still thinking of Cunningham poring over files at the London offices. Then he gathered himself together and asked when Suharto had closed his accounts with Harrier.

"I may have spoiled Tsang's Christmas," he explained. "I wound up my relationship with Harrier at the beginning of December."

"Very pleased to hear that, Bapak," said Sir James. "Thank you very much for your trust in this matter. I'll be cutting my ties very soon."

Suharto accepted the thanks with a nod and added, "You know, you were very clever asking Tsang about his *future* plans. He will need backers when he is exiled from the Finance sector."

Sir James was taking a sip of his whisky and nodding in agreement, but Suharto did not see. Staring into his own cup of green tea, he again used English and muttered, "Maybe my own exile is coming. I just hope the graffiti does not appear too soon."

"Pardon me Bapak? Graffiti?" asked Sir James.

Suharto returned his gaze to Sir James. "The Americans who helped me eradicate the Communists. Apparently, they used tactics they developed here for other operations. After they helped depose Chile's Allende, two of them came back to train some of my officers. They showed me photographs of graffiti that appeared across Santiago in the days leading up to the coup. 'Jakarta is coming' was painted on the city walls."

"You, my dear President, are no Allende." It was the best response Sir James could muster.

But Suharto didn't seem to have heard him at all. "I've been thinking about those photographs a lot recently. A generation or so later, and my own Jakarta is coming."

There was a long silence as Sir James contemplated that cryptic statement, and Suharto shut his eyes. When they reopened, his intense expression returned, but his voice was eerily calm. "James, you said we need a shadow play, or Wayang Kulit as we call them, to help us prevail."

He growled something to the translator. It took her aback, and the concentration in her expression suggested it was a very serious command.

"Our play will have two acts. Shadow puppets need light to bring them alive for an audience. Puppeteers, on the other hand, require shadowy darkness to work unseen. As you have already determined, Tsang is a puppet. His desperation, temper, and, most importantly, his Triad contacts are the levers you can manipulate to protect your legacy. You have already set the first act in motion by positioning Tsang and Cunningham."

Suharto leaned forward and smiled like he was talking to a grandchild. Sir James was inescapably drawn to him, but the feeling was deeply uncomfortable, like being pulled toward a vortex. "I will leave you to direct this act, Jim, so make sure you stay in control of your puppets."

His words were carefully translated for Sir James, who sat transfixed and felt helpless to do anything but nod.

Suharto looked at the translator, who confirmed she was finished. He said, "Good" in English before reverting to his mother tongue.

"I will decide what happens in the second act. But be in no doubt, James, you *will* be purged of your concerns about position and reputation."

He let the translator catch up, and with a trace of disdain, he used English to say, "Everyone knows how important those things are to the British."

His use of English had momentarily thrown off the concentration of the translator prompting Suharto to touch her shoulder gently and present her with a warm smile.

"I must now inform you that I already have a shadow at work," he continued. "This shadow is controlling your Major Speer. At first, it was just an act of surveillance, but for our play to work, the shadow has already created some compromising evidence that, if required, could deter him from leaving Asia too soon. With his military and finance experience, you and I can benefit greatly from his future redeployment. You get to reacquaint yourself with the riches of the arms trade, and from the shadows, I can begin to position my Republic as a resurgent force in this region."

Sir James stared with an uneasy admiration at the deeply troubled, old strongman. Pressures and doubts cloud our thoughts with uncertainty, and yet with all his problems, Suharto could still direct his focus with a level of clarity that was hard to comprehend. "I understand the gist of the two acts," he said, his voice quaking. "But I need to know more detail about your intended plot."

The President nodded solemnly. "As you wish. But I must warn you; I believe that seeing this through to fruition will require a greater strength of conviction than you have possibly ever asked of yourself."

The old Englishman went cold as the old General conveyed the detail he'd requested in a frighteningly matter-of-fact tone. It was almost as if he'd done this before.

Downstairs…

12)   Christmas Presents

Some 25 stories below the President and Sir James, Cain and Charlie were having a post-Christmas catchup in the Grand Hyatt's popular O'Reilly's bar.

Gili Trawangan was a catalyst for both of them. Cain and Ruby had spent a couple of blissful days together, but despite all the talk of visiting each other, things just kept cropping up till eventually, their communication slowed too. Charlie, however, went on to earn his Open Water Diving license courtesy of Sachiko. Initially, he only admitted to being 'royally Sachiko'd' over at the dive center on that last night. But over time, he revealed that he'd never been with a woman possessed of such sexual vigor, on land, over water, and even in it.

Cain and Charlie were still friendly enough at the office, but they didn't spend time together socially. Charlie's Gili Isle interests took him away whenever he had time, and Cain became more insular. His life revolved around work, the gym, and home as he sought comfort in the kind of routine he'd previously eschewed. The long hours he spent in the office, however, were anything but routine. Cunningham rescinded the non-smoking policy, and the appearance of ashtrays began to undo the uniform appearance of the office almost as much as the empty desks left behind by the many staff members who'd given up and gone home.

Climbing onto a barstool, Charlie bore a devilish grin and said, "Come on, Shaw, spill the sordid details. How was your Thai Christmas?"

"Are you still pissed off at having to babysit the office?" Cain responded, picking up on a faint whiff of bitterness in Charlie's voice.

"My flight cost a fortune, and I know you'll be saving a fortune with the bosses paying for your flight home at Chinese New Year to get even more money in those red packets."

"Indeed, my naïve, little Gweilo friend," Charlie sniffed. "But the obligation to give me money is a festering sore of irritation for my married relatives, and the price they'll exact is a shameful inquisition about why I'm *still* single. So… how was your Christmas? I still don't understand why you didn't go home like everyone else."

"Parents, mate," Cain began. "My mum loves to think that I'm a high-flying finance consultant but wishes I was doing it at home. My dad, on the other hand, really likes the fact that I'm all the way over here and trying to make a future for myself, but he hates my job. I remember telling him there was an Army officer in charge, but that only seemed to harden his attitude, so I didn't bother telling him anymore. You ask why I didn't go home. I didn't want to put myself in an unwinnable situation. Unlike you, I guess. You must be golden bollocks in your house."

Charlie gave him a look of disbelief. "Do you really reckon a son doing a job like ours could ever truly surpass the expectations of Chinese parents? For starters, my mum actually started going to temple when I moved to this 'land of Chinese haters,' as she calls it. And though I reckon my dad likes the fact that I'm doing well, he's not very… demonstrative with his affection."

"So, there are differences in the details, but overall, the picture's basically the same," Cain proffered. "Our parents are difficult to please and almost impossible to impress."

Seeing Charlie's expression of agreement, Cain gave him an outline sketch of his trip. "I didn't actually stay in Thailand. Flipping through my Lonely Planet on the flight, I read about an overnight train from Bangkok to a place called Nong Kai, where you can get a visa into

Laos. The capital was only a tuk-tuk ride away from the border, so I went for it."

"Laos?" Charlie exclaimed. "I thought you needed some fun. What's so good about Laos?"

"That's the kind of question that drew me to the place. I knew nothing about it except that the Ho Chi Minh Trail ran through it. I ended up in this amazing town called Luang Prabang...."

"Where?"

"You see, the whole country is pretty much a mystery, and that's what drew me to it. Luang Prabang is in the north. Very beautiful, very relaxed, loads of temples called Wats; and thanks to the French, the coffee and baguettes are delicious. I tell you, visiting Laos was like being in Asia 50 years ago."

"And there was me and the guys thinking you were giving it some hedonistic laldy at some Thai 'Full Moon Parties,'" Charlie admitted.

"Nah, I wanted to be by myself, and reading '100 Years of Solitude', I reckon the other backpackers got the message."

"You're a strange one, Shaw, but I'm glad you had a good time."
"Like I said, Charlie, it was just what I needed."

Charlie rubbed his small belly and observed, "You must have eaten healthily because you don't seem to have undone your hard work in the gym. New Year resolutions aside, I need to get fitter, and workouts might take my mind off tanking economies for a while. I couldn't believe that thirty billion was wiped off the Hang Seng, and I still haven't recovered from that nightmare day when trading was suspended on the Dow. It was a real battlefield, and the Fund lost a lot of ground. Can you remember Pyle's reaction, listening to Voice of America's report on the APEC summit in Vancouver?"

"I thought he was going to throw that radio out of a window," Cain recalled.

"Yeah, when he heard Clinton saying that 'Asia is experiencing a few glitches in the road,' Speer had to tell him to stop swearing because some of us had clients at the other end of phone calls."

Cain sighed; "The office was getting pretty messed up, to be sure."
"Speaking of which, how does it feel to be back?" Charlie inquired.

Cain tilted his head, thinking about his reply. "To be honest, it was a bit strange. You don't fully comprehend the decline in office numbers until you go away for a while. Then you notice just how empty the place really is. I was pleased to see that Lena's still around, though."

The mention of Temple-Speer's resourceful office manager boosted Charlie's mood. "Yeah, the place would fall apart without her. All those goodbye parties she arranged for the crisis quitters were brilliant. And to her credit, she really came out of her shell."

"Her parties were excellent," agreed Cain. "Mind you, I felt sorry for Walker and Kerrigan. All they got were catered sandwiches on their last day. I guess the sheer number of resignations eventually bred an air of disinterest."

"I'm not sure you know," said Charlie, "With so few of us left, Cunningham asked for a smaller office. But the landlord was so desperate to keep any remaining tenants, he just agreed to a massive discount there and then."

"Really?" Cain exclaimed, knowing how precious office space had been just six months earlier. He looked down at the bar top, remembering how lively the office used to be. "I do miss the likes of Cowie, Seymour, and Lofthouse. When they had a bet going, the abuse they gave one another used to be hilarious."

"Quieter now though," Charlie reflected as their drinks were served. "Just imagine how desolate it was over Christmas! Thank God Lena and Andy were around. And it was decent of the Major to work all the way through to Boxing Day. I believe he was on the first flight to London that Saturday to apologize profusely to his wife and kids for missing Christmas Day."

Cain had kept the Major's secret about the dancer from Tanamur and was therefore interested to find out what Charlie might know about his gossip-generating decision to miss Christmas with his family. Charlie, however, displayed an old trait, assuring him that his spirit had survived his non-Christmas. From complaining about being left in the office, he hardly drew breath before heaping ebullient praise on their current surroundings. "It was Andy who brought me here. The place is strictly pukka coz the hotel's owned by one of Suharto's kids."

Cain interrupted, having finally noticed the curtains covering the drinks behind the bar. "It's a great bar Charlie but what's with the curtains?"

"They're for Ramadan. If bars don't close, they essentially become 'Speakeasies.' The alcohol's hidden away, but they're still serving. Just one of many reasons to like this place. A solid professional crowd and the women are fine, but I'm not sure you notice them anymore."

Cain's laughter was caustic. "No, I still notice, but I'm content with things the way they are." "Still in touch with Ruby?" Charlie asked.

"Yeah, we still email each other, but we both see Trawangan for what it was."

"Just pen pals then," Charlie remarked. "And there was me thinking that nuptials were imminent."

Cain snorted, "With your faithful venerations at the altar of Sachiko, you'll be heading down the aisle long before me. Hey, maybe you could take her home with you for Lunar New Year. Her presence might thwart the family inquisition."

Charlie waved a hand dismissively. "It would be more than an inquisition. Me showing up for Reunion Dinner with a Japanese girl could start World War bloody three." Then slightly quieter, "And she just as much said the same thing about her parents. They can live with the alternative lifestyle of her being a dive master, but they still expect her to marry a nice Japanese boy."

While Charlie was talking, Cain reached down to his bag and handed Charlie a small box. "Well, it's a good job I got you this then. Nothing says Happy Christmas and peace on earth like a self-defense weapon for this hate-filled world. I got it in Singapore on my way back here."

Charlie thanked Cain, but opening the box, he became puzzled. "A torch?"

"Not just any torch. That's a Surefire. Not cheap. Even on sale, it still cost me over a hundred Singapore dollars. The Major carries one, and I thought we should too."

Cain took the torch. "You see this bezel sticking out to protect the glass?" He pressed the soft button at the back of the torch, creating a super bright flash that blinded Charlie. Then he punched the torch toward his friend's forehead as if he was going to strike him with the bezel.

"Wow!" Charlie cried, blinking away the blindness. "That's impressive." He snatched the torch from Cain, pressed the button, and did a mock strike that momentarily upset the conversations of several nearby O'Reilly's patrons. "That's badass! Thanks a million!"

Cain pointed at the torch. "As well as that, I also picked up some news about Singapore tightening the screws on companies like ours. It could really affect our HQ there.

Charlie looked serious. "You know, we might have to start planning for our own business a lot sooner than we thought. I have to admit that over Christmas, I mentioned it to Andy, and he really wants to be a part of it. I mean, if China is maneuvering to take advantage of the mess down here, as per Pyle's quite spectacular intel, the gravitational pull of its growth will be strong enough to drag all of East Asia's economies back off their arses. I'd hate to miss that."

"We've got a lot to think about," Cain reflected. "You know, I've missed all this. And while you couldn't join me for a workout, it was a grand idea to go for the buffet at the Crowne Plaza." Then he struck Charlie lightly on the arm; "Hey, Ruby works out, you know. If she ever makes it down here to cover the economic situation, maybe we could all do a night like this together. Ending the evening here would be a classy touch...." His face fell, and he added the dark afterthought, "It will also help us avoid running the gauntlet of beggars in the Hard Rock carpark."

"You're not wrong there. Me and Andy went during the so-called festive period, and there were more beggars than I'd ever seen before," Charlie recalled before the smile was wiped off his face. He was staring past Cain toward the bar's entrance and tried to whisper, "Bloody Nora! Now I know what the Major got for Christmas."

Cain followed Charlie's eye line. Looking over his left shoulder, he locked eyes with Speer, who was arm-in-arm with Feronika. Their moment of shared recognition meant it was now too late for either of them to avoid following through with some kind of greeting, no matter how awkward.

Charlie turned to his drink and tried to whisper without moving his lips, "No wonder he's been so laid back. One night with her would kill the average bloke."

Speer said something to the woman and walked purposefully to where his employees were sitting. "Hello, you two. I thought Wednesday night was a gym night followed by a Hard Rock supper."

Charlie winced and rolled his shoulder. "The old shrapnel wound's playing up, boss," he joked with a cheery firmness borne of uncomfortable overcompensation.

The moment ached for introductions and coerced Speer into breaking the ice that was freezing all their expressions. "Gentlemen, this is Feronika, a woman who's become rather special to me."

Cain was relieved because Charlie's initial response should have confirmed to the Major that his secret had been safe until now. But he had to wonder what had happened to make the Major believe that he could be seen and, as luck would have it, be caught in her company. What happened in the Speer household over Christmas? Did he get his marching orders?

More drinks were ordered, and with a confident word from Feronika to the bar manager, the four of them were escorted to a reserved table. There was a lot of post-festive season catching up to do, and that made conversation easier to come by.

Usually, so very in control, the Major seemed to be deferring to his exceptionally confident companion. When he havered about Christmas, it was Feronika who insisted he tell them about the time he spent with his family. While he spoke, it was as if she was hoovering up information from Cain and Charlie, watching every move and reaction and yet not apparently looking. It was really quite unsettling.

When Feronika entered the conversation once more, Cain stole a look at the Major because that was all he felt he could do without bearing his entire soul to her scrutiny. He saw real pride on Speer's face as Feronika demonstrated her worldliness, speaking with charm and ease.

"I hear you studied Interpol at Aberystwyth," she told Cain, only slightly mispronouncing the name of the seaside town. "I was going to go there, but I heard the department really isn't what it used to be, for instance, when you must have been there. But it's still a useful Mi5 recruitment center for students who show promise." Cain had only heard rumors about that and was riled by the thought of obviously not being talented enough to be considered.

But here he was, once again, in the very informal company of the man who had implied that he still held promise and could be offered another chance to prove it. The Major was almost a generation older than everyone at the table; he looked relaxed and was clearly enjoying the happy, youthful spirit of their company.

That was until his mobile phone rang. His face fell, and he excused himself with no more explanation than uttering the word "work."

In his absence, Feronika turned the conversation to her relationship with Speer, during which she reprised her brazenly honest, conversation-halting line, "A man like David should have a wife."

Then for their added discomfort, she added, "Because, since his return from his wife, he is much more… vigorous." She must have noticed their jaws drop, but she moved on as if she'd said nothing particularly outrageous. "And I need that in my man. Before David left, he was far too stressed."

While she was so very bold about her relationship with Speer, Cain noted that neither she nor the Major had ever mentioned Tanamur.

But as he'd never seen her dance there before the night when Speer must have met her, maybe that was a one-off thing. Covering for a friend, maybe.

When Speer eventually returned, he didn't even sit down. And when he spoke, it was clear that the call had poured anger, weariness, and anxiety into the vacuum created by the departure of his all-too-brief, relaxed joy.

"That was Ernest Cunningham. He just informed me that Sir James is in the city and will be attending tomorrow's morning briefing."

The evening's merriment was over. Cain was confident that the Major knew Feronika's existence would remain a secret at the office courtesy of the 'platoon of two.'

Speer paid the tab, and they all headed home, wondering what tomorrow's meeting might entail.

13)   "Fuck the Meek"

Cain had never met Sir James. He'd seen him on TV and read about him, but the pinstriped Knight of the Realm was rapidly undoing his status as an enigma.

Sporting a Panama hat and an uncanny suntan, Sir James was lecturing the entire team when he suddenly turned an unblinking stare on them and snarled, "Fuck the meek!"

As if he'd provoked a fight, he instinctively raised his chin, daring anyone to defy him.

"That's right, I said it. Fuck the meek. Because, gentlemen, these are testing times, and you have soldiered on like battle-hardened heroes to make sure my fund and my firm annihilates the competition." He looked around the room. "Am I right?"

They hadn't expected this morning's main event to be an interactive performance. He bellowed angrily; "Gentlemen, am... I... right!"

They shouted, "Yes!" but with a lack of conviction that failed to convey the definitive affirmation Sir James was looking for.

His tone became quieter, but the menace was all the louder. "The market is perhaps the last meaningful bastion of Jungle law, the 'survival of the fittest.' Forget the old book that claims, 'The meek shall inherit the earth.' Because, I say to you," the snarl returned, "They'll never inherit it while I've still got breath in my body."

Sir James widened his stance. Shocked but unimpressed, Cain redirected his attention to Ernest Cunningham, who looked like he'd just put something distasteful in his mouth.

"The world is ours. All we have to do is want it badly enough."

Sir James also glanced at Cunningham. He must have seen his expression because he cocked his head and looked away with an air of real animosity.

"You work here in Jakarta. But global finance has no boundaries. So, you're working in the same historically long, cock-hardening bull run as my Glenrovia team in London. Apparently, there's a New Economy on the horizon, and whatever that means, it's our God-given right to conquer it.'

Cain suspected that after defending Sir James' company in a five-month financial siege, the Jakarta team members were all numbed to bull market bullshit like this. His line of sight fell upon Speer, and he felt even more disheartened. 'Jaysis, he's actually lapping this up.'

He tried to make sense of the farce playing out all around him, accepting that Sir James was a CEO who paid people to make him money, not to question him. That was probably why he felt able to sell this misdirected spiel; rather than earning their attention, he'd bought it.

"The market tests men, and Temple-Speer has seen good men fall. Good men, yes, but the team I see before me now, you are the best of men. Tested but not thwarted. You are the men…. I'm sorry…. and women," he smiled patronizingly at Lena, "Who will power this company through the current tumult till market confidence returns. For my part, I'm committed to making sure the company is here for you as long as you are here to fight for its continued success."

Cain smirked; when he was training in Singapore, Cunningham had pointed out that being 'committed' to something doesn't actually mean anything. "'I will' is the definitive phrase, Shaw. The fact that it's fallen out of fashion does not speak well of the times we live in."

Sir James continued, "There are very few things that would force me to reschedule a visit to my orphanage in Phnom Penh, but that's how important you all are to me. So today, I will instead be flying to Hong Kong to guarantee more funds that could be used to assist Temple-Speer in these testing times." He glanced at Cunningham again and added, "As some of you may know, this will not be a straightforward task; and to call the man I'm dealing with impulsive is a supreme understatement. I trust that you'll wish me the same success that I wish all of you because, as I said, the world is ours. Thank you."

Sir James looked puzzled. Cain wondered if perhaps he was expecting the team to erupt in fervently appreciative desk-pounding, the way they used to react when Speer or Cunningham delivered good news in the halcyon days before the crisis. But that kind of elation was long gone, and so too were many of the Jakarta team members. Six months earlier, Sir James' audience would have numbered more than forty. As of January '98, the partners, David Speer and Ernest Cunningham, along with 'Technical Director' Terence Pyle, were backed up by the economist 'Big' Rob Watson and his two remaining analysts. There were only half a dozen Financial Advisors, including Cain, and the Fund team had been ravaged to the extent that Charlie's assistant Andreas was obliged to act in a capacity that fused and sometimes confused the roles of Researcher and Portfolio Manager.

The other key team member was Lena, who, to her eternal credit, began to clap. Her face-saving action belatedly prompted her colleagues to join in, and its timeliness wasn't lost on the old grandee. He walked over to Lena and kissed her on the forehead, exclaiming that she was a 'shining credit to the firm' before retiring to Cunningham's office with his senior management.

Cain and Charlie thanked Lena for clapping. "You really saved us from the deafening silence after that bullshit," Cain said in a hushed voice.

"It's my job," said Lena. She shuddered, made a face, and joked, "I took that kiss for the team."

After a brief chuckle, she relayed her observation, "You boys are… How do I say this in English?... You are getting more inside your own heads. You used to be funny. Now it's different."

"You're right, Lena," Charlie replied. "Thanks for the reality check. I'll try to be less uptight from now on."

"That will be much better, Charlie," Lena confessed whilst vigorously shaking his shoulders in a playful manner. "I have missed your jokes, and I have missed you." Then she turned to Cain. "Same to you Cain. You are not such a joker, but you have been too serious recently. I hope to see both of your nicer characters soon." Then she clapped her hands. "I must get to my desk. Thanks to Bapak Sir James and his… 'bullshit,' as you call it, I need to catch up with my work."

They waited until she'd sashayed off, having overcome her blushes.

"One minute Sir James is fucking the meek, and the next he's saving Cambodian orphans?" Cain wondered out loud. "I mean, fuck the meek?" he repeated Sir James' line again, shaking his head. "You know Lena's got a First-Class Honors Degree, right? And she's taking home a pittance. I hope she inherits the world," He turned toward where Sir James was talking to his top team and surreptitiously jerked his fist back and forth. "And gets to take it directly from the grasp of wankers like him."

"Man, she's good. Almost had me tearful," Charlie admitted. "She was a great help while you lot were away. And she's a damn sight better than the guy we ultimately work for. Why do old farts like him always wear Panamas?"

They were just about to sit down at their desks when Andreas approached with Big Rob. They both looked very anxious.

"The Rupiah is tanking!" warned Rob. "I mean really tanking."

Andreas added, "As you know, my President is announcing the state budget plan today, and there are rumors it won't comply with the IMF's prescribed reforms. He's probably trying to protect some of the family assets."

Charlie interrupted, "And everyone will say that Indonesia should do everything the IMF requires because it needs the multi-billion-dollar aid package that was promised on Halloween last year."

"Exactly!" replied Rob. "I wonder how Suharto will maneuver? Family or country?" Then he pointed at Cunningham's office, saying, "I have to go."

Cain looked at Charlie and sighed, "Looks like the meek really are going to get fucked."

Charlie tilted his head toward an approaching Lena, who inquired, "Are you talking about the Rupiah?"

They nodded.

"My mother just called. She told me everyone was going food shopping because prices were shooting up. She was worried that soon there would be no food left."

Cain was the first to respond. "We could get Pak Lubis to drive your mum to the shops so that she can buy and carry more. Where do you live Lena?"

"My family lives way out in Bekasi. It's a good idea, Cain, but there's only one company car these days. Maybe Pak Cunningham or the Major will want to use it later to escort Bapak, Sir James."

David Speer emerged from Ernest Cunningham's office, so Charlie called him over and explained what they were talking about. Speer cautioned that even though Sir James had his own car, they should avoid using the company car. "I suggest you reserve a Golden Bird limo cab I've been using recently. Ask for 'Eddie 123,' and if he's available, tell the operator that, on behalf of Major David Speer, you will need Pak Eddie for the rest of the day."

Lena looked perturbed and a little embarrassed. Cain gave Charlie the same 'what the fuck' look that Charlie was giving him. They knew Lena could never afford a Golden Bird in a million years, so they both took out their wallets.

Maybe he'd just been a little thoughtless, but seeing their wallets, Speer quickly told them to put their money away. He counted out one million rupiah and handed it to Lena. Her smile returned, and she thanked him profusely before running to her desk with the twenty 50,000-Rupiah notes, a wad that was two notes thicker than her monthly salary.

"Nice one, Major, said Charlie. "Getting Lena decent transport with a good driver will really help her family out."

"Least I can do. She's a valued member of staff, and I think things are soon going to get quite difficult for people like her. In fact, one of you should go with her."

Despite everything, Cain could not break the instinct to impress, but Charlie beat him to it. "Better that I go. My Indonesian's better than Cain's. Plus, he's on his own handling clients, whereas I've got Andy, who can definitely look after things while I'm away."

More than a little put-out, Cain joked unconvincingly, "The way things are going with my shrinking client list, I might end up helping Andy."

"You're doing fine Shaw. Don't lose heart," Speer said firmly.

All Cain could do was nod glumly. He felt like he'd seen through the Major, and the word 'superficial' came to mind. He might have given Lena the money for her cab, but perversely, he'd lapped up the bullshit Sir James was spouting. He'd shown no sign of following through with his indication that he wanted to help Cain progress at Temple-Speer. And on top of all that, he was running around with a disconcertingly confident woman who was half his age.

Eddie 123' was available for the rest of the day. The expat exodus that began with the initial shocks of the Asian Financial Crisis had, in turn, resulted in a massive reduction in bookings for the luxury service.

Cain and Speer waved off Charlie and Lena. And as they walked back through the lobby area, Speer revealed, "You're lucky it was only me who saw the crude little gesture I think you were directing at Sir James. You kept my secret, so I'll let it go this time, Shaw. But I suggest you control your temper in future… and your hands."

[ ]

Bekasi lies to the east of Jakarta, where a dense residential population lives in disorganized harmony with the factories and plants of many domestic and international businesses. Several Temple-Speer Fund investors ran companies out here, but this was Charlie's first visit. Eddie, thankfully, knew every street in the greater Jakarta area, and it was only when they were close to Lena's house that he required directions.

© Steven Clark 2023
Lynnburn, Amisfield, Dumfries & Galloway, UK

"What time do you leave the house in the morning to get to work?" Charlie asked Lena, checking his watch and noting that they'd been driving for 45 minutes.

"I usually leave the house by 6:15 am," Lena replied. "I take two buses. But if I am running late, I ride an Ojek motorcycle taxi."

Charlie began to appreciate how comparatively easy his commute was. "I've never been on an Ojek, but I bet that when you take one, you ride side-saddle."

"Of course. I must ride like a good girl," Lena teased with a cheeky tone in her voice. "Some ojek riders are crazy, but it's the fastest way to get through the traffic." Seeing her house, she said, "Excuse me, Charlie," and leaned forward to tell Eddie to stop the cab. "Pak, tolong berhenti di sini."

Lena's house was at the end of a street of small but neat, semi-detached bungalows. There were plenty of people milling around, and the black Mercedes drew a lot of attention on a street that had never hosted one before. Lena explained that she'd like to invite Charlie in but knew her mother would be embarrassed as the house hadn't been prepared to receive a guest.

Charlie hopped out and into the front seat as Lena went to collect her mum, who appeared on the doorstep, dressed for a family event rather than a supermarket scrum. She was made up and wearing a Kain batik sarong skirt, topped with a black silk kebaya blouse, tied with a brooch.

Mother and daughter strode toward the gleaming Mercedes, and Charlie dutifully hopped out to open the door for Lena's mother. "Hello, Ibu," he said.

Lena's mother extended her hand but withdrew it quickly, eyes scanning the neighbors on the street. Her smile was replaced with a questioning, quite frightened expression, and she stepped backward, bumping into her daughter.

Lena yelped when her mother's heel almost punctured her foot. Pained but smiling, she introduced Charlie, and her mother's hand was haltingly extended once more. Charlie knew what was happening. Dismayed, he forced a smile while he shook her hand and then held the door while both women climbed into the car.

Lena directed Eddie to a nearby shopping area with a small supermarket. It may have been a luxury car, but the short journey was decidedly uncomfortable. Charlie hadn't anticipated this when he volunteered to help.

Lena leaned forward between the two front seats. "Charlie, I am sorry. My mum was just surprised that you were Chinese. It was my mistake, and I thought that because you were my colleague, everything would be ok. Please believe me, it *will* be okay. She's actually quite embarrassed by her reaction, that's all.

Whilst he didn't appreciate the anti-Chinese attitudes of some Indonesians, Charlie was well aware of the reasons why Lena's mother had reacted the way she did.

Under Suharto's 'New Order,' Chinese Indonesians were required to speak Bahasa Indonesian, take Indonesian-sounding family names, and were prohibited from openly celebrating their culture. For upholding their part of the bargain, they could expect to live and work without too much interference. Enforced assimilation, however, tends to produce lip service, if not whispered hostility; and the Chinese were also suspected of harboring chauvinistic tendencies of their own. Whether their community really thought they were superior and kept themselves separate; or were held at arms' length by the suspicions of indigenous Indonesians, their ethnic distinctiveness fomented varying degrees of intolerance. Charlie tried to comfort himself with the thought that Lena's mother's prejudice inhabited the less harmful end of that egregious spectrum.

The neighborhood supermarket they visited had already been cleaned out. The few remaining items on the shelves were now being sold off through the store's iron shutters, and as Lena's mother found out, the prices had been jacked up to levels her housekeeping could not accept.

The awkward atmosphere in the car was gradually displaced by a rising fear that there wouldn't be any more food available. When they arrived at the next supermarket, Eddie was forced to park his car a short distance away. Shoppers were straining to carry the proceeds of their panic buying, and near the entrance, people were gingerly stepping over a multitude of shards from a broken plate-glass window. Charlie sensed danger. He wanted to turn around and leave, but Lena's mum was quite distressed, and from what they could see, the store still had goods to sell.

As the three of them approached the store, they became aware of a woman crying. Like many others, she'd only been wearing flip-flops, and her right foot was bleeding after cutting it badly on the broken glass. She had two bags of groceries and a big bag of rice. Charlie winced when he saw the amount of blood on the pavement where she sat, trying to bind her foot with a cloth. Lena and her mother were focused on getting inside to buy their groceries and barely glanced at the woman as they passed. Charlie wanted to help her but, on balance, decided he'd better stay close to Lena. With his mood darkening even further, he sniped, "I guess love thy neighbor isn't such a big thing around here after all."

The door served as both entrance and exit, and the store layout was designed to draw shoppers straight onto the first aisle. The checkouts were some 20 feet away to the right and partly obscured by a rack of display shelves that had been cleared of discounted items. Just as Lena and Charlie, pushing a trolly, started to follow her mum down the first aisle, their eyes were drawn to the right, where behind the checkouts, a group of men had forced a man and woman to the floor. They'd tied them back-to-back and were tormenting them, threatening them with sticks and curved-blade machetes called parangs. A cackling laugh prompted Charlie and Lena to peer around the discount shelving display. It took a moment, but Charlie soon noticed the shoppers were paying the yobs for their shopping as the cashiers were nowhere to be seen.

Lena slowly took Charlie's hands off the trolley handle and stood in front of him, using her slight frame to obscure him as best she could. He immediately understood why. The couple on the floor, most likely the supermarket owners, were Chinese. Terrorized as a child by stories of how his father's shop had been destroyed, Charlie froze.

His eyes flinched as a blood-curdling series of screams emanated from the woman who was tied up on the floor. One of the gang members had taken a parang to her clothing, and in her futile struggle to defend her modesty, she'd been cut several times. Her ripped white apron was turning red at an alarming rate, but that didn't stop the brute from pulling at her top and bra to add humiliation to the searing pain he'd just inflicted.

Her screams were mercilessly silenced by a swift blow delivered with a club across the woman's head, leaving her face misshapen and bloodied. She let a tooth and a mouthful of blood slip from her swollen lips. Her husband writhed frantically against the tether that bound him backward to his wife. He was pleading with the gang to stop. His wife had been hit so hard that she was incapable of any form of resistance. She just stared with hollow eyes at her cruel tormentors as if willing them to put an end to her pain and humiliation once and for all. Her body shuddered, and her eyes rolled back as she passed out and slumped against her terrified, wailing, powerless husband, his face awash with a wretched mix of blood, tears, and watery mucus.

Charlie's mind juddered back to life. The horrible spectacle had taken less than 30 seconds, but he realized it was both a miracle and the bravery of Lena that had allowed him to remain unseen that long. He pressed his body hard against the discount shelving to hide himself even more.

The club-wielding thug began shouting at the husband to 'shut his mouth.' Charlie winced as he began to lift the club once more. But before he brought it down on the pleading store owner, he and Lena were wrenched backward, jolting their vision away from the pitiless scene.

Charlie was struck with terror, but it was Lena's mother. And she didn't stop pulling and pushing them till they were out of the store. There they heard the crack of wood on bone followed by a rasping, gurgling wail that sounded more animal than human.

Still in a state of shock, Charlie saw that the woman with the bleeding feet was standing, probably fearful of what she could only imagine was going on inside the shop. She tried to walk, but her legs buckled in pain, and she fell. Charlie stepped forward and pulled her back to her feet. But as sounds of wild laughter, obscene shouts, cracks, and thuds emerged from the store, he glanced back to the window behind the checkout area. Two young men were staring directly back at him. One of them raised his machete, and Lena yelled, "Run, Charlie!"

The two men were gaining ground, but Eddie had already started the car, and as soon as they were inside, he sped off. Lena's mother was shouting orders to Eddie, speaking with incredible speed. Afraid that his heart was about to burst, Charlie stared into the wing mirror. The two machete-wielding thugs ran down the road for a few more seconds before giving up when they accepted their quarry was beyond reach.

With the car racing off, Lena translated the more salient parts of what her mother was saying. Charlie was shaking wildly but could still feel the tenderness of her touch as she held his hand.

With barely any time to recover, they approached a line of traffic waiting for a red light to become green. As often happens in Jakarta, a bunch of men singing with a small ukulele-type instrument were trying to elicit money from drivers. Eddie took a cap out of the glovebox and told Charlie to put it on. Lena added that he should take off his suit jacket and tie as well as pull the shirttails out of his trousers, resembling the way a batik shirt might be worn.

Charlie did what he was told, but he was gripped with anger. "Where the fuck are the police? He cried. "Where were the security guards? Those places always have them. How in the fuck could those bastards just carry on stealing from those poor people? Shopping like normal and passing money to those scum? Bastards! That has to be the most fucked up thing I've ever seen."

Lena moved her hand and lightly grabbed Charlie's shoulder. "Cool it, Charlie. Keep your head down till those guys move past us. We are sitting in a luxury car. They will think we have money. You saw what was happening to that Chinese couple back there. Don't let these guys see you."

Eddie hit the central lock button as the group of 'entertainers' approached, peered through the car's tinted windows, and began to sing. Charlie lowered his head. Lena let them sing for about twenty seconds and then wound down her window just an inch, allowing her to pass two 1,000 Rupiah notes through the gap. This was a very common scenario for car drivers and passengers, but given what Eddie's passengers had just witnessed, no one in his Mercedes dared to breathe. One of the singers took the notes from Lena and even said thank you.

When the cab started moving again, Charlie thrust the cap back to Eddie, saying, "Is this how it's going to be with you people now? I have to hide and cower. Until this afternoon, I loved Jakarta."

A tear ran down Lena's face as she leaned forward again and rubbed Charlie's upper arms from behind, saying, "Come on now, Charlie. You know that not everyone here dislikes Chinese."

Charlie turned and stared at Lena's mum for an uncomfortable moment and then turned around completely so he could see Lena. She stared at him, imploring him to cool down with a sweet smile that Charlie couldn't ignore. He could see the glistening trail left behind by the tear.

He sighed and said, "You're right, Lena. Of course, you're right. But I really have to put up with so much shit in Indonesia. I thought it was bad enough in London, but down here, the bigotry is really in your face. And sometimes it's bloody deadly!"

Lena tried to soothe him. "I know, Charlie. What we saw was terrifying and horrible, but it was also very unusual. You are angry, and I am worried. I'm worried because I have a terrible feeling that life here in Indonesia is going to become very difficult." She reached forward for his hand again, and more tears fell from her eyes. "But the majority of people in Indonesia are like me. They don't care about racial or religious differences. And people like me will be scared that people like you might leave us and never come back."

It was Charlie's turn to absorb what he'd just heard, and after a short pause, he stared at Lena and said, "You are amazing. What you saw was so horrible, and yet you can say something as beautiful as that. And so you know, I've got no plans to leave anytime soon."

As he wiped away her latest tear, he noticed that Lena's mother was watching. He awkwardly returned her concerned smile; "Hello, Ibu."

Lena shook her head as if just remembering her mother was there. "Charlie! I never properly introduced you. My mother's name is Indah."

He decided to break the ice by asking how she was doing now. "Ibu Indah, sekarang apa kabar?"

"Kabar Baik. Terima kasih Pak Charlie," she replied, telling him she was okay. Her expression warmed, and Charlie felt that they'd all moved beyond the incident outside her home.

Lena mouthed a silent 'thank you' to Charlie, who forced a lopsided smile and winked. "Where can we go that is safe and likely to have food?" asked Lena.

"We can go to the Isetan or Metro supermarkets in Plaza Senayan. I can't guarantee you'll find everything you need, but at least we should be safe there."

"Oh Charlie, we can't afford to shop from that rich man's mall," Lena protested.

"No worries, Lena. I know it'll cost more than you usually spend, but I'll make up the difference," Charlie promised. "And we'll get at least enough food to see you to the other side of Ramadan."

They told Eddie to take them to Plaza Senayan. He admitted that he was relieved to be heading back to the more familiar territory of his typical passengers.

Eddie drove off after dropping his passengers at the Mall's atrium, but not before assuring Ibu Indah that he'd wait for them. His promise cheered her up, and she became happier still when she remembered she was dressed in her good clothes for this unexpected visit to Plaza Senayan.

Highly polished marble floors and walls invited shoppers in from the heat outside. Brands like Yves Saint Laurent, Gucci, Kenzo, and Prada were housed alongside two large department stores, a food court, cafes, and a cineplex to create a beautiful retail playground for well-off Indonesians. And although Ibu Indah would have liked to see the musical clock come to life at the top of the hour, she and her daughter had urgent business to take care of. Charlie led them through the mall to Isetan supermarket beneath the Japanese department store of the same name. It was busy but totally different from anything else they'd experienced that day. Seeing goods on the shelves, Charlie, Lena, and her mother grabbed a trolley each and piled them high with staple goods.

Charlie grabbed a ten-kilo bag of rice for himself in case things got really bad. He also filled up a handbasket with snacks for Eddie 123, who'd need something to break his fast with. All in all, the shopping expedition had been more expensive and much more dangerous than any of them could have believed at the start of their day. But they'd achieved their goal and were still in one piece.

Eddie thanked Charlie for the snacks and promised to take the women home so Charlie could return to the office and Tuan Speer.

Charlie waved them off and called Cain, who asked, "You alright, mate?

Charlie couldn't stop the feeling. He started to well up, and his voice broke. "I'll tell you all about it later. Bottomline is, Ramadan or no Ramadan, I need a night out."

Hanging up the call, Charlie wiped a tear from his cheek and looked around at all the people in the Atrium. Rich people were getting in and out of SUVs and luxury sedans, while others hopped in and out of taxis. He felt terribly alone and fractured by the terrifying events of the day.

Grimy, with his shirt hanging out over his trousers, his suit jacket in one hand, and a bag of rice in the other, Charlie was uncommonly casual. There were no Silver or Blue-Bird cabs, so he walked past the long line of queueing President taxis and jumped into an Express cab.

He told the driver where he wanted to go and asked him to turn up the aircon. The driver grinned apologetically and explained that it was broken. Charlie wound down the window and sucked in the food-scented air of early evening Jakarta.

"What a day," he groaned to no one in particular.

14)   J T H

The workday was almost done when Cain was summoned by email to Cunningham's corner office and asked to close the door behind him.

"When I heard what Charles and Lena had endured, there was no way I was letting either of them come to work today," said Cunningham. "The weekend's coming, so an extra day off should be welcome. How is your friend coping, Shaw?"

"I went round to Charlie's apartment last night, and as he was still a bit out of sorts, we stayed in and got some food delivered."

What Cain didn't want to reveal was that just before he'd received Cunningham's email, Charlie had called to remind him that he wanted to go out on the town.

Cunningham told him, "Probably the best thing you two could have done under the circumstances. And it was very nice of you to give up your night at the gym Shaw. I must compliment you on your much-improved physique. Maybe you could convince Charles to join you. It might help him move past that horrible episode."

Cain was just about to say that he and Charlie had already agreed to that when Cunningham added, "And if I may say so, having a training companion might also serve to lighten your mood, Shaw. I've observed that you've been somewhat carnaptious for quite a while now. Is there any way I can help?"

Cain almost laughed at the way Cunningham's Edinburgh accent drew out the vowels in 'carnaptious.' But he didn't find himself in the old man's office very often and appreciated that he'd been handed an unexpected opportunity to ask why the usually meticulous sage had sent two willing but barely able employees to Hong Kong with such slapdash preparation. Remembering how Cunningham had looked at Sir James during his "Fuck the Meek" speech, he couldn't escape the feeling that Cunningham had his own agenda for not using professionals to find out what was troubling Harrier Bank. And from that belief, his angry imagination had conjured up some very dark motives over the last few months. There was, however, a more plausible and less damning suspicion that he felt he could voice. The inherent trust and knee-jerk urge to please had been significantly eroded during the strain of the last few months, so Cain returned his boss' question with one of his own. "Mr. Cunningham, are you retiring?"

Cain's oblique response ruffled the usually imperturbable business sage. He jerked forward in his chair and closed a folder on his desk. His odd reaction revealed the front cover labeled 'JTH 77-81'. This bought Cunningham some time to decide how to answer, but it plainly wasn't enough, so he stood up and sat on his window ledge. Cain watched.

He ran his hands up his thighs as if massaging them. "With these knees, maybe I should have retired long ago, Shaw. But why do you ask?"

There was nothing else for it, so Cain told the truth as he remembered it. "When I was in Hong Kong being grilled by a banker who turned out to be Harry Tsang's nephew, I was struggling to cope, Mr. Cunningham. It's so unlike you to be ill-prepared for anything, yet there I was in Hong Kong, totally out of my depth without the requisite detail to carry a plausible lie. I've thought about it ever since and wondered if you maybe just didn't care that much because you were planning to leave anyway. I mean, way back in Singapore, you told me Jakarta would be your swansong."

From calculating whether to say anything at all, Cain had said much more than he thought he would. Cunningham also seemed surprised.

"Your candor is commendable, Shaw, but your suspicion is misplaced. Of course, I'd have preferred to compose more comprehensive 'legends,' but if you recall, time was not on our side. With more time, I could have written; and for that matter, you could have committed to memory, legends with the requisite detail. I can assure you that the carelessness of an old man with his foot halfway out the door wasn't a factor in what I admit were hastily devised preparations."

Cunningham looked unusually pained at the inherent accusation, and without too much thought, Cain said, "Sorry, Mr. Cunningham, it's just that I've been really worried about the terrible outcome of that trip. Ruby Miller invited me back to Hong Kong, but I'm actually scared to go there."

Cunningham moved from the window to sit against the side of his desk next to Cain. He patted the young man on the shoulder. "It's me who should be apologizing. We had Terence's intel about Washington and Peking, and I learned some valuable information when I met Suharto. You heard Sir James say these were testing times, didn't you, Shaw? We felt it was imperative to investigate Harrier to help Temple-Speer survive the 'testing times' that even he belatedly recognizes have so damaged the economic trajectory of the region."

Cunningham rolled his eyes when he quoted Sir James, and it wasn't lost on Cain, who'd witnessed his reactions during Sir James' speech. He looked at Cain for a moment. "Your assignment was ultimately botched even though you managed to divine the intel we sought. I promise to make it up to you both someday. I simply wish Sir James had closed his Harrier account as soon as he'd been apprised of the information you gathered. I worry that too much time has already passed."

Cain knew Cunningham wasn't known for saying anything without a purpose. Promising to make it up to him and Charlie was heartening, but it was his statement about Sir James that was more telling. Unfortunately, he wasn't quick-minded enough to probe further as Cunningham had moved to the door, saying, "The weekend is nigh, Shaw; you and I should be pushing off."

He tried to read the older man. His explanation had been somewhat reassuring, and Cain considered telling him about an email Ruby had sent him earlier that afternoon. A photojournalist had given her a photo of Sir James and Harry Tsang smiling and shaking hands outside the Harrier Bank offices as Sir James was getting into his car.

He decided against sharing that news for now and enquired: "All this talk of legends, Mr. Cunningham, were you ever in the intelligence services?"

His boss smiled and reached back to his desk to pick up the JTH file, holding it with the title clearly visible. "Tedium, terrible remuneration, and the prospect of a greatly reduced life expectancy? A dreadful career choice, as I see it, Shaw. With those words, he ushered Cain out of his office. "I was going to drop this into our American friend's office. Would you be so kind?"

[ ]

Hard Rock Café Maître D, Ginung Bandjar was instructing his staff to clear the first two rows of tables as the Friday night crowd grew and began to encroach on the dancefloor. He stopped for a moment to watch with pride as Nisa Kuwat moved quickly and effortlessly through the crowd to deliver a couple of beers to Cain and Charlie.

"Here's your beer, boys," the accomplished waitress announced. Cain thanked her, saying, "These will be a grand start to our night."

"I'm sure they will," Nisa replied in a honeyed tone. "These are on the house. Pak Ginung is so happy you are here and have not already left our troubled Indonesia."

Ginung waved, and his two favorite expat customers stood, raised their glasses with one hand, and saluted him in a comical fashion with the other.

As Cain sat down, he watched the waitress talking to her manager. "You know, I think Ginung has a thing for Nisa. Even from here, it's clear to see he's rejected Hard Rock's 'Love All Serve All' theme in favor of a more singular philosophy.'"

"I reckon she might be worth it," Charlie remarked before shouting across the table to Cain as the music got louder; "It's been bloody ages since we stayed on here after dinner."

Cain agreed, "Well, you deserve a decent feed and a good night out after what you went through with Lena yesterday."

Charlie shuddered; "You're not wrong there. I just want to pretend Thursday never happened." He looked at Cain and added, "But at least it managed to get you in front of our boss for what sounded like a rare display of openness. As for those dodgy legends, I'm still not sure I totally believe his explanation. But I'll admit that I actually *want* to believe him now."

"I feel the same," said Cain. "But there's another thing that's been bugging me about that chat today. Nothing was said, but the old boy seemed to be doing everything he could to let me see the front cover of a file labeled 'JTH 77-81'. It all felt a little....."

Charlie fed Cain the word, "Staged?"

"That's as good a word as any," Cain accepted. "He asked me if I'd pass it to Pyle, which of course, I did. I was going to have a peek inside, but Pyle was actually on his way to Cunningham's office, so I bumped into him before I got a chance. It was just a thin manila folder called JTH 77-81". He repeated the name to help him remember and wondered out loud, "What was the old bugger up to?"

With that question wedged in his mind, his face turned to the crowd. It was reaching the point when a critical mass found itself on the dancefloor and transformed the restaurant into a nightclub. He moved his chair closer to Charlie, enabling him to talk without having to shout over the resident band's attempts to cajole the crowd onto the dancefloor.

"Ruby reckons Harrier's on the brink. Of course, no one at the bank will give her the time of day. Her former admirer Jeremy Lyons and your pal Stokesy were given the heave-ho. But Jared Hing's family connection seems to have guaranteed an iron-clad employment protection policy. Mind you, Ruby heard on the journalists' grapevine that Hing's been spotted several times on coke-fueled benders, flashing money around in Wan Chai and screwing Filipino bar girls two at a time. Of course, no one else knows why he was doing it, but Ruby reckons he took our little stunt very personally."

Charlie exclaimed; "If that's how the nephew reacted, I wonder how Sir James handled the uncle? He must have got his money because you said Ruby's photo showed the pair of them shaking hands after their meeting."

With a faraway look in his eye, Cain affirmed, "Yep, when I called her a little earlier, she said in that very posh drawl of hers that it all appeared rather smiley and convivial."

Charlie grinned mischievously; "You love that posh-girl stuff, don't you?"

The band finished their first set, and the DJ opened his with House of Pain's 'Jump Around.' The anthemic madness of the tune finally kicked off the dancing as the crowd started bouncing around the dancefloor. The older expat barflies remained in their seats, but their younger girlfriends with negotiable affections, grabbed one another and giddily skipped over to the dancefloor to have some fun.

To Cain's surprise, Charlie declared his love for the tune and started jumping around with a bunch of Indonesian kids and some young-looking expat lads that neither he nor Cain had seen before.

As Ginung collected payment for their meal, he shouted, "Great to see you and Charlie enjoying yourselves here again."

"It's good to be here," Cain shouted, straining to make himself heard over the music and the noise of two hundred people jumping around as per the song's lyrical diktats. "And thanks for the beers. I'm relieved to see that business looks as good as ever."

"So far, so good," Ginung replied. "But this is not an easy time. Suppliers are already raising their prices because of shortages. And as it's Ramadan, we have to close at 1 am like the hotel clubs. On top of all that, some of my university student part-timers are taking a lot of sick leave. I worry that they are actually part of the rumors I've heard about students organizing protests.

Cain placed a sizeable tip on the table, saying, "Sorry to hear that, Ginung. It's a credit to the tight ship you run that those strains don't show."

Ginung laughed; "I hope you continue not to notice. Please enjoy yourselves tonight."

Walking to the dancefloor, Cain saw that Charlie had progressed from jumping around to jostling with the young expats, who seemed to have understood this as moshing and joined in. Their aggressive dancing was causing others to keep their distance or leave the floor altogether. Charlie's face looked strangely angry, and he'd already started sweating as he threw himself around with his fellow dancing combatants. Cain didn't know what to make of Charlie's unusual physicality, but it looked like it was on the verge of getting out of control, so he joined in.

"Charlie!" he yelled as they were both pushed around, "Calm the fuck down!"

But Charlie just stared and pushed him hard. Keeping his feet, Cain watched as his friend spun through the others and lost his balance, banging his head hard on the floor.

One of the expat lads stopped and helped Charlie up. He looked a little bit dazed and unsteady, so Cain ran over, and they held him up against a speaker at the edge of the dancefloor.

"Your friend, he is crazy," the young stranger said in a heavy French accent. "This place is also crazy. I love it!"

Cain shouted, "Hey, thanks for your help," before turning to Charlie and shouting, "What the Fuck was that all about?"

"I don't know. Just trying to fight off the memory of the other day," Charlie replied. He held out a trembling hand. "I'm shaking like I've got a fever, and this bloody speaker isn't helping. I need a Coke."

The three of them picked their way carefully through the crowd. Cain apologized to everyone they came across because he'd seen plenty of pissed-off looks from fellow clubbers who had obviously felt pushed around by a bunch of rowdy foreigners.

Cain bought some drinks, and the French guy introduced himself as Laurent. He explained that his friends were colleagues and they all worked for a mobile phone manufacturer. It wasn't long before more of his friends joined them. Cain understood enough of their language to learn they were actually checking Laurent was okay in the company of the pushy Chinese guy.

They all started talking about the clubbing scene in Jakarta, and Laurent asked about CJs at the Mulia hotel. As it turned out, Cain and Charlie hadn't been to Jakarta's latest club sensation either. They all agreed to meet there for the final hour before the 1 am Ramadan closing time.

[ ]

Whilst the Mulia Hotel had been built at breakneck speed to be ready for last year's South-East Asia Games, no expense had been spared, and it boasted a thousand of the biggest rooms in Jakarta. The lobby featured large Egyptian-looking ornaments to greet the many Middle Eastern, modern-day 'Pharaohs' who came to Jakarta hoping to have some fun in a more moderate, Muslim-majority country. Equally, the lion, leopard, zebra, and other animal prints on the décor added an African high note befitting the hotel's address on Jalan Asia-Afrika.

"Blimey, this is what it must be like to live inside Gianni Versace's handbag," Charlie exclaimed as he and Cain ventured through the lobby and up the central staircase toward the entrance of CJ's.

The club was in full swing with an American band belting out modern chart-topping tunes, as well as making admirable and much-appreciated attempts at several Indonesian hits. Drinks in hand, Cain and Charlie explored and soon discovered they'd forgotten how brutal an Indonesian club could be on the lungs. Cain spluttered. "It might be all Versace in the lobby. But in here, it's more like being inside one of Ronnie Wood's lungs!"

Just then, Laurent slapped their shoulders with a beaming smile, declaring, "This place is magnifique!" Pointing over the island bar to the dancefloor, he shouted, "Come and join us."

Cain and Charlie turned to where Laurent had pointed and saw his colleagues dancing with a group of women. Cain hadn't been out in ages and felt a twinge of reticence.

Charlie sensed it, and with a glint in his eye, he grabbed Cain's forearm and urged, "Come on, Cain, I need this. I haven't seen Sachiko all year!"

Cain retorted, "All year? It's January 9th! Jaysis but that woman's put a spell on you."

"She has indeed, but here's the truth. Sachiko's back in Japan. With so few tourists, the dive center closed down shortly after she got her Dive Master qualification. She told me she wants to go back, but God knows when that might happen."

Cain looked quizzically at his friend. "What was going on with you in Hard Rock? You were dancing like a madman."

"It took me by surprise a bit, too," Charlie revealed. "I reckon it was some kind of pent-up emotion after that horror show I witnessed the other day in that supermarket." He pondered a moment, looked at his friend with a wounded expression, "I just got this angry energy that I had to get rid of."

"And did you?"

"I bloody hope so mate. I would never have the energy to keep that up."

Cain laughed. "Come on then. But let's keep it all friendly, right?

© Steven Clark 2023
Lynnburn, Amisfield, Dumfries & Galloway, UK

They had a great time. There was something pleasantly joyful about hanging out with a bunch of guys their own age. The Ramadan early closing time, however, brought the evening to an abrupt end, causing a long queue for cars and taxis at the Mulia's entrance. Cain suggested they should let the queue die down and get a nightcap at the hotel's 24-hour restaurant.

The club's music was still ringing in their ears, but the restaurant was quiet, allowing Cain and Charlie to explain how Jakarta's party crowd typically club-hopped all over the city during the eleven non-fasting months. They also swapped business cards, and Cain even managed to arrange a meeting with some of them to discuss offshore investment portfolios.

The taxi queue had all but disappeared when they finally decided to head home. In the cab, Cain's stomach growled so loudly that Charlie suggested stopping at a 'Circle K' minimart. There wasn't much on the shelves, but they saw a few packets of Indonesian brand biscuits called 'Good Times.'

Charlie grabbed and held up a packet like he was acting in a commercial, "They may be Good Times, but they're certainly not the best of times."

It wasn't particularly funny, but something clicked, and the pair of them ended up on the floor laughing uncontrollably.

"Ah, Jakarta. I love this old town," Cain proclaimed between fits of the giggles.

15)   A Bank of Prey in Freefall

"Hey Charlie!" Cain shouted across the roof of the Silver Bird. "Over here."

Charlie waved when he heard his friend's voice and picked up his laptop bag. Watching him run across the atrium from the office tower entrance where his client had an office, Cain couldn't help but be impressed. His friend was working so hard to mask the extraordinary effort he was making to cope with what he and Lena had seen last week.

"Good to see you," Charlie said while opening the cab door and climbing in. "Nice timing, too, considering the traffic around here. How was the meeting with our French pals? Any new clients?"

Cain told the cabbie to drive to DPL Tower, which housed Temple-Speer, and settled himself in the back seat. "It was a weird kind of morning. All I've done the past few months is placate and try to hold on to clients, so I'm really out of practice at performing the sales pitch. And this morning, I really didn't like doing it."

Charlie smiled knowingly. "The fact that you befriended the French guys before you pitched to them couldn't have helped." He looked skyward, made the sign of the cross, and contrived an Irish accent; "Tell me your sins, my son, and they'll be absolved."

Cain looked doleful. "It'll take more than three Hail Marys to absolve my sins. The sin of omission, for a start. You know, avoiding any explanation of fee structures and Hanthorpe's penalties for not sustaining their payments."

"Yeah, but there's nothing unethical there," Charlie insisted before asking if Cain had used the less-than-ethical technique that was quietly encouraged at Temple-Speer; "You didn't need to 'churn' any of them, did you?"

"You were right about Laurent, Charlie. He's older than the others, and as you suspected, he already has a portfolio. Poor guy even brought in his documents."

Charlie screwed up his face; "Documents! Cunningham used to call them the perfect props to build a case for a churn. Poor Laurent really walked into that one."

Cain confessed, "Scruples never used to bother me. I could have easily convinced him to cash in his portfolio and use the money to inject into Hanthorpe. And the commission for churning his $65,000 would have come in handy."

He felt Charlie's gaze on him. "Sounds like you had a crisis of conscience, my friend."

Cain couldn't shake off the surprise visit from his conscience. When Cunningham was schooling him in the art of the sale, he bought it hook, line, and sinker. Get them signed and get them for as much as possible. But while trying to reel in the French lads, his conscience got in the way. Without pushing, he'd just left the papers with them to think about.

Cain was glad his parents didn't know about Temple-Speer's modus operandi. His mother would be beside herself if she knew, and his father might even disown him! During one of their arguments, before he came out to Asia, he called service 'the highest form of work for any man.'

His mother had stuck up for him, arguing, "He's not like you, Andrew. He's university educated and would be wasted in the army."

Undaunted, her husband countered, "You might be right there, Elizabeth, but maybe it's the education that's wasted on him." He unreservedly assumed that Temple-Speer was a shady enterprise that should have been beneath the likes of his well-educated son.

An awful thought occurred to Cain; 'Imagine if he'd heard Sir James' the other day?' "'Fuck the Meek?" Jaysis son, you work for a wastrel like that?"

Charlie said something.

"Sorry, Charlie, what was that?"

I said, "You did the right thing. I wouldn't want to 'churn' those lads either."

Cain talked away the thoughts about his father; "You know, they're convinced they'll win the World Cup this year. I think it was their soccer-mad joie-de-vivre that kept my spirits off rock bottom during the meeting."

About to respond, Charlie was interrupted by the Silver Bird driver; "Hey, mister, you like Indonesian food?" Cain and Charlie both answered in the affirmative. Then he asked if they liked alcohol because he liked Scottish whisky. Noting another affirmative response, he then asked if they liked Indonesian women because he loved them and had many girlfriends as well as a lovely wife. The guys dutifully answered, saying they thought Indonesian women were beautiful, which pleased the driver no end.

Charlie nudged Cain and said to the driver, "Mas, you tell us you like Scottish whisky, and you also tell us you love women, but you're a Muslim man, correct?"

The driver thought about this. Sizing up the two foreigners in his rear-view mirror, he smiled knowingly and declared, "Ah, I see your meaning. Yes, I like whisky and women, but I only standard Muslim, not fanatic!"

The driver giggled, and surprised by his answer, Cain and Charlie were soon laughing quite uncontrollably.

[ ]

The sobering news that greeted them when they reached Temple-Speer, however, knocked their unexpected good cheer on its head.

Cain gave Charlie a look of hopelessness; "It's only Monday, and my nerves feel like they've been on a rollercoaster for a week."

The Hong Kong assignment had been commissioned in relative secrecy, but the fallout had quickly made it common knowledge at Temple-Speer. So, when news broke that Harrier Bank was going under because of bad loans, it spread like wildfire through the greatly diminished staff headcount.

Terence Pyle emerged from Ernest Cunningham's office, followed shortly thereafter by the man whose name was on the door. They looked grim.

"Gather around everyone," Cunningham announced. "You too Lena."

"As you're probably aware, Harrier Bank has folded, and Sir James has conveyed some disturbing news. Despite his representations to the bank's founder, it appears that he may have been too late to secure his invested capital."

Charlie asked, "Was that because the management took exception to what Cain and I did up in Hong Kong? Some kind of revenge?"

Cain knew Cunningham wouldn't appreciate him airing the company's dirty linen, but still…. "We tricked them and then worked out that they'd invested in Safe & Sound buses, of all things. That can't have gone down well."

Cunningham was stony-faced. "Believe me, Sir James would have let me know, in no uncertain terms, if that was the case," he insisted.

Chief Analyst Rob Watson asked the question that laid the situation bare for everyone in the room. "If Sir James couldn't recover his money, then where does that leave Temple-Speer and our fund? If you remember, he said some of the money he'd recover from Harrier would be used to temporarily buoy up our operations here."

Cunningham's eyes darted from Cain to Rob, maintaining the same steely focus. "I must be frank, Robert, it's unlikely that Sir James will recover all his money. In short, he informs me that he'll need to wait for the outcome of the receiver's processes."

There was a loud collective silence. Heads were bowed or looking around in disbelief. Cain and Charlie had spoken about starting their own business one day in the future, but he'd always thought that he'd need to resign from Temple-Speer, not that his employment would be terminated. He worried about how that would look on his CV.

Inhaling the silence as deeply as he inhaled the aroma of his favorite brand of kreteks, Cunningham exhaled with words that, while realistic, were about as welcome as second-hand smoke. "I must emphasize that *nothing* is confirmed at present, but I feel that it's incumbent upon me to call your attention to the clauses in your contracts concerning notice period duration and the proper recording and claiming of reasonable repatriation costs."

He paused, looking around for reactions, but there were none. "Robert's recollections also oblige me to remind you that in his address, Sir James never said Temple-Speer's future was contingent upon his recovery of funds from Harrier. His intention was simply to park some of those funds into our firm to guard against the worst this economic crisis might throw at us. Now if you'll excuse me, I must inform Major Speer of this development if I can reach him on the telephone."

Cunningham returned to his office, leaving Terence Pyle to face the stunned team. But Pyle had questions too. "Have any of you seen the Major? He hasn't shown up for work yet, and there's been no word from him."

Cain and Charlie looked at one another. They'd agreed to say nothing about Speer's extra-marital social life.

Rob Watson looked rattled by what he'd just heard. He asked Pyle what his plans were.

Extravagant client dinners had clearly agreed with Pyle's palate but not his wardrobe. He undid his belt and pulled at a nearby office chair to sit on. "Well, guys," he said, addressing everyone, "in truth, I'm retained as a consultant, not really an employee. I think I'll just take a break and then return to freelance journalism, as there's not much in the way of competition in Jakarta. I'll tell you something, though, whenever I interviewed Tsang back in the day, he was a royal pain in the ass. No wonder he goes through support staff like Clinton reportedly goes through interns and cigars."

Pyle thought his joke was funny, but no one laughed. He looked over his shoulder to Cunningham's office and sighed heavily. "Although Ernest denied it, I really believe Tsang would definitely want to screw Sir James for that stunt we pulled last year."

With the word 'stunt' ringing in his fears, Cain posited, "Nothing to lose, so, like Samson, he brings down the whole temple."

"Or Temple-Speer," Pyle pointed out. "You may be right there, Cain. And somewhere in that line of thinking, there's an excellent headline. Thanks, buddy."

The subsequent discussion about personal plans and what to do with clients only compounded Cain's worries. Everyone at Temple-Speer could be out on their ears, and who would give a shit about a bunch of expat finance consultants when Asia clearly had more pressing priorities.

Standing next to Rob and lost in his own thoughts, Cain was shocked when the big man pointed at Cunningham's office and exclaimed, "That old queen promised me everything would be okay when I told him I wanted to leave last October. Back then, myself and Jenny would have been ahead of the returning expats, and I might have even been able to secure a job to feed my kids. He struck a table; "Fuck! What am I going to do now? They better pay for my bloody repatriation coz I'm calling Santa Cruz for an estimate today!"

"I see you've been informed about what's happened," Speer remarked, viewing the extraordinary scene in the office, his mobile phone still in his hand after taking Cunningham's brusque call.

Rob exploded; "Oh, Loverboy's finally turned up. How's the girlfriend?" Cain couldn't believe what was happening. Rob knew about Speer too?

Speer bristled and lunged at Rob, delivering two hard and fast blows to his face. But Rob had played first-team rugby at university, and after being knocked onto the back foot, he grabbed his boss with massive hands, locking him in a vice-like grip, and dragged him across the room. Speer's struggling body scattered chairs and rattled desks before Rob threw him heavily against a wall and watched his boss slump to the floor. Speer should have been out for the count, but the fury coursing through him, powered him back to his feet for another strike.

Cunningham flew out of his office and bellowed, "Stop your bloody nonsense, the pair of you!"

Momentarily shocked, Cain and some of his colleagues rushed forward to hold the two men apart. Rob easily shook off his restrainers and pulled himself together. "Ernest, I'll be in touch about repatriation fees, but as of today, I no longer work here. You'll have this in writing, but right now, I need to go home and see my family."

The big man stomped over to his desk and started packing his belongings.

Speer gathered himself and his attaché case together. Both had been thrown across the room by Rob. Cunningham glared at Speer and Pyle and ordered them to his office for a 'chat.'

"Not now, Ernest," Speer said curtly.

Neither Cain nor Charlie had ever seen their bosses so agitated, and it was really unsettling.

Speer turned to Rob and said, "First, I need to speak to our Chief Analyst and owner of an exceptionally strong right arm." He grimaced, rubbing what must have been a very sore shoulder, and asked Rob to please come to his office.

Rob looked quite nonplussed by the invitation but still had the gumption and wit to ask, "Surely you don't want another go at me, David?"

Speer reassured Rob that he knew better than that, and the two men left the room. Within seconds of disappearing, Speer stuck his head out from the door, asking Lena for two coffees, jolting her back to life from a state of confused shock.

An hour later, Rob walked out of the Major's office. He chatted comfortably and cheerfully with everyone telling them he'd work his two-month notice period plus one more month as an independent analyst. 'But right now, I need to think, so I'm headed home."

Seeing Rob walk out, Cain and Charlie agreed that they should also slip away for a while to chat about their own futures.

First, they approached Lena. "Would you have dinner with us tonight?" Charlie asked.

She looked puzzled, so Cain said quietly, "Come on, Lena, I think we all need some time together to blow off some steam while we offer you a position at the company we're planning to launch."

With the cold threat of unemployment lifted, she cheered up and wiped a tear from her cheek. They'd planned to take her to a nice restaurant in Kemang, but she asked to go to Hard Rock instead. "I know you go there often. It's been a long time since I last went, and it would be a fun venue for such a happy event."

They acceded to Lena's request saying they'd pick her up later.

[ ]

The café they visited was owned by the wife of a former Indonesian diplomat who'd replicated the Pacific Northwest coffee culture vibe in a large Kuningan district bungalow.

The two young expats sat in leather armchairs by a large bay window, sharing their astonishment and disappointment at how quickly their bosses had crumpled at the first sign of trouble.

"It's like a lyric from a band I used to listen to called The The," said Cain. "All the people I looked up to are no longer there."

"You mean you actually looked up to any of those blokes?" mocked Charlie.

"Oh, come on," urged Cain. "We both know Cunningham can be difficult, and somewhere in my mind, I can't shake the feeling that there was something underhand going on with our Hong Kong gig, but the old man's business credentials are solid. The Major, on the other hand, is a bit of a disappointment but Pyle… well, he turned out to be much better than any of us thought he'd be. And Ruby *really* respects him."

"I like the man too, but as he said, he won't be around for long," Charlie recalled. "That will leave us back at square one with Cunningham and Speer, and neither of them is the same bloke we worked for before Hong Kong. Cunningham's been acting weird for months, and now that it's common knowledge, it's only a question of time before the Major's indiscretion bends him out of shape even more than Big Rob did."

"Yeah, turns out he isn't the gentle giant I had him down as. But something else dawned on me, Charlie. You know Ruby's got that photo of Sir James and Tsang looking all friendly?

Charlie nodded.

"In Hard Rock, you assumed Sir James got his money because Ruby described the photo as 'friendly.' Why would he be smiling and shaking hands with Tsang if, as Cunningham announced, he actually didn't get his money?"

Charlie shrugged and smiled slyly, "Maybe they share a philanthropic interest in Cambodian orphans." Then a sudden realization prompted him to clasp his hands. "Hey! Maybe that photo was taken *before* what must have been a bad-tempered meeting. Was Sir James getting out of the car or getting in? Arriving to close his account or departing? We don't know the real context of the photo, and neither does Ruby."

Cain looked over his shoulder. The hardwood floors and high ceilings lent themselves to helping sound travel around the café. He softened his voice. "Precisely. The context determines the nature of the photo, and we don't know what it was. But whether the truth lies closer to Ruby's understanding of that photo or Cunningham's announcement, our business plans are more pressing than ever. Given what's just happened, did you talk to Andy again?"

"I did," Charlie confirmed. "Said he'll get family connections to fast-track our business application with the Financial Services Authority. His family will also be principal investors. We'll need to do their bidding for a while, but as we prove ourselves and the economies around here start growing, we could look into starting our own Equity fund."

"Our team will be small but capable," Cain predicted. "And Lena will be a great asset."

"Too true, mate," Charlie agreed. "In a smaller firm, she'd be capable of a whole lot more responsibility. Something I reckon she'd really welcome."

Charlie rubbed his hands together excitedly and continued, "Cool. I know you want to be a bona fide fund manager, and that day *will* come. Meantime, I'll get Andy to have a quiet word with the office landlord. The building's so empty; I'm sure he can score us a good deal."

Cain's mobile phone rang. "Ruby! Hello."

© Steven Clark 2023
Lynnburn, Amisfield, Dumfries & Galloway, UK

"It's happening Cain! Harrier's collapsed. I've actually been on camera, covering it for the channel, and my editors are saying I've devastated the competition."

She was giddy with excitement, and Cain could barely get a word in to congratulate her.

"Of course, I'll keep suggesting stories from Indonesia, but I can't imagine that happening very soon as I need to establish myself on air with this story as long as it lasts."

The plan to come to Indonesia had been in the background ever since Gili Trawangan, but this was a massive step in the right direction.

"First things first, Ruby, you've made it on air, and I know you'll be brilliant. I couldn't be happier for you."

Excited as she was, Ruby asked how he and Charlie were doing.

'We're just sitting in a café planning our own venture down here. Seems like today's been a big day for all of us."

His news clearly took her excitement to another level. "Gosh, how exciting. You and Charlie deserve every success. Cain, I'm sorry, I've got to go. Another live hit in five minutes. Bye!"

When Cain hung up, he became aware that, as well as Charlie, two women enjoying their afternoon coffee, had also heard the high-energy conversation with its commensurate volume. Cain said: "Ma'af sekali," to apologize, but they just returned their attention to their magazines.

"That sounded positive," Charlie commented, before only half joking, "But if she ever does make it down here, you'll need to do your best to prevent her producing a feature on us," he paused, then added with a deep movie trailer voice; "The industry insiders who blew Harrier apart."

"Jaysis!" Cain exclaimed. "I've told you how ambitious she is, but surely she'd know better than that." Saying it out loud, however, did give him pause.

[ ]

Cain and Charlie lost all track of time talking about their new business. Thankfully Andy was more than willing to drive Lena to Hard Rock.

Introduced to Ginung and Nisa, Lena quickly picked up on the waitress' accent and established that their families came from the same area in central Java. That revelation prompted the pair of them to chat every time Nisa got a moment's break.

Despite the economic turmoil affecting the entire region, the four young, would-be business partners were decidedly upbeat about their future. "After all, the way things are going, there'll be no bloody competition," quipped Charlie.

Andy suddenly became very animated. "Hey, you know how you wanted something that sounded 'elemental' for the name of the firm. What about 'Flint'? We are based in the 'Ring of Fire,' and Flint was the original fire starter.

Charlie's face also lit up; "Shit yeah, we have to call it Flint for all the reasons Andy mentioned. But think about it. The full name of the company would be 'Flint Independent Financial Advisory.' We'd be working at FIFA! Come on, Cain, the French lads would definitely invest in that."

Laughing along, all Cain could do was nod his head, saying, "Hell yeah. Let's do it."

16)   Reformation Genesis

When Lena met Nisa at Hard Rock a couple of weeks ago, they'd somehow started talking about how their grandparents had struggled against the Japanese before fighting the Dutch for independence. Lena was amazed at how the kampung girl had been able to link the fight for independence to a struggle against the IMF, which was forcing their beloved Republic to give up its food and fuel subsidies. She called it a form of Neo-colonialism, prompting Lena to wonder where she'd picked up her very political vocabulary.

Lena had always tried to ignore politics, but Nisa had stirred something in her the very same day she'd been told that she may lose her job. The dependable office manager was, therefore, more easily persuaded to attend the rally than she might ordinarily have been. And with all the remaining Temple-Speer staff so preoccupied with their own futures, she came to the forlorn conclusion that no one would really miss her.

Lena had never attended a political protest, and she was quite nervous. Bapak Suharto was the only leader she'd ever known, and it was the same for many other Indonesians. Like their tightly controlled media, they'd never think of questioning their President's more questionable actions; and if they ever did, his secret police would ruthlessly deliver the state's response.

Nisa was excited. She told Lena that today's protest was the result of endless secret meetings and introduced her to several activists, including Denny, her village 'brother.' Of a delicate build, he was intelligent, opinionated, and boyishly handsome. Nisa said, "Our families agreed that we should travel to Jakarta together," and Lena could see why. Jakarta must have been as remote in terms of mindset and lifestyle as it was of geography.

The demo was organized to oppose the IMF austerity policies designed to reset Indonesia's economy. The government stridently promoted the measures as being prescribed by foreigners. People who obviously didn't understand the feelings of the Indonesian people because they included the staggered elimination of Indonesia's politically sacrosanct food and fuel subsidies. Protesting the IMF's austerity policies was, therefore, highly virtuous. But the inherent nuance that the protest was critical of the President and his implementation of those policies rendered it both remarkable and extremely dangerous. In truth, however, the anti-Suharto aspect of the rally was much more than just a nuance. Whilst loudly denouncing foreign intervention, the activists were also whispering about endemic corruption and domestic reform.

The morning's papers had been full of praise for Suharto's big announcement, but even Lena had her doubts. Nisa parroted what she'd heard from her fellow activists, shouting over the noise of the city center traffic; "I can't believe Suharto chose Habibie as his VP. He might be okay as our Technology Minister, but not as Vice President."

Hearing Nisa's dangerously naïve delivery, Lena's eyes nervously scanned the pedestrian bridges spanning the roads that fed into the iconic Selamat Datang roundabout. She replied in a significantly quieter tone. "Watching the Rupiah plummet, even the Bulés at my office think he's just a Suharto clone. My mum told me that shops were trying to shut as people fought to get in and buy things before the prices sky-rocketed again."

Money was apparently not an issue for the protest leader. Ikraem was a Ph.D. student, and according to Nisa, he made sure his activists were well-fed. At the evening meetings during Ramadan, he'd arranged bottles of water and large packets of Nasi Goreng Istimewa for everyone's breakfast. And as the end of the fasting month approached, the activists' bodies were already accustomed to enduring the daylight hours without food while holding their anti-IMF placards aloft and shouting their opposition to the austerity plans.

Lena wiped her brow. The rainy season may have slightly cooled the daytime temperatures, but it also drove up the humidity. "I hate this time of year," she told Nisa. "I love my shoes, but the weather cannot be trusted, so I wear these flip-flops instead."

Nisa agreed, "It didn't take me long to notice the drains in my village are better than here in Jakarta. And the flood water often stinks because it's mixed with sewage."

"Then there's the mold that creeps across the walls at my home," Lena added. "We don't have aircon, so there's nothing to do except wait for dry weather before we can get rid of it properly."

"Getting my laundry dry is so difficult!" exclaimed Nisa. "Sometimes the material starts to smell."

Lena sighed; "I know what you mean." At least once a year, that smell reduced her to tears as yet another precious item of clothing fell victim to the archipelago's brand-unconscious rainy season. Standing by the side of the roundabout, she was thankful that it wasn't raining. But the humidity was sapping her energy and making her clothes stick to her skin. She'd left her beloved Balenciaga bag at home, stuffed with newspaper to absorb moisture. In its stead, she was using her brother's daypack into which she'd packed a spare blouse, though right now, she was wishing she'd also packed another skirt.

The rag-tag group of demonstrators blew whistles and yelled, refocusing Lena's attention. Some of the passing drivers declared cautious support from the safety of their vehicles. Every time they tooted their horns, it bolstered the spirits of the demonstrators, and they roared their appreciation. However, when a large SUV with blacked-out windows parked nearby, there were conspicuously fewer horn blasts.

"I am not sure I'm very comfortable now that we're almost certainly being watched," Lena told Nisa, motioning with her eyes that she was talking about the SUV. "That must be a BAKIN car. Inside there will be state intelligence agents taking photos of us."

Nisa was about to respond when another voice intervened. It was Ikraem. "No need to worry about them. It's the ones you can't see who we need to worry about," he cautioned while draping his arm over the shoulder of a gleeful Nisa. Lena's disapproving eyes followed his skinny arm over Nisa and maintained their vigilance as he uncomfortably withdrew it again.

Dressed in black from head to toe, Lena wondered how long it had been since the Che Guevara wannabe had washed his jeans. Her critical observation had been prompted by their awkward introduction earlier that morning. After Nisa had gushed about how he paid for their food out of his own pocket, Lena reasoned that as she earned a decent wage, she wanted to make a small donation. But Ikraem's response bordered on condescension in the way he refused to take her money and basked in Nisa's glorification. That was when she grasped how easy it must have been for Ikraem and his followers to mold and fashion Nisa's political awakening. She'd been given the vocabulary but were her convictions truly political, or were they simply a by-product of wanting to make friends in a big city that was totally alien to everything she'd previously known?

By contrast, Lena loved chatting to Ikraem's deputy, the infectiously likable Denny, about their nearby kampungs and the local characters. She told Nisa, "It was so nice to hear you call Denny 'older brother' the way we do at home, using the word 'Raka.' But I don't understand why you two are not a couple?"

Nisa responded in a manner that Lena implicitly understood; "Aiyoh, Denny is like a brother to me." Then noticeably quieter, "Or maybe a dear sister."

Lena knew that Denny would have been completely stifled growing up in a kampung where there's often little chance to be by yourself; never mind, in his case, to actually *be* yourself, and began to understand why he was living life so whole-heartedly here in the capital.

Denny was keen to see their protests grow and told Lena of his confidence that he and Ikraem could join with others to get thousands of students onto the streets. "Speed is crucial. We need to achieve a critical mass of defiance before the government makes good on its warnings and bans all demonstrations."

His passion was undeniable when he spoke about what he called 'Reformasi,' and just like Nisa, Lena was soon calling him 'Rayi' or younger brother in their shared dialect.

But there was something Lena just didn't like about Ikraem. It was obvious that Nisa could barely contain her excitement whenever he was near, but as no relationship had been mentioned, Lena wasn't going to ask. Instead, she told Nisa that the traffic fumes were making her feel ill, and shortly thereafter, she was wishing everyone the best of luck and saying goodbye.

She knew there were showers in the executive bathrooms of the Temple-Speer building. The friendly security staff would surely let her use them to wash off the grime from her very first protest. With that thought in mind, she hopped onto an Ojek, somehow maintaining her elegant side-saddle position as the motorcycle weaved through the traffic.

[ ]

The wonderful, warm water shower washed away the residual effects of the morning's dangerous and very uncomfortable activity. Feeling refreshed, she returned the executive bathroom key to the kindly, middle-aged security guards who always treated her like a favored niece.

At her desk, Lena made her usual preparations, thankful that no one saw her arrive. The tranquility of the office seemed stark after the traffic noise and protest chants she'd endured all morning. She walked to the far end of the reception desk and peered into the void of the main office. A couple of portfolio managers were in a meeting with Pyle and the Major in the conference room. And just within earshot, Andreas and Cain were chatting. Listening to their conversation and having spent the morning with people who wanted an end to foreign interference in her country, she was reminded of the huge gulf between life in this office and the struggles of her own family. She suddenly felt quite angry and exhaled sharply as if trying to expel the unusual emotion. Eavesdropping, she muttered, "Well, at least you're trying to see things from our point of view, Cain." But her anger wouldn't subside. "Between this office, your fancy apartment, the gym, and the nightclubs, your expat bubble totally insulates you from feeling my country's pain."

Even though she was across the room, she could tell Andy was trying to word his conversation politely. "Yes, it's true. Indonesian men do notice how arrogant some Bulés get when they are here. It's like they don't understand their position is temporary."

Cain said something about a book he was reading called 'A Passage to India,' and Lena remembered seeing the movie on television. He said the book had bored him at school, but reading it in a foreign land, made it more interesting because he could see parallels in his own life.

Lena pretended to be busy looking in some cabinets. Cain's voice became louder. "And it was published in 1924? That's 74 bloody years ago, and nothing's changed! There's a scene where some Indian characters are sitting around talking about the English, and they agree that when most of them arrived, they were actually okay. But then they go on to discuss how quickly they develop their snooty – or 'sombong' – attitudes and basically become arseholes."

Lena muttered under her breath, "You need a book to tell you that?" The door to the nearest small meeting room was ajar, so she walked quietly over and let herself in because from there, she could see and hear them more clearly.

On her way, she heard Andy say, "I guess you're beginning to understand why some people in South-East Asia still don't like Westerners. Colonialism is still in living memory, and there was nothing glorious about empires from our perspective. You should read 'This Earth of Mankind', by Pramoedya Ananta Toer for an Indonesian view. To us, colonialism was a horrible period in our country's history. It can't be forgotten within a couple of generations."

Cain interrupted, "You don't have to tell me that, mate. England's oldest colonies are Ireland and bloody Scotland. We're pretty bitter too. The thing is," he continued, tactlessly putting Andy on the spot, "I'd love to hear your own opinion on expats over here because you must have seen the situation from both sides after studying in the US."

Andy scratched his head, searching for an answer. "I'm not sure my view will be so different from yours, Cain. What you have to understand is that we Indonesians can be just as sarcastic as anyone. So, when we see Bulés strutting around like they own the place, we make fun of them because we know expats like them will come. But more importantly, they will leave."

Lena watched Andy scratch his head. "I'm trying to understand you," he continued. "The expats we are talking about are not my people, so

I don't see their behavior as letting me down personally. Maybe that's why I can ignore them more easily than you. And yes, while some Bulés go off the rails, many more settle down eventually. Like yourself, if you don't mind me saying."

"Really?" said Cain. Lena smirked because Andy had clearly surprised him. He hadn't expected to be personally included in their chat.

Andy explained, "I guess your ego was stroked when you arrived, but Charlie told me you weren't a typical 'Gweilo'. You didn't screw around, and you are younger than most expats here, so I'm sure you got offers."

Cain nodded awkwardly. "That so-called attraction of the Bulé boyfriend has always puzzled me." Lena tutted as that tedious old topic was brought up. "I've heard some women even get pregnant trying to hold onto their relationship, despite the incredibly high probability of the expat beating a hasty retreat home."

Andy leaned in a little closer. Lena did the same. "I spoke with my sister about this. She told me that some women really want a Bulé husband, but if they can't have that, they are happy to have a half-Bulé child who might eventually bring them an income as a model. You must have noticed how so many ads here feature mixed-race, Eurasian models."

Cain nodded. "Yeah, and selling stuff like skin whitening creams."

Andy pointed excitedly as if Cain had made a point for him. "You really need to read Pramoedya's book. What he wrote about social standing being based on the amount of European blood in a family tree is still way too relevant today."

Lena thought the interesting part of the conversation was over and decided to take a circuitous route back to her desk, over to the other side of the office, and behind the boys. On her way, she saw Andy point toward her reception area and didn't know where to put herself when she heard her name. "Lena used to work with a girl called Anna. She was determined to get a Bulé husband. That is probably part of the reason she came to work here. But Lena's different."

Lena stopped and pretended to tidy the desk closest to her.

"She's smart and wouldn't settle for just anybody. The thing is, her exposure to foreigners and their possible influence on her could put some Indonesian guys off. It's tough for such girls. They walk a real tightrope when it comes to men."

"You don't know the half of it, Andreas Prakowo," Lena grumbled, bending over and pretending to look at something on an empty desk's blank PC screen.

It was Cain's turn to scratch his head; "Sheez Andy! I never appreciated the pressures faced by women like Lena. It's really not fair. Mind you, sometimes, I think Charlie and Lena would be a good match."

Lena was quickly arriving at the conclusion that listening to colleagues talking about her was excruciating. She had to put a stop to it. She stood up and breezed by Andy and Cain on her way to the reception as if nothing had happened.

[ ]

Making up for her lost morning, Lena hadn't noticed Charlie walking out of the elevator and was shocked when a large bag of rice landed on the reception counter.

"I've just seen some Indonesian kids protesting against Suharto at the Selamat Datang roundabout," he announced. "Considering how risky it is, they're pretty brave to criticize the President like that. Brave and hungry, I guess. As it's Ramadan, they've probably been out there all day with empty stomachs."

Lena couldn't believe that in the last hour, she'd been the topic of two conversations. She dismissed an initial pang of paranoia, telling herself the timing was all wrong and that Charlie couldn't have seen her. But it bothered her when he said that the protests were Anti-Suharto because she'd understood it as anti-IMF. How many other people had misunderstood their protest? There was little comfort for her in Charlie's description of the protestors as 'brave.'

He was now looking at the bag of rice as if he'd just remembered it was there. "Oh yeah, after my meeting, I got lunch in Plaza Indonesia's basement 'warung' and then popped into the supermarket. It had been pretty much emptied out, but this was sitting on the floor. I reckoned your family could put it to good use."

Lena was overcome with happiness at Charlie's kindness. He'd done this a couple of times, despite that awful first meeting with her mother. She never thought she could be attracted to a Chinese guy, but maybe Cain was right because there was just something about Charlie.

She leaned over the desk, checked no one was coming, and gave him a peck on the cheek. "Pak Charlie, you are always so kind to my family. My mother says you should come for dinner sometime. God bless you."

Charlie winked. "Got to take good care of my future business partner." Then, pointing toward the main office, he asked, "By the way, is Pyle in there?"

Lena nodded affirmatively as he thanked her and walked past her into the office. She chuckled, noticing a big white dust mark running down his back, no doubt the result of slinging the bag of rice over his shoulder.

Charlie waved to Cain and pointed at Pyle's office to indicate where he was headed.

When he reached the American's door, he could see the room was empty. He was almost going to turn around when he saw a big box file labeled JTH sitting on his desk. He looked around and went in.

Cain had described the file as being thin, but its thickness was the main reason it had been so visible from across the room. He was also sure that Cain had called 'JTH 77-81', but standing over Pyle's desk and looking at it the right way round, Charlie noticed the '81' had been replaced by the number 93.

His nerves were on edge, and he became aware that he was even grinding his teeth, but the draw of the file was irresistible. If those numbers denoted years, then no wonder it's so much thicker, he deduced while taking a look. Inside, the first thing he saw was the thin manila folder Cain had spoken of with the 77-81 label. More folders lay beneath, and the last one was labeled 90-93.

He peaked through the office door. Thankfully the only person he could see in the office was Cain. He exhaled slowly and began to leaf through the 77-81 folder. All the typed pages featured the names of Asian, African, South American, and Middle-Eastern countries, along with legalese about end users and lots of code numbers. But there were also many hand-written notes in the margins that appeared to be explaining those codes. Charlie screwed up his face as if squinting would help to decipher them, but they were far too technical for a layman.

From the recurrence of his name on the pages, however, Charlie confirmed that the folder name 'JTH' was clearly a reference to James Templar Hawes.

A noise from outside disturbed him. He quickly closed up the box file and bent down, pretending to get something out of his bag, as someone – he couldn't see who – walked by.

He had to get out of there. He walked toward the door, writing a text to Cain asking if the coast was clear. He waved cautiously. Thankfully Cain noticed and saw the look on his face. He sent the text. Cain looked at his phone, nodded, got up, and walked to meet him halfway.

Charlie took a deep breath and walked out, looking straight at Cain. When he reached his friend, they tried to act and chat casually till they were sure they'd got away with it, but no one was paying the slightest attention to them.

Charlie whispered, "I've seen that JTH file you were telling me about. It's in Pyle's office, and it's a bloody sight thicker than when you last saw it.

Part 3:

The Quickening – 1998 April - May

17)   Beware of Yanks Bearing Gifts

A beleaguered Temple-Speer limped along for a few months, but everyone knew it was the end of the road. Terence Pyle left and spent an extravagant Chinese New Year in Singapore with his 'golden handshake.' Returning to Jakarta, he rented an apartment while he waited for the interior décor to be completed in the large penthouse he'd purchased. Factoring in the Rupiah exchange rate, he joked that he should have bought two and tried to breed them.

Apart from his investment, nothing else he did was particularly forward-looking. After several conversations on the subject, Cunningham passed him a thick dossier full of information about Sir James' business affairs over the last quarter century. But Pyle had swiftly fallen into a debauched existence since losing his job. At first, he frequented the bars at the 5-star Shangri- la and Mulia hotels, along with trips to Tanamur and JJs. But as time went on, he strayed to the back streets of the Blok M area, where drink, drugs, and women could all be bought at rock-bottom prices. Whilst there, he'd heard about a bar in the Mawwar hotel catering to all manner of desires.

Good to his word, Chief Analyst Rob Watson stayed to work through his notice period. In return, Ernest Cunningham secured a partnership for him at a newly established financial advisory in rural southwest Scotland. The firm was hoping to cash in on a surge of new properties being renamed 'Dunroamin' as more and more well-heeled retirees moved into the large county of Dumfries & Galloway.

The Major had worked tirelessly to build the company, but his strength of purpose had diminished with the arrival and apparent influence of Feronika. To her credit, she also seemed to have relaxed the man, and that had allowed him and Rob Watson to become closer than they'd been even before their brief but vicious brawl. Together, they worked well with Cunningham to start winding down Temple-Speer's operations.

Cunningham was much more content, and at times, he was even good-humored. In telephone conversations with Sir James, he tried to avoid retirement talk, but curiously, it was often Sir James who introduced the topic by reminiscing over their shared history. Cunningham was obliged to make noises about missing the work, and Sir James promised to 'see him right' after acknowledging his regrettably slow response to the ample warning Cunningham had provided ahead of Harrier's downfall.

In a most unexpected fashion, the process of closing Temple-Speer became one of the Firm's more carefree periods. Cain and Charlie added to that blithe spirit when they announced they were starting their own company. Declaring that they'd happily take on Temple-Speer clients with Hanthorpe portfolios just made things easier all round.

Back in late January, Charlie upset his mother on several counts during a difficult phone call when he told her he wasn't coming home for Chinese New Year. He explained that he could lose his job later in the year, but instead of coming home, he was staying on to set up a new business venture. In subsequent calls, whenever news broke about trouble in Indonesia, she threatened to fly out and, if need be, drag her son back to London.

Cain had spoken with his own parents once or twice but didn't share the news that he and Charlie were starting a business of their own. He didn't want to give his father any ammunition by telling him about the demise of Temple-Speer. But he was still in touch with Ruby, who was struggling to pass Indonesia stories by her editors. Ruby's frustration only served to heighten Cain's own sense that he was actually living within a massive news story. He was in Jakarta at a time of historical flux. He still believed it promised a bright future if only he and Charlie could get the new business up and running by the end of this month.

Lena was helping everyone when she could but was also spending more time at home helping her family make it through an extremely tough time. Well, that was the story she spun at the office, and there was truth in it; but she was also dividing her time between home and the student protests, which she'd started to find irresistible. Nisa, Denny, and the others spoke so passionately about forging a new future for the Republic that even Lena began to believe they might just actually succeed. Her innate sensitivity ensured that she really did feel the anguished pain generated by the contradiction between her life at work with privileged foreigners and on the street protesting foreign neo-colonial interference. Thankfully, she could draw on a deep reservoir of personal strength to help conceal that pain. Her natural intelligence lent her the capacity to recognize that she was being tested and, therein, try to maintain a measured perspective.

The mettle of the Republic was also being tested. Indonesia needed a bailout, but there was a sense that the country had already bitten the hand of those who would condescend to feed it. Suharto agreed to implement IMF reforms such as the closure of crony banks and institutions, but the government-stoked outcry over the end of fuel and food subsidies emboldened him to brand those particular reforms as unconstitutional. The IMF retaliated by delaying a three-billion-dollar tranche of a 40-billion-dollar loan package, and its Chief, Michel Camdessus, appeared to adopt an unsubtle strategy of divide and erode. Pitting Indonesia against its neighbors, he claimed Suharto's intransigence could undermine their fragile recoveries. The old General was clearly in the crosshairs. He was now being blamed for the woes of the entire region.

Public protests had been banned since February, but on March 11th, thousands of students from more than thirty universities held protests, claiming their government was doing nothing to ease the nation's hardship. Those protests took place the day after the People's Consultative Assembly added insult to a catalog of injuries already inflicted upon the electorate when they re-elected the unopposed Suharto for a seventh term.

[ ]

Sir James arrived in Jakarta yesterday. He'd flown in a private jet from Seletar's small airport in northeast Singapore to Jakarta's old Halim airport, where he boarded a chopper for a short hop to the Hyatt. Suharto's staff felt this route was necessary if Sir James was to avoid witnessing the capital in tumult on his way to the Presidential suite that had once more been granted to him.

Not long after Sir James' arrival, Speer had taken Cain aside. He seemed quite excited. "Just wanted to tell you that I've managed to get you into a meeting tomorrow with myself, Ernest, and Sir James. It's at the Hyatt, and we're meeting the new Finance Minister, Fuad Bawazier. Always felt I owed you one for Hong Kong... and for keeping my secret. Admittedly, it'll be observation status only, but you'll definitely find it interesting." He paused and wagged his index finger at Cain. "I just need a promise that you won't repeat the hand gesture you gave Sir James when he visited the office. Promise that, and we're good to go."

Cain was excited about the meeting, but as a gesture of goodwill, it fell far short of the expectations the Major had bogusly encouraged him to accrue.

Admitting he was jealous, Charlie rationalized Cain's good fortune. "Speer always had a soft spot for you. I put it down to the military connection. But couple that with a dose of Tanamur dancer, mid-life crisis guilt, and he's likely just trying to make amends with himself as much as with you."

He'd then wagged his finger at Cain, "Just make sure you get some good contacts for us when we break out on our own."

[ ]

Cain had never seen the Grand Hyatt's massive lobby so quiet. Apart from himself, Speer, and Cunningham, the only other people he could see were hotel staff and, from a distance, what looked like three Asian businessmen deep in discussion. But when the Temple-Speer trio were escorted across the lobby to a private elevator with just one floor option, Cain noticed the businessmen had left.

The unusually fast elevator rocketed upwards to the Presidential Suite. When its doors opened, Speer looked at Cain, who was trying to appear unmoved. But he couldn't help himself and silently mouthed the words, "Thank you."

Deputy Finance Minister Arif Suyatno greeted them. Hand stretched out, he quickly explained, "Apologies, gentlemen, Finance Minister Fuad Bawazier has been called away, but I am eager to talk with you."

Cain didn't have time to be disappointed as Suyatno shook his hand, saying, "And you must be Mr. Shaw."

Sir James had been following the Deputy and timed his approach perfectly. "Glad to see you chaps made it here unscathed. My feet have barely touched the ground since I arrived, and my gracious Indonesian hosts have gone to quite extraordinary lengths to keep me safe."

He shook their hands one by one; "Ernest. Major. And Cain Shaw. Good to see you again."

Cain was dazzled by the rarefied atmosphere he'd been catapulted into. "Sir James, pleased to see you again." Thankfully, his insincerity was masked by his endearingly overawed tone.

Sir James suggested they sit as he and Minister Suyatno had been enjoying a thought-provoking conversation.

And Suyatno didn't waste any time. "Gentlemen, after keeping 40 billion from our country, the Americans now have the impertinence to tell the world how charitable they are by announcing their intention to send 70 million in food and medical aid. Emergency aid for an emergency they are nurturing! It's a point that Bapak and Minister Bawazier are going to make very strongly in Cairo at next month's Group of 15 meetings."

Sir James struck the arm of his chair. "Excellent news! I hope Bapak sends a powerful message to the world about America's mendacity."

Cain was bursting with pride. Here he was at a meeting, the like of which he'd only ever read about in textbooks or newspapers. Sitting bolt upright, he was scared to move in case he woke up and discovered this amazing scene was nothing more than a dream.

Sir James continued, "The Trojans famously cautioned, 'Beware of the Greeks when they are bearing gifts.' But at least the Trojans knew their enemy. In your case, Minister, the true enemy may be harder to determine." He leaned forward. "And it's not the Greeks, that's for sure. But strictly speaking, it's not the Americans either. We at Temple-Speer believe the White House is acting at the behest of Peking."

Minister Suyatno's eyebrows rose, widening his eyes before he consciously narrowed them, his voice becoming quiet and serious. "I fear you may be correct, Sir James. If you are examining the same data as me, then you too will have noticed the considerable uptick in Chinese purchases of American debt. Clinton needs a decisive end-of-tenure victory and could even balance the US budget at some point next year."

Cunningham took advantage of the ponderous silence. "When one considers the apparent lack of logic in the advice being dispensed by the IMF, one must assume there's another motive in which the destabilization of an ideological ally like Indonesia can somehow make sense."

Suyatno sprang back in his chair. "It's just as Pak Bawazier and I have been telling Bapak Suharto. The IMF's advice is incomprehensible! Thank goodness their latest correspondence indicates that Bapak Suharto's forbearance has been vindicated. Tomorrow he will agree to dissolve more of the Republic's banks, and In Shaa Allah, they will concede more time before we must dismantle food and fuel subsidies."

A door opened, and a voice called out, "Pak Suyatno, are you talking about me?"

Suyatno scrambled to his feet, as did Cunningham and Speer, who hissed, "Look lively, Shaw."

Suyatno was already telling his President what they'd been talking about when Sir James finally stood up too. Cain couldn't believe what he was seeing. He stood at ease, soldier-like, with his hands behind his back, just like Speer. No one had expected this.

Suharto took Suyatno's seat. "Sir James. Pak Cunningham. Thank you for confirming our growing suspicions about Washington and Beijing."

He told them all to sit, and his translator explained that the President had been working in the other Suite but had been anxious to greet his guests.

Cain was beside himself and trying desperately to control his excitement. He looked at Suharto and saw the nation's history etched on the man's face.

He spoke. "Yes, my friends, it looks like the IMF is giving my Republic a light reprieve concerning the cessation of subsidies. Perhaps Camdessus feels he has already closed every option for my government." Then he sighed heavily. "To use Paul Keating's insult; I cannot fathom why they are not giving that old Malaysian 'recalcitrant' a tougher time."

Cunningham had heard a rumor about Malaysia's Prime Minister Mahathir during a recent visit to Singapore. "Mr. President, if I may."

Suharto showed him an open right palm. "Please, Pak Ernest. You are always interesting." Ernest bowed his head in appreciation.

Cain couldn't help but be very impressed that his mentor had received such a compliment from a man like Suharto and had done so with such grace.

"Mr. President. Prime Minister Mahathir remains popular for now, but maybe Camdessus knows about the rift developing with his Deputy Anwar Ibrahim. If so, he will wager that the unusual plan to discredit Anwar may result in the two men upsetting the country's political and economic prospects all by themselves."

Sir James picked up on Cunningham's comment; "Ernest makes a good point, Mr. President. You've just been re-elected, and you have successfully held out against the IMF. In so doing, you've won a great victory by maintaining the people's food and fuel subsidies, which was the student's central gripe. Once the news gets out tomorrow, they might stop their churlish little demonstrations once and for all."

Sir James had been on solid ground flattering Suharto, but he looked a little uneasy when his simple statement of facts had strayed into prediction. Cain couldn't help but see the contradiction between the supremely self-confident man he'd first met and the rather obsequious man sitting with him now.

Sir James tried to add a little depth to his shallow remark. "Over the last thirty years, students have forced their way onto the pages of history, but with the exception of Iran; from the US and Europe in the sixties, through Burma in '88 and Tiananmen a year later, those pages are riddled with the word 'failure.'

Cain thought that if Sir James had been trying to reassure Suharto, drawing attention to Iran was surely a mistake because it hadn't ended well for the Shah.

The President nodded slowly as he absorbed the translation before suddenly standing up and saying, "Major Speer."

As everyone else stood, Speer snapped to attention and saluted.

Suharto returned the gesture, albeit much less crisply. "Jim has been telling me some very good things about you."

Cain had never even contemplated that anyone might call Sir James 'Jim'. He pressed his lips to conceal a sardonic smile while Speer spoke of his time in the Army Air Corps, and Suharto cherry-picked from his own career to bond with the Major by mentioning his time leading the mobile air arm.

The President was now standing next to Speer as if inspecting him. "A man can leave the service, but the service never leaves the man. You project the very essence of leadership." With Speer beaming, he turned to address everyone; "Indeed, that is why I expect General Wibowo will do a fine job as my new Commander of the Armed

Forces. Firm but even-handed, I am certain he can maintain the essential balance between elements and personalities at this difficult time."

Suharto gave no further detail about those 'elements and personalities' and looked like he was going to leave, but Sir James pronounced, "Mr. President, I must say that in balancing elements in your administration, you made an inspired choice naming Pak Habibie as your Vice President. He may have no military experience, but he is a fine technocrat."

Suharto switched to English, saying, "I must thank you again for your advice in the matter, Jim," before directing his gaze at Cunningham. "And thank you, Ernest, for your wise counsel about my American friends and the Chinese." He then looked at Cain as if seeing him for the first time. Cain returned his attention with a very conscious smile and bowed his head ever so slightly as Cunningham had done.

Suharto clapped his hands together, saying, "Now, if you will all excuse me?"

As he left for the other Presidential Suite, an aide explained that "Bapak has an important meeting at the Istana." Then he turned to follow his President and the Deputy Finance Minister.

In the absence of the President and his staffers, Speer, Cunningham, and Sir James were free to outline their progress in winding down Temple-Speer and didn't seem to mind Cain's presence at all. Looking around the impossibly luxurious suite, Cain remembered how impressed he and Charlie had been with their rooms in Hong Kong. They were nothing like this, though.

Sir James recaptured Cain's attention when he declared, "Bankers talking about being innovative? Christ! The words 'innovative' and 'banking' have no place together. If the world wants financial artistry, it should look to the likes of us." He lowered his voice and looked at Speer. There are, however, other sectors where innovation is always key, and they need good men like yourself, David. I have some very good contacts if you're interested in another Asian role."

"Certainly something to think about," Speer conceded.

Then Sir James looked at Cain. "And you are planning to tough it out here in Asia, young man? I have to say how much I admire your pluck."

Cain was saying 'thank you,' but Sir James was already looking at Cunningham; "Oh, to be young and unencumbered by the baggage weighing us oldies down." Then to Cain, "I should like to come by the office and talk to you and your mate Charlie if I get a chance before leaving this Thursday."

Cain lied, "I'm sure he'd love that, Sir James."

Just as he'd spotted the old man's use of the word 'commitment' back in January, he'd also seen through the escape clause within Sir James' latest promise. Equivocation might not be his mother tongue, but Sir James spoke the language with habitual ease.

18)   First Blood from Shadows

Lena's exasperated mother claimed she looked like a peasant.

"Look at your skin! You used to have such a beautiful, pale complexion because you didn't spend all your time outside in the sun. We have all heard stories about so-called activists disappearing over the past year. I worry every day that my precious daughter will not come home. And what would happen to us if you lost your job?"

Showering in the office block's 'Executive' bathroom, Lena's smile at the memory of her mother's anxious face jarred against her recollection of rumors about the torture techniques used on activists. There was no doubt that things were changing fast. The President may have saved the food and fuel subsidies by standing up to the IMF, but the motivation for the demonstrations had moved on. The students now wanted nothing less than his resignation. Lena was also struggling with the pace of change in her own consciousness. Like her contemporaries, she'd grown up in a fog of denial about the regime's rumored excesses, but that fog was lifting.

As she walked through the Temple-Speer entrance, Lena noticed the office wasn't as empty as she'd expected it to be. There were a few former colleagues she hadn't seen for weeks. She could make out the huge figure of Rob Watson, and peering further into the room, she saw Terence Pyle. His hair was limp and greasy, and his skin was morbidly pallid. Lena chuckled, thinking that even her mother would have agreed that Pyle's skin was *too* pale. The Major was leading a meeting, and on closer examination, she saw a Panama hat and realized that the older man next to him wasn't Pak Cunningham.

Cain turned when she gasped, and Charlie called for her to join them. Everyone was looking in her direction, and despite knowing there was no future at Temple-Speer, she couldn't help but be worried about the reaction she was going to face for being absent. Her heartbeat raced as she walked toward the group. She dearly wished she'd remained at the demo.

The Major welcomed her; his tone was grave. "Hello Lena, I'm afraid I have some terrible news. Ernest Cunningham was found dead at his apartment this morning by his maid. The police were here just a short while ago. They believe he was murdered. They are investigating, but so far, all they've determined with any certainty is that he died at approximately midnight last night."

A dizzying composite of relief, fear, and sadness swept over Lena, causing her to grab the back of a nearby chair as she became faint.

Sir James told everyone to give her space while Speer rushed forward to keep her upright and sit her in the chair. Cain ran to get her a cup of water from the cooler.

He watched with admiration as Lena recovered. True to form, she composed herself as best she could, apologized, and thanked them all for their kindness before asking. "Who would want to kill a gentleman like Pak Cunningham?"

"That's what we're all asking ourselves, my dear girl," Speer replied.

Despite some troubling times with Cunningham last year, Cain's relationship with him had improved over the past few months. He'd never experienced death, never mind the murder of anyone he knew. So, whether he was numb or just didn't know any better, he asked, "Did Brigadier General Kusnadi tell you anything more, Major?"

Speer took Cain's question but addressed the room; "You will all have noticed that Ernest never spoke about his private life. Even though I worked closely with him for several years, I can't honestly say I knew much about him, apart from his intelligence and incredible work ethic."

Sir James piped up, "Same goes for me, I'm afraid. As for family, he has a sister who lives in Dorking." Then as an after-thought that he appeared to direct largely at himself, he added, "But I'm not entirely sure they got on."

With Sir James' voice drifting off, Speer cleared his throat and shared the further details of what he'd been told about Cunningham's death. "I think we all observed a... a respectful silence around Ernest's private life.

With the words 'Ernest's private life,' Cain knew this meeting was going to be difficult for the Major. That thought was confirmed by the way Speer looked around at the faces in front of him, "What I'm about to tell you must not be discussed beyond these walls. Ernest's body was found naked on the floor next to his bed... sex aids were scattered around the room... There was even a gay porn video in the VCR." Speer looked down. He was struggling, but when he recalled the rest of the details, he carried on. "There was a scarf tied loosely around Ernest's neck, but marks on his skin indicated that it, or some other ligature, had been tied a lot tighter." He drew a deep breath. "It was explained to myself and Sir James that some people like to be partially suffocated during sex as it makes the climax more intense."

Sir James had been shaking his head slowly during Speer's last few words as if trying not to hear them. He stood up from a desk he'd been sitting on to announce, "The Brigadier General says he's seen this kind of thing before. He's insisting on an autopsy."

The old man, who'd known Cunningham for decades, was then overcome and sat down heavily on the desktop again. Shaking his head and saying, "Poor Ernest. What a bloody mess."

Cain had seen a very different side of Sir James every time he'd been in his presence. Horridly self-righteous and shouting about owning the world, then quiet and compliant with Suharto, and now he looked like a broken old man finding it difficult to cope with the loss of an old pal. Cain remembered when his younger clients first considered their mortality during his sales pitch. None of us can escape that final moment of vulnerability, Sir James, no matter how bloody successful we think we are, he concluded.

Speer completed the police description of the scene. "Stoic to the end, Ernest managed to write 'Hi' on the title page of his Loeb Classics copy of Marcus Aurelius' 'Meditations,' but then appears to have passed out and never recovered. He must have been in agony because the two-letter word was written in a child-like scratch." The Major leaned forward a little and lowered his voice. "Now, while I'm quite sure that Ernest *was* homosexual, I don't think he was active here. I believe the scene must have been created by someone who wanted to discredit Ernest as well as kill him. This is why Sir James has asked his government contacts to get their best man to investigate. The Brigadier General was commissioned by the President himself to cover the case and to do so in a manner that won't draw any unwanted attention."

"That's correct," Sir James affirmed indignantly. "Ernest didn't deserve to die in such a violent manner, and he certainly doesn't deserve to have his memory besmirched by such an ignominious end. I want to do everything I can to protect his good name."

"More like protecting himself," Cain whispered angrily to Charlie.

Speer saw the whisper but ignored it. "We all liked Ernest, even though, let's face it, he could sometimes be a difficult man. But please remember that Sir James knew him longer than any of us. We have to keep an even keel throughout this torrid turn of events, protect

Ernest's dignity by maintaining our own, and help the police in any way we can."

Sir James thanked the Major for his kind comment, explaining that he was truly devastated.

Pyle looked like he was aching to say something and coughed by way of interruption. "Man, I know you Brits like your reserve, but I can't believe how little you know about the man who was the cornerstone of this whole fucking company."

Last year Cain correctly identified that Speer felt three was a crowd in Temple-Speer's management. For an instant, Speer looked like he would cut Pyle off, but in the presence of Sir James, he clearly thought it better to let the American talk himself even further out of the old man's good graces.

Pyle continued, "You know, I hung out a lot with Ernest during my time here and figured I got to know him quite well. He was one of those old bachelor asexual types. But who knows? There *are* places for gay guys in this city. By necessity, the scene is kept low-key. But let me tell you, Ernest would have been quite a catch, and if a local boyfriend somehow got jealous … Well, some of you may know from a client or even personal experience how nasty things can get when relationships don't work out down here. I agree with the Major. We have to be cool about what's happened, but we shouldn't overlook the possibility that this could have been a crime of passion."

Charlie chipped in with a supportive view of what Pyle had said but was actually shushed by Sir James. The old man's furrowed brow clearly conveyed that he was not at all comfortable with Ernest's lifestyle being subjected to this level of scrutiny.

Speer moved the meeting on; "Listen, everyone, as Brigadier General Kusnadi explained, his police officers will be in touch with all of us in the next day or two. We can infer from that statement that he expects us to remain in the city and be contactable. I know you all have a lot on your plates, and this horrifying news doesn't make matters any easier, but please try to be strong."

Sir James had to leave. His driver was called to ready the armor-plated government car and motorcycle outriders for the short journey to the Grand Hyatt. That journey was going to be taken via the Istana and another meeting with the President, but there was no good reason to share that with those present. Instead, he appeared quite lost in his sorrow and asked, "Where does one purchase Easter Eggs in a Muslim nation? It's Maundy Thursday, and I fear I may miss out on the entire Easter experience this year."

There was general bewilderment at Sir James' ability to switch off from the news about Ernest. Cain didn't like the man but reasoned that it was probably just a coping mechanism. "I'm sure the staff at the Hyatt can source Easter Eggs for you, Sir James. There's a mall next door to the hotel," he dared to advise.

After a couple of months of criticizing Sir James since he'd first met him; and being irritated that he hadn't been invited to the meeting with Suharto's surprise attendance, Charlie was more than a little exercised by Sir James' curiously disconnected and insensitive question. He whispered in Cain's ear. "I'd like to make sure the Panama hat-wearing prick gets the full Easter experience; Crown of thorns, wooden cross, and three big fuck-off nails."

Holding himself together till Sir James' departure, Cain began to feel quite emotional. The shock was giving way.

He rubbed his itching right eye and tried to expel the lurid image of Ernest's death.

At that moment, Rob Watson and Speer walked past, heading to the latter's office. Charlie's tone was almost timid when he asked, "I know the time is beyond awful, Major, but could myself and Cain speak with you?

"Certainly, Charlie," Speer replied. "As I said, we all have to remain strong, and talking things through will help. Give Rob and me thirty minutes, and then we can chat."

Hearing the Major's response, Cain told Charlie he was going to the toilet and excused himself.

He got into the lift and took it to the top floor, pushed a fire door open, and ran up a flight of steps to the roof. Pushing open another door, he heard the hum of the city far below. He gulped in the warm air and stumbled over to the old cigarette butts that marked the spot where people from the building's many different companies used to chat. He'd come up here to get out of the office for a moment and recalled a similar need after meeting with Edward Grant. Christ, but that seems like an eternity ago with all that's happened, he thought. Standing there by the wall that edged the roof, he gazed out at the city lit by hazy sunshine. A warm wind breezed across him, but far from refreshing his mind, he felt unsteady on his feet, obliging him to hold onto the perimeter wall.

He was horrified by Ernest's death and could not escape the image of its lurid details. What had Ernest done to deserve such a fate? These were difficult times for Indonesia. Back in January, Charlie and Lena had witnessed appalling brutality, and now Ernest had been murdered. Cain was banking his future on a city that had shown him the extreme breadth of fate it could bestow on anyone. He thought he was beginning to understand Jakarta. But at this moment, he was feeling very lost.

His mobile rang. It was Charlie asking where on earth he'd gone because the Major was ready to see them. Cain shook himself. "Sorry mate. I'm coming now."

[ ]

They discussed the shocking news with the Major.

"It's absolutely incomprehensible and surreal in the true nature of those overused words." the Major reflected. "I'll be honest with you. I'm shaking, and I can't quite discern the reason for it. Fear. Anger. Grief. I'm just not sure. But I am certain that no matter how awful this is, we can't allow it to grind us all to a halt. Indeed, the very nature of the tragedy behooves us to carry on maintaining an even keel. Ernest wouldn't tolerate anything less."

Charlie rapped the desk lightly, saying, "Exactly, Major, that's why we're here. We felt we should tell you our plans for a Temple-Speer-ish operation, albeit very slimmed down, of course."

Cain didn't return the Major's smile. He felt none of the intimacy he'd experienced in such moments during the brief period around Hong Kong. Those days had passed. He'd done his bit and received absolutely nothing in return, so he and Charlie were going to determine their own futures and not wait for the likes of him.

Cain began, "Quite frankly, Major," and he sounded very frank indeed, "When I last had an opportunity to churn a potential client, I felt sick to my stomach." The Major kept on smiling but leaned hard against the back of his chair and crossed his arms. "So, it's ethical investment funds for me from now on. It seems like the word ethical is being hammered into everything right now, so I'm just hoping there's an appetite for ethical investments too."

"Impressive, Shaw," Speer titled his head, "I also hope your specialization proves viable."

Hearing the praise after he'd adopted such a diffident tone, Cain felt, for the very first time, like he was at least on par with the man he'd previously looked up to.

Charlie took his turn. "Unlike Sir James with Harrier, my clients have recovered their profits from the Temple-Speer Fund and are eager to find new investments.

Cain was almost uncomfortable. Charlie had risen the bar on his own diffidence and almost sounded dismissive.

"Andy and I have been studying China data over the last five years and see a lot of potential in firms run by former People's Liberation Army officers. It's nearly a decade since Tiananmen, and businessmen over here seem to have moved on, as has China."

Speer didn't appear as impressed by Charlie's plans. "Maybe the time has indeed come for the world to move on from Tiananmen. Sir James made the same argument many years ago when we were looking to set up in Asia. I thought the world wouldn't forget. He argued that Deng Xiaoping had to send in the tanks to prevent China from reverting to its ruinous cycle of perpetual revolution and insisted that world leaders would affect the necessary amnesia when China's economic progress ripened."

Cain was usually wary of letting his feelings be known in the office, but he couldn't help himself. "Well, if Generation X thinks like Sir James, I should probably shelve my idea of selling ethical investments."

They were expressing themselves provocatively, but the Major appeared to be bending over backward to keep things cordial. "Your generation will be better than mine, I hope. You'll remember, Shaw, that after the Hyatt meeting, Sir James told you how much he admires you two. Shortly after, he confessed to me that he even felt a twinge of jealousy. Well, I share his sentiment, so I want to offer you all the support I can."

They'd heard that kind of thing before. Cain was going to utter some form of non-committal gratitude when Charlie asked Speer what his own plans were.

Looking relieved at the change of topic, Speer smiled and rounded on Charlie with mock anger, "Well, clearly, there's no job for me in your enterprise."

Cain countered just a little too coldly, "We couldn't afford you."

Speer rubbed his dry nostrils, tone deaf to Cain's weak attempt at effrontery. "I'll also try to remain in Asia. Can't say very much, but Sir James has opened a door for me in Singapore with an interesting firm."

He paused as if weighing his next words, "But what I can confidentially share with you is that whilst in Singapore, I will settle matters with my wife and family. You've both met Feronika, and another regional role will give me time to evaluate what I want for my future. To be honest, it's all a little too complicated for my liking, and I aim to simplify my life once and for all."

Cain felt uncomfortable and yet intrigued at this conversational portal into the Major's life, and he could see Charlie felt the same.

"So, just like you lads, I too have decisions to make," the Major concluded in a manner that suggested he was wrapping up the discussion.

© Steven Clark 2023
Lynnburn, Amisfield, Dumfries & Galloway, UK

He stood and suggested, "You two will need to offer your clients a sense of continuity. In that respect, you can use this office, the computers, and the telephones till you get your own. After all, it's proving quite impossible to withdraw from the office equipment agreements. I've called the vendors repeatedly and can't get through. Seems everyone's going out of business."

[ ]

They'd decided to go to the gym in an attempt to distract themselves. Stuck in the evening rush hour traffic, Charlie broke a long silence. "Everyone's starting to talk about the inevitability of change. Reformasi is the new word being whispered around town. But after today, I'd give anything to go back to the way things were."

Staring out of the cab window, Cain clenched his teeth against the discomfort he felt in his belly. "Same here, Charlie. But we can't stop the clocks." He remembered his thoughts when he was up on the rooftop. "God knows where this will end. Working in Finance, I thought I knew about managing risk, but look at what happened to poor Ernest. What on earth did he do to deserve that? And then there's Speer. Now he's been reckless for sure, but he's just the latest in a long line of Edward Grants that this city has created."

Charlie picked up the thread; "And from what I heard about Pyle; he's just been pissing his life against the wall since he left. Makes me wonder what he did with that JTH file coz he took it with him when he left."

Cain turned to look at Charlie; "That crossed my mind the other day. He's bought an apartment here, so if we see him again, there'd be no harm in asking, considering what's happened." He shuddered; "And what's happened is really unsettling. Jakarta certainly takes no prisoners, so we need to be really fucking careful from now on."

"Sod the gym," said Charlie. "Let's go to your place. We can order takeout, and I'll sleep in your spare room."

Cain nodded. "That might be the only way the pair of us gets any sleep tonight."

19)   The Coward's Weapon

Out of concern for Pak Lubis, after he lost his job with Temple-Speer, Cain had given him a call. Relieved to learn that he'd become a Silver Bird driver, he booked him for a ride to the airport and back because Ruby's editors had finally given the green light to her proposed Indonesia assignment.

Everything went smoothly. Ruby's plane arrived on time, and she made it through immigration smoothly. She ran up to Cain and hugged him tightly, telling him how happy she was to see him again. But then reality punctured the dream. She'd secured an interview with the new Finance Minister and needed to go straight to his offices. "The timing is perfect," she boasted. "Very soon, the IMF is reportedly going to resume its lending program and approve a billion-dollar payment to Indonesia."

Cain was so disappointed he didn't even feel like boasting that when he'd met Suharto, the Minister's deputy had already told him about the IMF.

She said she'd come to his apartment but cautioned that she'd arrive late in the evening. It had been three long, fretful weeks since Cunningham's murder, and whilst her arrival in Jakarta was never guaranteed, he'd pinned a lot on seeing her again. He hadn't known what to expect when he saw her but was all too aware of how unexpectedly sullen he was during the journey back to the office. Sitting in the back of Lubis' cab after his fleeting reunion with Ruby, his mind became plagued with thoughts of Hong Kong, Jared Hing, and poor Ernest.

Taking an unfamiliar route back to the city, Pak Lubis suddenly put such concerns on hold by replacing them with very real fears about the here and now. He pulled over, apologized, and told Cain that he better get into the boot of the car for the rest of the journey.

[ ]

Charlie, Andy, and Lena were all at Flint's new, smaller office. To help them provide the impression of service continuity, the landlord carved the space from the office that previously housed Temple-Speer. Logo, business cards, and letterhead had been created, and Lena was powering through all the other admin jobs while Andreas used family connections to accelerate the processes of business registration and visas for Cain and Charlie.

"The way things are going, we'll definitely be open for business very soon," Charlie enthused. His excitement even managed to lift Cain's mood after his disappointment at the airport and the frightening return drive he'd endured.

Of the two stories, he was more inclined to share the latter. Lena wanted to know how Pak Lubis was doing, so Cain started there.

"Well, he's as dependable as ever, Lena," Cain assured. "He was dressed smartly and claims he even keeps his shoes on these days when he's not carrying a passenger. To be honest, though, he did look like he'd aged."

Andreas looked concerned. "That's hardly surprising when you consider that he lost his job right in the middle of the worst economic crisis since Suharto came to power."

Cain cut in, eager to talk about his journey. "Lubis told me we should avoid the airport toll road, but I never thought that I'd end up nearly suffocating inside the boot." Now they were listening.

"I'll tell you, it was really frightening lying there in the dark, breathing increasingly bad air. Apparently, there are gangs who target expat families heading to the airport with cases full of precious possessions they didn't entrust to the movers. And it's a similar story for Chinese families heading for countries like Singapore, Taiwan, and Hong Kong. The robbers think they've all got suitcases stuffed with money to avoid the government's capital flight controls."

"Some of my clients told me similar stories," said Charlie. "Did you see the departure hall? I heard it looks like a campsite with scores of people trying to get flights out."

"No, I didn't, Charlie," Cain coughed to clip the wings of his colleague's potentially wide digression. "But getting back to my story. We've all seen Pak Lubis do it, but today when he touched the crucifix strung around his rear-view mirror, he did it with a reverence that was palpable."

He paused to draw breath, but there were no interruptions. "We didn't take the toll road. After leaving Soekarno Hatta, we drove west, *away* from the city, before turning south. But when we got closer to the city, I think we were in Tangerang. Lubis told me to get in the boot till we reached the CBD! I couldn't believe what I was hearing, but he was really fearful of vigilante checkpoints."

Cain's story prompted a lengthy discussion about how normal life was breaking down across the city, but eventually, they all settled down to work. They made plans for the theater of making clients feel comfortable and yet important when they arrived for their appointments at the new office.

For now, Flint would still handle the Hanthorpe investment products for transferred Temple-Speer clients, but it primarily offered a Scandinavian investment platform called Icekand. New clients would be offered Icekand, and old clients would be told about its higher returns and greater flexibility. Charlie and Andy also knew that some of the clients would be ripe for a 'churn' from Hanthorpe to Icekand, which could significantly speed up Flint's revenue generation. After his experience with the French expats, Cain didn't want Flint to use the practice, but he was eventually talked around by the fiscal practicalities of their situation.

Lena took a call and informed the guys that Brigadier General Kusnadi was on his way. She was excited to meet BG Kusnadi. He looked very handsome on television and seemed to have the same self-assuredness as Major Speer, comporting himself in a manner that made him appear much more mature than Cain and Charlie, who were only slightly younger than him. But she didn't share this with her colleagues, even when Andreas was telling them of Kusnadi's remarkable rise to prominence.

"Everyone calls him 'the BG,' and despite having no military experience, many expect him to command the national police force before he's 40. Achieving that would be amazing because it might pave the way for the police to finally become independent of the military."

Cain had described Pak Lubis as quite well dressed, but the BG was immaculate. He was courteous and charming, and while Lena was chatting to him, Cain whispered to Charlie, "We could learn a thing or two from this bloke."

Kusnadi went on to outline what he'd already learned. "I understand that no one was particularly close to Mr. Cunningham. Several of your former colleagues believed he lived for the job and had no social life at all. When I consider those statements against what I found at the scene, it very much decreases the likelihood that Mr. Cunningham's death was a misadventure borne of passion. Though someone went to great lengths to make it appear that way."

Charlie agreed, saying, "Major Speer told us what you found. But to be honest, from what I know of Ernest, he'd think auto-erotic asphyxiation or 'breath control play' was unhygienic."

Kusnadi tilted his head, absorbing Charlie's candor. "Yes, your former colleagues basically concur with that reasoning. "Whilst keeping an open mind, I'm starting to suspect that the very exacting Mr. Cunningham was the victim of a professional hit. The murder scene was intriguing. The killer, or killers, left no fingerprints, and it was only after very close scrutiny that subtle signs of a struggle were uncovered. So far, I've had the results of two autopsies. The first found nothing except a slight burning of the lips, tongue, and throat. Mr. Cunningham had vomited, and we also found dried excrement."

Cain was imagining the scene again and wondered if, at the end, Ernest would have been aware of the horrible things that were happening to his body. He must have made a face because Kusnadi picked him up on it.

"Yes Mr. Shaw. Hollywood films tend to avoid such details. Poison might be the coward's weapon, but death by poisoning is often a painful and unpleasant process."

Cain thought he detected a slight wince on Kusnadi's face and wondered if he was recalling the gut-wrenching smell of the scene that he himself was imagining.

"It is very horrible to think that Mr. Cunningham died like that," added Lena, clearly upset.

Kusnadi handed her a tissue and continued. "I was recently in China as a guest of the Guangdong Province police force. They were investigating a spate of Triad murders using poison. Southeast China is developing very quickly, so inevitably, there's a lot of dirty money sloshing around. In every case, the poison was the same, a liquid of very pure Aconite."

Cain was just about to ask when the BG added, "And, of course, Aconite is more commonly known as Wolfsbane."

And once again, pre-empting questions and other time-wasting responses, he barreled on. "Anyway, I remembered how the Guangdong cases tallied with the burning, the vomit, and diarrhea, so I requested a second autopsy, and the lab techs found traces of enough Wolfsbane to have killed two people."

"This is getting surreal!" proclaimed Charlie. "Old Cunningham, killed by Wolfsbane? I'll tell you, BG Kusnadi, whoever killed Ernest knew nothing about him. There's no way he'd be into Russian roulette masturbation."

"Well, that's a start," said Kusnadi crossing his leg and allowing himself an uncomfortable smile. "Mr. Cunningham must have been in tremendous pain when he regained consciousness and managed to scratch the letters 'H' and 'i' in that book. We can safely assume he wasn't writing 'Hi' as a greeting. Any idea what he might have been trying to communicate?"

Cain, Charlie, Lena, and Andy all bowed their heads, deep in thought.

Kusnadi checked his watch. "Please be in no doubt that I am very focused on this case. Some powerful people are anxious that I solve it before the media gets hold of the story. And in respect of that, I am hoping to speak to an eyewitness in the coming days who might provide valuable new information. I must, therefore, kindly ask you not to leave Jakarta. And in the meantime, I will have my own officers increase their patrols of your respective neighborhoods." He looked at Andy, "Well, apart from your already very secure neighborhood Pak Prakowo."

Handing out business cards, he told them, "My handphone number is there. If you have any thoughts about this tragic matter, do not hesitate to call me. I have a hunch that whoever killed Mr. Cunningham might still be around. And if someone wanted him dead, then what about other members of Temple-Speer's management?"

If he'd meant to unsettle them, his parting shot hit the mark. Cain, Charlie, Andy, and Lena went for coffee which none of them particularly enjoyed. They all felt uncomfortable and returned to the office, hoping hard work might supply enough distraction from the memory of Kusnadi's words.

At the airport, Ruby told Cain she wouldn't finish work until late in the evening because her timely interview with Indonesia's Finance Minister had to be broadcast the next day. Before that, the best soundbites had to be translated, time-coded, and transcribed before the tape could be express couriered overnight to Hong Kong for editing. With that in mind, Cain wasn't in the slightest bit bothered when they all realized they'd worked right through till 7:30 pm.

Lena had to get home to her family as there were worries in her neighborhood about people stealing out of sheer desperation. Her father and brothers were taking turns to sleep on a mat in the kitchen to protect their food stores. With the BG's words of caution about the killer haunting all their minds, Andreas called a family driver to pick them up. He was to drop Andy, Cain, and Charlie at Hard Rock, take Lena home, and then return to Hard Rock. "This driver is well-trained to use the gun he keeps in the glove box," Andy reassured and worried them in equal measure.

[ ]

Ginung apologized to his guests as he explained that many dishes weren't available. "And it's going to get worse before it gets any better," he warned, not for the first time. "I was speaking to the

McDonald's guys downstairs. They were wondering how to market what sounds like nothing more than a rice and egg meal because they can't get the ingredients for their usual stuff."

"Wow, even their standards have fallen," Andy sniggered. "How are they going to market that?"

The question gave Ginung the chance to share the McDonald's manager's dark joke; "The McFamine Happy Meal."

Andy chuckled as Ginung left them, but he soon stopped when a sullen Cain exhaled loudly and said, "I like Ginung, but I'm in no mood for gallows humor like that today."

Charlie looked surprised but agreed, "I know what you mean. I must be hungry by now, but I've got no appetite." Then in his disjointed stream-of-consciousness manner, he exclaimed, "Shit! Rice! I've got a big bag of it for Lena's family in my apartment. I must remember it tomorrow." Then he let loose again; "Hey! We're still working with the landlord on the office structure, right?"

Andy and Cain looked at one another, both clearly puzzled at Charlie's outburst.

Not waiting for an answer, he explained, "I reckon we need to add a small room to act as a stationery and equipment storage cupboard. It'll need to have a lock and strong shelving."

"Okay," said Cain in a slow manner, clearly indicating that he thought the intensity of Charlie's declaration was a little over the top. "We could also…"

Interjecting sharply, Charlie said, "Hold on, mate, I guess I should explain. We can also store food there. You heard what Lena's family is going through. If we have a lockable pantry of sorts, it might come in handy for all of us. Especially if things get as bad as Ginung reckons."

Andreas was onboard immediately. "That's a great idea, Charlie! "And we should put a safe in that storage room too. My father reckons the banks might soon become less reliable. If he's right, we need to keep money out of the banks here. And when we are in business properly, payments to us by clients, by Hanthorpe and Icekand, should be deposited in a Singapore bank account. Interest rates will be much lower, but the money will be safe."

Cain approved; "Grand stuff Andy! I was thinking along the same lines myself. In fact, you should see the fridge in my kitchen. The freezer's full of money I withdrew from my account here. I just defrost a wad of Rupiah whenever I need one."

Andy laughed. "Well, get defrosting then. Dinner's on you!" Charlie chuckled, but all Cain could do was smile weakly.

[ ]

Walking into his apartment, Ruby declared, "I'm totally knackered. I need wine and a decent bed."

But 10 minutes later, sitting at his kitchen table with a glass of red wine, she was displaying unfeasible amounts of energy, arguing, "Oh come on, a story about Cunningham would be fantastic."

Sleep-deprived as he was, Ruby's energy surprised Cain almost as much as her insensitivity riled him. Kusnadi's words about keeping the story from the media were now ringing in his head. He'd mistakenly believed that Ruby was somehow exempt from that media blackout.

"All I need is a link between Ernest's murder and the wider financial chaos I'm supposed to be covering," she mused, confirming the mistake Cain knew he'd made. His mood was darkening.

He listened and managed to resist passing comment, but he did begin to bristle as Ruby's new plans gnawed more deeply into his disquiet.

"I called Terence Pyle, and we're going to meet as soon as poss. Said he was busy, but he sounded a tad off on the phone, probably because of your boss's death. By the way, I'm going to North Sumatra on Saturday morning and then to Bali on Tuesday till the following weekend. That could all change, but we'll just have to go with the flow. Doing a feature on how the financial crisis is affecting people all over Indonesia, and thought I'd go to the far reaches of the country that an international audience is more familiar with. Tomorrow I'm shooting a piece on the 'Safe & Sound' bus company's role in Harrier's downfall, so I need to make an early start and head over to the Hilton to hook up with my crew. Could you get me one of those Silver cabs for 6 am, darling?"

The question at the end of such a febrile delivery caught Cain off guard. Scrambling through the detail of her revelations, he hadn't expected an opportunity to speak, never mind an invitation.

"Huh, oh yes. I can do that," he stammered, catching up with everything Ruby had said. He'd quietly hoped they'd spend some meaningful time together, but was this it? Hello, goodbye and call me a cab, would you? He didn't even know if he'd get to see her again while she was in the country! He was tired and knew the last thing he needed was an argument that would inevitably result in an angry, regretful, and probably sleepless night. But here he was, trying to act normal when he'd been told that there was a killer out there! Maybe some psycho who'd lost a lot of money and blamed either Ernest or Temple-Speer. If it was the latter, then he might also be a target. And that thought frightened him and Charlie because they both knew how out of their depth they were after stupidly agreeing to go to Hong Kong last year.

"You'll need to be bloody careful in Medan," he warned, "It's in Aceh province. Andreas' dad led some brutal attempts to crush the independence movement up there. Combine that with the protests against Jakarta for this economic mess, and it'll be a real powder keg of tension right now."

Ruby pouted ostentatiously, "You should have told me about Andy's father. His story sounds even more interesting than your late boss."

Cain was losing his grip on any kind of composure. "I was really looking forward to seeing you again. But you're clearly only interested in the story, Ernest, Andy's dad, and the economy."

"Jesus wept!" she cut in. Yes, I've been trying forever to get the go-ahead to come here for the story, but I also came here for you."

"Seriously?" accused Cain. "After today, that's really hard to believe. You arrive, you tell me you're taking off again, and then I'm getting friggin instructions to book you a cab? Jaysis, when do you ever switch off?"

Ruby simmered as she stared across the table at Cain. "I honestly can't believe you either. I've had one hell of a day. You know, I thought you were different. But actually, now I think of it, you were just as petulant on the way to the Gilis. Dress it up any way you like, worried about your future, your job, or wanting more time together; you're just... you're just a needy little boy."

It was Cain's turn to stare as she picked up her unopened overnight bag and turned to him. "Sumatra will be difficult, but I'll call you from Bali or when I'm back in Jakarta. Maybe you'll be worth talking to by then. Remember, I came here because of you. But right now, I'm leaving because of you."

She walked out and left the door open. He listened to her heels clicking down the marble-floored corridor and heard the elevator arrive and take her away. Head in hands, his jaw clenched with rage, every sinew in his body seemed to quiver. The door could wait.

[ ]

Due to the lateness of the hour, David Speer completed the journey from his apartment to Jalan Fatmawati in less than 20 minutes, thanks to Eddie 123. He'd heard about the so-called delights of the Mawwar Hotel as it had gained a lively notoriety among certain expats. But he didn't think he'd ever actually go there.

Speer had received a call from Pyle, who was clearly out of his mind. He couldn't get any sense out of him, and eventually, a woman took over to explain that; "Pak Terry is behaving badly and needs to be taken home." She told him where Pyle was, and Speer guessed that Eddie would know the place. While he had no obligation to extricate Pyle from whatever mess he'd gotten himself into, he couldn't help himself. Select with his words, he told Feronika, "I need to go and make sure that idiot Pyle gets home safely."

Speer was up and quickly dressed. He saw Feronika's concerned expression and smiled. "Don't worry, darling. I can take care of myself."

As he made his way to the door, she rose from the bed and threw his discarded work shirt over her naked body. He paused, and they kissed. As he walked away, she leaned against the doorframe and said, "Be careful, mister."

He turned back and lightly touched her face. "I'll be back soon, darling." And with a peck on the lips, he was off.

Eddie said he'd taken clients to the Mawwar before and advised Speer to take an elevator up to the tenth floor and then climb one more flight of stairs. Traveling upwards in a tiny elevator, Speer remembered feeling a similar sense of grave unease following Pyle into Tanamur. When the elevator juddered to an unconvincing halt, he climbed the flight of stairs as instructed and entered a dark bar full of sofas and young women, all wearing the same tiny black dress.

A rank potpourri of beer, cigarettes, laundry, and cleaning fluids, assaulted his senses. Through the smoke-filled darkness, he could make out three Asian customers being 'entertained' on sofas at the far end of the room. None of them appeared very interested in what was going on, putting them in stark contrast with two loud Australians who were drunkenly pawing at a couple of girls.

Speer sighed when he gathered Pyle wasn't in the room and went to the bar where he was pounced upon by two squat, overweight bargirls with their hands all over him. When he managed to free himself, he explained that he'd come to collect 'Pak Terry.' "Come with me," cooed another young woman.

Down a corridor with yellowing, textured wallpaper, and a carpet that made Speer thankful he was wearing good shoes, the young woman informed him that Pak Terry was a regular visitor, but tonight they were worried about him. Speer asked if money was the problem. She said no, but explained, "He was in a fight with two other customers because he was taking too many of our best girls."

They paused outside a door. When she knocked and announced her name, Speer heard Pyle's voice and a bunch of women shouting gleefully for her to join them. The door opened, and there was Pyle, lying prostrate across a bed with naked women writhing all over him.

Pyle saw Speer, but far from being concerned, he slurred, "David! Girls, this is David. Show him some love."

Three giggling girls peeled off their client and approached Speer until the young woman who'd brought him to the room said something to make them drop their sexy diva acts. They smiled sweetly and began to pick up 'Pak Terry's' clothes. Pyle obviously sensed that his little orgy was coming to an end and whined like a child who doesn't want to go to bed. Despite his considerable size, he was powerless to resist the young women who were sitting him up and dressing him.

Two of the hotel's security guards arrived to help escort him from the building as his body was limp with alcohol and whatever else he'd taken. But Pyle's good humor proved indomitable, and leaving the room, he threw money at the women who stopped getting dressed and scrambled to catch it. Passing through the bar area, the Aussies had gone, but Pyle made a point of saying goodbye to the Asian guys. Speer tutted and yanked him away, angry that Pyle was drawing even more attention to himself, but thankfully everyone seemed to ignore him.

The Major didn't want to be left on the street with Pyle in such a state and was thankful that Eddie had managed to park next to the Mawwar's entrance. Eddie knew where Pyle lived and sped off as soon as he and Speer had managed to lay him out across the back seat. From the front passenger seat, Speer tried to get some sense out of him.

Through a fog of gibberish, Speer deciphered the American's night of wanton hedonism as best he could. "I've been on a bender, as you Brits say. Tonight was a reward for all my hard work. For the last few weeks…." He stopped and scrutinized Speer as if trying to weigh him up. Narrowing his eyes, he moved his head a little closer to his former colleague and wiped his nose across the back of his hand. A shake of the head and a dismissive grunt served as the punctuation marks he needed to redirect his slow train of thought. "Well, anyway, tonight was a well-deserved reward that I deserved."

Speer wasn't impressed by Pyle's claims of hard work. The man was a mess.

"I wanted to say goodbye to the guys, but they couldn't hear," Pyle whined. Mok and Wang were super friendly, and the young one with the very fine blow was called 'the Kid'?"

Pyle noticed Speer glaring at him. "Major!" he exclaimed, waving a finger in an attempt to be reassuring. "Don't be too concerned, Major. Those guys wanted to share their beer jugs, but you and I both know that in a place like that, you don't drink anything you haven't opened yourself."

Speer scoffed; "What a genius you are, Terence. You happily snort their coke but are lucid enough to drink your own bottled beer."

"You know it, Major. We know how to look after me. We know..." Then he started to snore.

"Ah, Christ!" Speer winced, envisioning the difficulty of hauling an unconscious Pyle into his apartment. But as he snored, Speer sniggered, noting that 'call-me-Terence' was fondly known as 'Terry' at the Mawwar. And while he'd heard tall tales about the place, Pak Terry had obviously taken its 'delights' to a whole new level.

© Steven Clark 2023
Lynnburn, Amisfield, Dumfries & Galloway, UK

20) TGIF

In the strange half-light of the coming day, Cain stirred from a restive sleep. Most of the night, his beleaguered brain was fired up and re-analyzing the short but decisive fight with Ruby. He'd upset her, and she'd basically told him to grow up.

Needy little boy? What did she know? "If there was any immaturity on display, it was coming from you," he growled, reliving the argument like a heckler on the bus home who'd failed to get the better of the comedian.

"What the hell?" he told himself for the umpteenth time. She may have been excited at the prospect of her first overseas assignment, but Ruby's reaction to the news about Ernest was reprehensible. She'd hurt him, and he was right to confront her.

He'd eventually nodded off to the drone of that defensively blinkered line of reasoning. Ruby had pissed him off with her reaction to Cunningham's murder, but the other facet behind his outburst was selfishness, and that was shameful. Ruby had waltzed into town, told him she had no time for him, and then announced that she was off. And when she was called on it, she'd basically paraphrased his bloody father telling him to get a grip. He'd been used by the Temple-Speer bosses and spat out into the world to look after himself; his mentor was dead, and now he was reliably informed that he could be the nutter's next victim.

There was no message from Ruby on his phone. He contemplated spending the day in bed but quickly grasped that being alone with his thoughts was probably the worst thing he could do.

[ ]

Woken up by the eclectic repertoire of Myna bird song, Lena stepped over her younger brother, who was asleep on a thin piece of foam on the kitchen floor. Last night was his turn to guard the food stores against would-be burglars. She gathered up a cast-aside sheet, placed it back over his body, and crept onward for her morning mandi. The washroom comprised a squat toilet and a big barrel filled with water from a pipe that had a tap screwed on the end of it. Closing the flimsy concertina door, she slipped off the baggy Tee-shirt she used as a nightie and lined up her toiletries. Removing the lid from the barrel that prevented mosquitoes from laying eggs inside, she dipped a plastic jug into the mandi water. Pouring it over her head, the coolness of the water momentarily tensed all the muscles in her body. Lena caught her breath and repeated the action until sufficiently doused before applying soap and then washing it all off with several more jugs of water.

She was now quite an accomplished protestor. She routinely wore trousers for a possible ojek ride, and she dressed casually. Smarter office clothes were lovingly placed in a daypack along with toiletries so she could wash and change at work. She told Charlie she was taking her mother to the doctor that morning. The excuse would only give her a few hours at the protest, but as it was Friday, she preferred to avoid any potential trouble following congregational prayers.

[ ]

Feronika brought tea into the bedroom for 'her David.' She opened the balcony doors, and they sat up in the early morning light, listening to birdsong and drinking their tea as Speer shared his version of Pyle's ridiculous behavior. "I left him on his bed. He stank so much that I didn't even undress him. The man was a fucking mess. Drugs, drink, and whores. Makes me wonder why someone like Ernest would ever hire such a man. That Mawwar place was awful."

Feronika said she knew of that 'so-called wellness center.' She grabbed Speer between his legs and giggled, "Don't ever let me catch you in there, David."

[]

Charlie wasn't a natural early riser. Switching off his alarm clock, he put his body into auto-pilot and went through the motions of being awake. He switched on his coffee machine and then headed for the bathroom. All the while, he rubbed and squeezed his nose to loosen the hard, dusty matter that edged his nostrils after inhaling dry air-conditioned air all night.

Stepping out of the shower, he realized he'd forgotten to shave. Boy, did he miss the days when he and Cain routinely performed 'Nancy's overhaul.' The shave he went on to attempt resulted in fragments of toilet paper being applied to his chin. "Thank God it's Friday," he said to himself as he took his first sip of the smooth Sumatran coffee that jolted him awake and helped him remember to bring the sack of rice for Lena and her family. Pak Lubis arrived to take him into Temple-Speer. No, he beamed; Pak Lubis was taking him to Flint Independent Financial Advisory. The driver laughed when Charlie explained the FIFA acronym. Lubis revealed that he'd always wanted to stand in the Kop at Liverpool's Anfield football ground. Charlie was astounded at the depth of his knowledge about the club, and the pair of them ended up singing 'You'll never walk alone' to take their minds off the rush hour chaos.

[]

Brigadier General Kusnadi received his morning brief about the burgeoning number of students taking to the streets in North Sumatra's autonomy-seeking city of Medan, as well as the historic seat of Javanese royalty in Surakarta and, of course, Jakarta. For some time now, the students had been making explicit calls for the resignation of President Suharto; and today, there were concerns that some Imams might preach politically charged messages at their midday prayers, contributing both numbers and anger to the protests. The Brigadier General was careful not to specify which Jakarta protest site he'd visit later that morning, trusting that the ambiguity would compel his officers, armed with nothing more than rubber bullets, to maintain their admirable restraint across all the sites. Muddying the clarity of his orders somewhat, the commanders of specialist riot teams and elements of the military had also been placed on standby.

Kusnadi's office was contacted yesterday by the security company at Ernest Cunningham's apartment block. The old guard who'd been on duty the night Cunningham was killed had finally returned. He'd gone completely off the radar whilst visiting his family in a village somewhere near Yogyakarta but would be available for an interview later that day.

[ ]

Ruby and her crew were filming at a traffic pinch-point on the toll road that ran through West Jakarta. A 'Safe & Sound' bus passed her cameraman, who shouted in Cantonese, "Half its windows are missing, the wing mirror is a guy hanging out from where a door should be, and the exhaust is held by wires and spewing out black fumes!"

The soundman pulled his scarf away from his mouth briefly, "Some of our minibuses are bad, but I've yet to see a bus that would be allowed on the road in Hong Kong."

Ruby was making a valiant attempt to put last night behind her, eager not to be dismissed by her crew as a struggling rookie. When she saw what her soundman had done with his scarf, she searched for a shawl in her bag and shouted, "This city desperately needs a Hong Kong-style MTR system."

The young Indonesian fixer helping secure interviews and locations was called Awing. He passed Ruby a small packet explaining, "It's an N95 mask, boss," before adding a quip he'd learned from an Australian crew. "Tying a shawl over your nose is as useless as an ashtray on a motorbike."

Ruby chuckled politely, and he reported, "I'm hearing of a standoff developing between students and police at the Trisakti University campus just up the road. Do you want to get some demo shots while we're nearby? We'll definitely still be able to make the interview this afternoon."

Ruby replied, "Sure thing, Awing. And we can escape this exhaust pipe pollution for a while."

[ ]

Cain had used a clipboard for the team meeting. The agenda was hardly a test for his memory, but he'd needed it to help him focus his thoughts as last night's turmoil was still so raw.

"Okay, so that's where we are right now. Andy, thanks a million for getting the landlord to build a storeroom with extra-strength walls. Charlie, the landlord even told Andy he'd help us find a safe! Right, Andy, it's confirmed; you'll be accompanying Charlie and me to Singapore to open that company bank account as soon as we get the okay to travel from BG Kusnadi. Lena, please don't come to work when we're away. Spend the time with your family."

Lena thanked them for their kindness, and Charlie suggested that in Singapore, they should buy two more of those Surefire torches for Andy and Lena.

"Roger that," Cain affirmed. He'd also planned to get one for Ruby, but they were expensive, and for all he knew, he might never see her again.

He rubbed his palms together to get his mind back on track and reminded his travel companions that they might be meeting David Speer. "He'll be in Singapore wrapping up the last of the Temple-Speer paperwork and attending a job interview."

"Right then, any other business?" he concluded, sitting down at his own desk and trying to keep thoughts of calling Ruby at bay.

Charlie stood up. "Yes, as a matter of fact, I have the business of thanking you three for your incredible support in getting Flint up and ready so quickly. Given everything that's going on right now, I recognize the leap of faith you've all taken and I'm very grateful. I just can't help but feel that together this little team has a real chance to steal success from this economic crisis when everyone else is looking elsewhere."

He looked at his colleagues. They were attentive, but he was already frustrated with his delivery. It wasn't him, and it sounded hollow. He changed tack.

"Look. I'm not gonna start spouting the old fortune cookie philosophies that Gweilos love – sorry, Cain. You won't hear me trying to be wise and enigmatic by talking about how the Chinese word for crisis, 'Wei-Ji,' comprises the characters for danger and opportunity because it's absolute nonsense. 'Wei-Ji' actually means something like a perilous moment when crucial change can take place. So, with that put aside, what I will say, is that with the world having written off Indonesia, at least we'll be here to catch the inevitable economic bounce... We need to..."

Cain could see Charlie was struggling. He tried to prompt him by stating what Charlie had told him when they planned the meeting. "Like the fund managers who mentored you in London said, 'We need to strike dexterously when the iron is at its coldest.'"

Charlie still looked lost. "Yep... yeah, that's right... To maximize the chances... Just give me a moment..."

The problem was that they were trying to start a business in a crisis the depth of which Charlie's mentors had never experienced. Momentarily knocked from his own internal strife, Cain started to see how drained Charlie was. He'd been the sole driver for office morale, but even his spirit was starting to wane amidst the growing tension that accompanied daily life in Jakarta these days. Its unremitting constancy was quite perversely something one could almost get used to. But it was starting to open fissures in the very bedrock of the nation's soul, releasing poisonous vapors of hatred into the capital city's already polluted air.

Charlie wiped his brow and looked up at his audience of three. "That economic bounce might take some time to happen. But in the meantime, we have some strong backers, and we have one another. The fundamentals for success are right here in this office. We just need to make sure we're ready when the market's fundamentals start falling into line too."

They clapped, applauding Charlie's determination to make his point as much as the point itself.

[ ]

There were jeers from the demonstrators as Kusnadi's car drew up. He walked over to the police cordon drawn up outside Trisakti University's campus gates where, ironically, many children from Jakarta's elite families, who'd benefitted greatly from Suharto's rule, read their degrees. He commanded the senior officers present to reiterate his message of restraint, and as he did so, he saw a TV crew amongst the protestors. He ordered an officer to get photos of the crowd only to be told that some BAKIN agents were already doing that. Such news was predictable but unwelcome. He told the officer to take photos anyway for their own documentary evidence. His gaze drifted past the officer. He gave the order to take clear photos of the TV people and the students they were talking to and get copies to him as soon as possible. Then he thanked his officers and returned to his car.

[ ]

Pyle was awakened by the sound of a vacuum cleaner being switched on. Head thumping, he rubbed his bleary eyes and sat up in bed. He was fully dressed, and his nostrils railed against the stench of sweat, smoke, booze, and sex. "Jesus H," he muttered, scarcely believing the wild time he'd had at the Mawwar.

He smirked while he muttered a Churchill impression, "Never in the field... of human carnality ... has so much been done to me... by so many for so little." The joke prompted the memory of fighting with the obnoxious Aussies and the amazing blow he'd shared with the Chinese guys.

How he'd gotten home was still a mystery. He got out of bed to look for some kind of clue. Every lumbering movement was accompanied by a sound effect. Slowly the memory crawled out from somewhere in his foggy mind that Speer had dragged him out of the Mawwar. "Well, I guess I owe you one, Major." Then he froze and spat the word "Fuck!" as he remembered the documents strewn all over his study. Had Speer seen them?

© Steven Clark 2023
Lynnburn, Amisfield, Dumfries & Galloway, UK

258

Just about open his bedroom door, he stopped and shook his head. "Sheez man, get it together," he muttered to himself as his mind fog cleared a little more.

Breathing a sigh of relief, he remembered that the lengthy document he'd written was already packed into an attaché case, along with his notes and all the documents Ernest secretly passed to him. He smirked, thinking how apt it was that he'd passed an attaché case to an embassy attaché who'd agreed to have it placed in a diplomatic pouch and deliver it as instructed.

He'd been slow off the mark, but since Ernest Cunningham's death, his research into Sir James' life had gathered significant fear-induced momentum. Ernest had passed him lots of information, and his page notes were written in a fashion that was perfectly legible to the Vietnam vet. Last night's debauchery at the Mawwar had been a reward for his diligence. And whilst it wasn't a particularly polished draft, Pyle had sketched a fairly cogent outline of how young Jim Hawes had so ruthlessly become Sir James. And it didn't reflect well on the British Establishment either.

Reassured that everything was actually in order, he decided to take a shower and then call Speer to thank him. He peeled off his stinking clothes and put on a pair of shorts as his maid was obviously cleaning the apartment.

With a dull ache in his head, he opened the bedroom door and was hit by the full effect of the vacuum cleaner, which was just standing by itself in the hallway. Then he noticed plastic sheeting all over the floor. He stepped out to switch off the noisy device. "Sheez, what the…"

The plastic rustled, and he felt a terrible crack across his skull. It took another to fell him. Lying on the plastic, more strikes landed faster and haphazardly across his body. The last few felt distant, barely part of him.

The violence stopped as suddenly as it had begun. The vacuum noise was gone, but it had been replaced by a piercing noise in his head. Paralyzed, he didn't know if his eyes were open or shut. All he could see was white light.

A disembodied voice as distant as the last few blows mixed with the searing white noise. "They'll never find you."

[]

Megaphone in hand and standing on a pile of wooden pallets, Ikraem was calling for the removal of President Suharto. Lena still didn't particularly like him, but she couldn't stop herself from chuckling when he joked that the President's son Tommy, must be running up gambling debts in Vegas again as his sister 'Tutut' was putting up more highway tolls around the city to bail him out.

She turned to Nisa and saw her gazing at the man she clearly adored. "I wonder if the TV people will interview Ikraem," Lena shouted.

Nisa turned and confessed, "That would be wonderful. I'm so proud of him."

Lena smiled sweetly and turned to Denny, who shouted at them both, "Well, this might get them interested in us."

And with that, he stepped up onto the pallets. Ikraem helped Denny up and passed him the megaphone. Lena felt for him as he stared at the crowd, hesitating for a moment. "Come on, Denny," she muttered, willing him to put aside his kampung inhibitions.

And he didn't disappoint. "Hey! 1968 was the year when American and European students tried to change the world." Then, he pointed at the crowd and sang the line, "You say you want a revolution," before shouting, "Like '68, '98 is the year of our revolution. Flip the six; 98 is Indonesia's 68!" Then he started singing, "For the times, they are a changin."

The audience joined in and began to sway. As Denny led the crowd, Ikraem stood stock still, fist punched into the air. Lena tutted and turned back to see the TV camera. It must have moved because it glinted in the sun. Denny's voice went quiet as he turned away from the megaphone to look over his shoulder. Singing and holding Nisa's hand, Lena's eyes followed Denny's body movement, and she saw two men clad in black who'd pulled up on a motorcycle just meters behind the impromptu stage. The pillion rider threw what looked like a small sack. Lena followed its trajectory over Denny and Ikraem into the crowd behind her. Petrifying fear gripped her. Eyes squeezed tight shut, she curled her body with her hands over her ears, waiting for an explosion.

There was no boom. She started to be jostled, and then the screaming started. She was knocked hard against the pallets where Denny and Ikraem were no longer standing.

"Lena!" she heard Denny cry. He was lying next to her. They grabbed one another and fought against the stampeding crowd to stand. It all happened in seconds, but shock, fear, and the effort to stand and remain standing totally drained them.

As the crowd cleared, they saw Nisa lying on the concrete just feet away from two very agitated cobras and a small hessian sack. Denny walked slowly toward her. He grabbed her nearest arm and slowly dragged her away from the writhing cobras. Lena then helped Denny lift and carry Nisa. He pointed, "Over there. There's a room with water and medical supplies."

A couple of medical students quickly revived and took care of Nisa. Lena had carried the girl, and there was nothing to her. She must have been kicked around like a rag doll in the melee.

Ikraem arrived, arm around a male student who was hopping. "Salleh's been bitten," he cried.

Another medical student attended Salleh. Ikraem tried to be reassuring, "He should be okay. The police usually milk the snakes' venom. It's just a scare tactic."

Lena dismissed Ikraem's words as pompous and cavalier. Thankfully she heard the medical student insist that Salleh be taken to the hospital. Stroking Nisa's forehead, she looked at the clock. She'd been here too long. "Denny, call Hard Rock and tell them Nisa won't be at work tonight," she instructed.

She walked with haste to the other end of campus and onto an Ojek. Wearing trousers, she didn't need to sit side-saddle, and she asked the rider to hurry.

[ ]

Andreas was getting lunch for himself and Charlie, who was feeling better. Cain said he wasn't hungry, and Charlie was just beginning to understand the source of his friend's suppressed appetite.

"Bloody hell mate. I've never seen you snap, so maybe you just didn't know how bad your outburst would have sounded. We both kind of admired old Cunningham, but Ruby was probably just as tired as you. She'd have been excited about doing her first overseas assignment and getting a chance to see you again. That combination of exhaustion and excitement might have caused her to say things she ordinarily wouldn't have. And I mean, calling you needy isn't the worst thing, is it? I know it was totally superficial and, at times, exceptionally kinky, but I miss having Sachiko wrapped around me."

Cain knew his friend was trying to lighten his mood with that last line and felt obliged to smile. He needed help, but telling Charlie about being called 'needy' was as far as he went. He couldn't admit that there had been a very selfish and needy streak within his anger, so he didn't bother. "I just don't know where the anger came from. It's really starting to screw with my head. Sometimes I even think it's the heat getting to me. Whether it's work life or personal, every time I take a step forward, the universe kicks me backward."

Charlie snorted; "The heat can get to you Gweilos, but not in your case, mate." He checked that they were still alone; "Right, I don't normally like getting all Oprah with the kind of crap you get in self-help books. This is just between us, right? The platoon of two."

He waited for Cain to nod before he continued. "We were thrown together at Temple-Speer, but we'd have gravitated to one another anyway because we're basically the same. Because of the pressure my parents put on me, I blamed them for every tiny setback and put myself under even more pressure. There were quite insane performance expectations when I was working in London, but I managed to pile even more stress onto myself. Failure terrified me. That's why I jacked it in when the Major offered me the job out here. If I was going to fail, then I'd do it far away from my parents and their judgment."

Cain had sat motionless, staring at the floor, so Charlie continued. "Well anyway mate, what I mean to say is, it's not the universe, your family or friends or anything else that's holding you back… it's you. You can't rely on any favors from the universe coz you're responsible for yourself, the good stuff, and all the faults, fumbles, and tumbles. Understand that, and you'll be much more content."

Cain took a moment to respond. "You're right, Charlie. Our similarity is the reason we're friends. You say failure terrified you, whereas I've always been scared of mediocrity. And being away from home really sharpens that fear for me. We've been expatriated from everything that's familiar to us, and while we try to be cool and nonchalant about it, we're all kind of naked out here." He thought for a moment and added, "I guess that's why so many guys try to clothe themselves in some form of personal reinvention."

Charlie snorted, and Cain thought he was about to be rebuked for bringing up the old reinvention chestnut. But that wasn't the case. "Don't get trapped in that personal reinvention shite the way I did. I thought the cheerful chappie and Mockney stuff would help me fit in whilst still managing to stand out. Utter bollocks! Life's much easier when you keep it real."

Cain had stopped short of being open and honest about his feelings, and there was Charlie showing him the way. Of course, the accent and swagger were much diminished these days, but this was the first time he'd really opened up about any change having taken place at all.

He wanted to tell Charlie how brave he'd been, but while searching for a word other than 'brave' because it was too touchy-feely, Lena arrived. She sang out her greeting from the doorway, but her voice sounded cheerless. Charlie asked how her mum had got on at the doctor's. She looked vacant for a second. Her colleagues thought it was anxiety, but she'd actually forgotten the excuse she'd fabricated for her absence. After a pause, she thanked them for their concern and explained, "She's been given good medication and is feeling a little better."

Lena busied herself at her desk, and Charlie whispered, "Talk about keeping it real. That poor girl's the sole breadwinner in her family. She's holding down a job and holding her family together. She's amazing."

[ ]

David Speer's mobile phone rang. The call was short, and upon hanging up, he told Feronika that Brigadier General Kusnadi was asking all the remaining former staff of Temple-Speer to meet at the new Flint office at 4:30 pm.

"It's okay for him; he's got outriders and sirens," Speer complained.

Looking at her watch, Feronika agreed, "And the unofficial half-day created by Friday prayers doesn't help. If you're going, you better leave soon."

"We can go together," Speer offered. "After Rob Watson told everyone about us, there's no reason why you couldn't come with me. And I'm tired of hiding you."

She stroked his arm and kissed his cheek. "That's sweet, David but one of us has to make sure we are ready for our trip tomorrow. You go. I'll make sure the house is ship-shape and that I have packed clothes that guarantee you won't want to hide me when we are in Singapore."

"You do that, dear, and I'll call Eddie. I hope he's okay after last night's fiasco."

[ ]

It was like a small Temple-Speer reunion. Rob Watson was returning to the UK the very next day, but he and some of the former advisors showed up, along with Speer. Cain, Charlie, and Andy were the genial hosts and had ordered up some curry puffs and kueh from the coffee shop in the lane behind the tall office block. Lena, who would normally be in her element at such an occasion, was so withdrawn that it prompted Speer to ask Cain what was going on.

"Not exactly sure, Major," Cain admitted. "Her mother's been unwell, but she may have other worries too. These are difficult times."

Speer shook his head solemnly. "The economic mess is biting hard. And there's a drought in the Nusa Tenggara region, east of Bali. Those people will starve if their crops fail."

Cain absorbed the Major's gloomy prediction and asked, "How is Sir James bearing up?"

"The short answer is, he's not," Speer replied. "Until recently, he was in London licking his fiscal wounds. I guess he was doing his own version of your so-called 'Nancy Overhaul.' Daily visits to the Turkish baths, then off to Curzon Street for a shave at Trumpers, followed by a brisk walk to his Mayfair Club. I know he took himself off to Cambodia to check on that orphanage of his, but right now, he's currently in Singapore, anxious to get Ernest's body back to England for a proper burial. But that will be contingent upon the Brigadier General's success or otherwise."

Kusnadi arrived and was greeted by Charlie and Andy. He informed them that he'd uncovered some new information and greeted Lena as he made his way through the gathering to address them. She tried to respond by saying, "Hello, BG Kusnadi," but her voice failed her, and she shrank away to the back of the room.

Kusnadi began, "I had initially wanted to scan the CCTV tapes from Mr. Cunningham's apartment complex, but even if the security guards had switched the system on, the tapes were moldy and useless. The security guard on duty the night Mr. Cunningham was murdered returned to the capital today. His interview was quite revealing." He looked around the room. "I just hope it prompts some thoughts from you."

It had been more than nine months since the Hong Kong assignment, but Cain and Charlie gasped in unison when they heard the BG say, "The security guard said he saw Mr. Cunningham with three Chinese men. Two of them looked like they were in their mid-30s, and the other one was younger. He had a slimmer build, and when I pressed the guard for more information, he remembered the younger man's spectacles because the frames were brightly colored. He said they looked like spectacles a woman might wear."

Cain blurted out, "You said Ernest wrote 'Hi.' He must have been trying to write 'Hing!'"

"Hing?" Kusnadi queried.

"The description of the glasses," Charlie explained. "It sounds like a banker called Jared Hing. Cain and I met him in Hong Kong last August. Did the guard mention green eyes?"

Kusnadi's tone was even more serious. "No mention of eye color, but the frames on the glasses were bright green." He moved on; "Hong Kong? That might explain his two associates. Did you meet this Hing socially or professionally?"

Speer felt he had to interject and explain the background to the Hong Kong trip, after which Kusnadi turned back to Cain and Charlie. "And you two found out about Safe & Sound. Did you use any coercion to extract that information? Because this is all beginning to sound rather dubious, if not illegal. Not your usual line of work, I imagine."

They both shook their heads. Cain explained, "It was actually just a conversation we had over dinner. Looking at it now, I can tell you that the bankers didn't really say anything. It was just something in their tone when they said the investment would be safe and sound. There was no coercion or anything like that, Brigadier General. It was just a sudden realization, which we then had checked out by the financial researchers who were working for Temple-Speer at the time."

"And Harrier bank collapsed earlier this year," Kusnadi recalled. Then the momentous events of the previous month of April became more apparent. "Ernest Cunningham was found dead just a couple of months after the bank's collapse and about seven months after this Hong Kong adventure. That's enough time for a viable buffer of plausible deniability. If this is the thread we should be pulling at, it's beginning to sound like a professional hit."

Rob Watson added, "When you also factor in the point that Harrier's boss withheld funds from Sir James, fatally damaging Temple-Speer, then this is one horribly twisted piece of revenge theater."

"Okay. All of you, please listen carefully," Kusnadi entreated. "There could be three killers out there. You need to be aware of the danger for all of you."

Cain looked at Charlie, thinking, 'Jaysis, it was us who tricked Hing and his pals. We must be targets too.'

Speer had been quiet for a while, and he didn't look comfortable at all. He fidgeted and cleared his throat; "I think I saw Hing and his associates last night at a hotel called the Mawwar."

Cain spoke before he thought. "The Mawwar! Ernest is dead, there are killers on the loose, and you were in a place like that?"

Speer had clearly been angered, but he kept his cool. "If you'll allow me, Shaw, I was just about to explain." He tugged his shirt flat and threaded his fingers in a clasp he settled on his lap. "I went there after I got a call from Terence Pyle. He was drunk and, for some ungodly reason, decided to call me. Well, I couldn't just let him rot there, could I? So, I went to get him and make sure he got home safely. He told me about some Chinese trio he befriended, and I think I saw them when I was there. It was difficult to see, but one of them appeared to be younger and, well, a bit softer looking."

Kusnadi asked, "Major Speer, where is Mr. Pyle now? Was he okay when you left him?"

"He's fine," Speer affirmed. "I got him home safely and put him to bed. Right now, he'll be sleeping or nursing a very bad hangover."

Cain knew his judgment had been a little harsh. "I'm sorry, Major, I've been sleeping badly, and I think this is getting to me."

Speer replied: "I understand, Shaw," but interrupted himself. "My God!" he exclaimed. "Shaw, did you see them? They were in the Grand Hyatt lobby too! The day we met the President! It must have been them."

Cain was relieved to have moved passed his ill-judged condemnation. "Jaysis, yes, Major! There were three of them, but as we walked past where they'd been sitting, I noticed they'd gone. If it was them, Hing would guess that I'd recognize him, so they all must have left."

Kusnadi exclaimed, "Finally, a possible break. Right, the security cameras at Mr. Cunningham's apartment were worthless, but the Hyatt should have captured images of our suspects who clearly have unfinished business."

The BG looked at his audience; "Okay, we have three suspects. They probably traveled here separately under false names, but I will run checks on this Jared Hing."

Speer interjected, saying, "Actually, they might be aliases, but for what it's worth, Pyle told me the other two were called Mok and Wang."

Cain could tell that Kusnadi was having a busy day. He looked stressed but thanked them for their assistance. "I will get the footage from the Grand Hyatt. I will need to ask you, Major Speer, and you, Mr. Shaw, to verify the faces you saw. This evening if possible." Addressing the Major, he added: "My forces are stretched. Otherwise, I'd arrange more security for you and Mr. Pyle…."

Speer interrupted him, "Thank you, Brigadier General, but I'd be obliged to decline security even if you could offer it. I leave for Singapore tomorrow." Then he looked at Cain, who couldn't mistake the faint sound of disappointment when his former boss said, "Guess I'll see you later, Shaw?"

[ ]

Lena escorted the BG to the elevator, where he asked her to accompany him down to the lobby. As the elevator door closed, he asked, "Ms. Ngurawan, how long have you been associated with the Trisakti student protest leaders?"

Lena was surprised that the BG knew her family name and that Ikraem and Denny were known to him too. She took so long to digest the question that Kusnadi carried on. "The students have been very effective so far but cannot control the anger they are generating in populations beyond the campus grounds. It is ironic that students, who are the people with the most time ahead of them, are usually the people in the greatest hurry. I, too, feel that change is coming, but it will do so without anyone needing to push too hard."

"I think you are correct, BG Kusnadi, and those are very wise words. But my friends think they need to keep up the momentum and the pressure," Lena explained. Until this moment, she had been rather star-struck by the BG, and if she'd understood him correctly, he wasn't exactly condemning the protests. All of a sudden, he wasn't the famous police officer from the television; he was an extremely intelligent gentleman who seemed to care for her opinion and even possibly care for her.

He asked, "How did you get involved? You are not a typical candidate for such activism?"

The elevator door opened, and they spoke in the lobby as the Brigadier General's Land Cruiser drew up in the atrium, accompanied by two motorcycle outriders. Knowing the BG was a busy man, she simply told the truth; "Denny and his friend Nisa come from a village near mine in central Java. I met Nisa at Hard Rock Café the day Cain, Charlie, Andreas, and myself agreed to create the Flint advisory."

 Kusnadi listened closely, never taking his eyes off Lena. He was one of those people who could make you feel like you were the only person in the world, and Lena loved how his very important man took the time to listen to her.

"Forgive me, Ms. Ngurawan; I must be brief as I need to get back to HQ. Please be very careful with your friends. I tell you this because I want you to be safe. I fear we may soon witness more of the frightening scenes you may have experienced today. And finally, I must also assure you that those snakes were not thrown by my men."

Lena had seen him briefly at the protest but didn't think he would have seen her. She didn't doubt his sincerity and stared at him thoughtfully. She whispered the word "BAKIN."

Kusnadi nodded and adopted a very caring tone. "Call me if you ever feel in danger."

Riding the elevator back up to Flint, she smiled, remembering how Kusnadi had looked at her. No one as important as the BG had ever truly spoken to her like she was an equal. Like she mattered. He was

Indonesian like her, but he'd managed to shed his VIP persona and make her feel every bit as special as she believed him to be.

She wasn't back in the office for two minutes before she was brought back to earth with a bump. The breakthrough with Pak Cunningham's investigation meant that she needed to book Monday morning flights for Charlie, Cain, and Andy before the travel agents closed for the night.

[ ]

Speer arrived at the Brigadier General's offices first, so by the time Cain got there, they didn't have a chance to talk before they positively identified Hing and his associates.

Waiting for Kusnadi to finish briefing his aides, they were, however, obliged to sit together and overheat in a stuffy corridor, becoming ever more irritated by the clanking noise of a broken air-conditioning unit that no one else seemed to notice.

Speer looked straight ahead. "You honestly think I'd indulge myself in a place like the Mawwar?"

After his earlier misunderstanding, Cain had been wary of being alone with the Major but still found the strength of his accusatory tone very uncomfortable. He'd never spoken honestly about his view of the Major's relationship with Feronika. He'd done quite the opposite, in fact, by helping conceal and even encourage the affair in its early days. But Speer was no longer his boss, and something needed to be said.

"I'm sorry I spoke out of turn, Major," he said, trying to cope with his dry throat.

Speer's face began to soften as his former employee paused, but it was soon hardened again when Cain spoke his mind, albeit as politely as he could.

"I know you would never go to a place like the Mawwar, but I am worried about you. I looked up to you as a man who had everything. Distinguished careers in the military and finance. World travel and a self-assured manner fashioned by your success. I'm just starting out and saw you as a role model. Now I'm worried that you might be throwing away everything for a woman you can hardly have much in common with." He'd said a lot, and he needed to take a breath. Speer said nothing, so he carried on. "This is all very hard to say, Major. I know clients who've had affairs and lost everything. I honestly wouldn't want that to happen to you. It's not my business, and yet, I couldn't look myself in the face if I didn't take this chance to tell you. I hope you understand."

He took a deep breath and looked directly at the Major, ready to get an earful.

But Speer, who'd been sitting so rigidly, let his posture collapse with a heavy sigh. "From the mouths of babes, eh Shaw. It's not like I've been acting blindly. Like you said, I've got years on you. I should have learned. Indeed, I have learned. And yet, sometimes life just throws a bunch of things at you at the same time. They knock you off kilter, and you learn that you're not impervious to the world. For all the experience I may have over you, this is all new to me."

Cain interrupted; "But it's reckless, Major. Think about it. You had everything already."

Speer stood up and tried to fan his chest with the material of his shirt by tugging at the loosened collar. "I'm aware of all of that, Shaw, I really am. But I've strayed down a path, and let me tell you, from the viewpoint of someone with 20-something years on you, I'm still trying to find my way. No matter how old I get, I'm still just finding my way."

Cain wanted to say more, but Kusnadi was approaching. "I mean this in the best way, Major. I truly hope you do find your way before your present impacts your possible future."

With Kusnadi close, Speer whispered, "Thanks Shaw," out of the side of his mouth.

21)   Amok

These backstreets would provide the gritty shots Ruby wanted. The intense May sunshine ensured that the dirt roads filled the air with a thin haze of dust that settled everywhere, including the yellowed laundry that hung lifelessly on lines and clothes horses.

Staring at a shop window rendered opaque by the ubiquitous dust, Ruby's perspiring brow furrowed. "That's about the fifth time I've seen this daubed on a building, Awing. What does 'milik pribumi' mean?"

Awing had been ignoring the graffiti, hoping his clients wouldn't ask about it. "It means owned by indigenous Indonesians," he replied, omitting the fact that it was actually a warning to the Chinese occupants to get out. Instead, he peered through the sunlit dust into the shadowy doorways from where unusually taciturn adults and children watched the Chinese crew at work. He wondered if anyone could be persuaded to give a soundbite to his clients.

There were times that day when he believed it was only the presence of their camera that had saved them from real trouble. Awing had tried hard to get voxpop interviews, especially in the wake of the police station attack, but no one wanted to help. Young men scowled, and some even spat when he asked them if they wanted to go on camera. Women simply walked away from him without answering. After a few paces, they'd look back, their faces full of contempt. With crews he'd worked for in the past, little kids would always play and jostle cheekily for the attention of TV people. But as his current clients went about their business, they were either hauled away by adults, or they just whispered and pretended not to watch from a distance, unsmiling.

Ruby was directing Seetoh to focus his camera on the graffiti when the sound of metal pounding on metal reverberated through the neighborhood, accompanied by screams and shouts. The doorway onlookers slammed their doors shut, leaving the crew outside and alone.

"Boss, we should get out of here," Seetoh advised, with Awing and soundman Goh readily agreeing.

Awing hoped Ruby would listen to Seetoh, but he'd also learned how important this assignment was to her. She clenched her fists by her sides as if trying to gird herself. "We missed the police station attack this morning," she paused to swallow. "We can't afford to miss this."

Awing and the crew looked at one another, and Ruby took charge, instructing Goh to mic her up. "I want to record a piece-to-camera with some overlay footage to send to HQ as soon as possible."

Goh tucked the wireless mic pack into the back of her trousers. Ruby took the cable from him and fed it under her top to her neckline, but Seetoh stopped her. "No. Don't use a clip mic. Use a handheld one. People will see more clearly what you're doing and hopefully leave you alone."

Seetoh was clearly more experienced than Ruby, and Awing agreed that was a much better idea. He could feel Ruby's gaze on him. The same unspoken cry for support she'd given him after sharing her plan to come here. He'd turned her down initially, explaining that the Acehnese in North Sumatra didn't like the Javanese because it was military officers from his island who'd inflicted unspeakable violence against the independence movement. Ruby had listened, but her response was to offer another fifty dollars a day, an offer he currently wished he'd rejected.

They approached a street corner where a thicker fog of dust could be seen spewing from an even smaller side street. Ruby asked, "Where exactly are we Awing? I'll need to mention it."

"Tembung market district," he replied, putting the cumbersome tripod down and rubbing his sore shoulder.

They turned the corner, their hearts quickening, demanding more oxygen and faster gulps of the dust-riddled air. Wary, they moved closer to the fury driven by highly combustible, individual energy that was, in turn, being grotesquely super-charged by the collective savagery of the mob.

Seetoh shouted that he'd film from his shoulder and that she could start anytime as he was already rolling. Awing pressed himself into a doorway opposite, out of shot. It was incredible; between the fleeing dust and the frenzy of the mob, Ruby appeared to move freely.

Speaking directly into the lens, she painted the scene with her words and actually stepped through the big wooden frame that, minutes before, had housed the jewelry shop window. Awing gasped, thinking that she was pushing her luck too far, but people were running and jumping through the window frame, in and out of the shop with their booty, as if they were blind to Ruby and the camera.

Despite the chaos, Ruby fended off looters as they bounced off her, doggedly maintaining her engagement with the camera. "...and violence like this has been erupting across the North Sumatran city of Medan where mobs run amok in neighborhoods like...."

There was a blur, and Ruby disappeared. Awing ran forward a few steps but stopped abruptly when he saw the two men frantically trying to grab Ruby. She was lashing out in all directions to fight them off. Awing couldn't move. More men surrounded Ruby. She screamed for Seetoh and Goh, who were already running to her. All this had happened in an instant, but they were too late. Ruby was struck across the head with a club. The fight was taken from her, and she fell heavily on the broken glass that covered the floor.

With their equipment falling from their bodies, the crew started to kick and punch Ruby's assailants, but shouts of 'Chindo!' let the rest of the mob know they had two Chinese men at their mercy. Awing knew their luck had run out. Still recording, the camera and sound equipment lay on the floor alongside its operatives. Two men dragged Ruby's body across the broken glass and further into the shop. Awing, absurdly driven by his terror, walked into the shop. He held himself against a wall. Blood streaked from Ruby's body as glass shards ripped into her back and legs.

Awing froze against a demolished counter and saw the attackers peel off Seetoh and Goh to return to the business of ripping the shop apart. Legs quivering, Awing lurched further into the shop where Ruby had been dragged. He pressed himself into a corner and witnessed evil. Ruby's clothes were ripped from her body. Violence had driven her assailants beyond all morality, civility, or humanity. The first attacker slashed through the waistband of her underwear, ripped the delicate garment from her body, threw her legs apart, and seconds later, he was pushing inside her. Withdrawing, he looked at the other men around him, grabbed the inside of Ruby's left thigh, and using it to spin her round, he passed her on. He looked directly at Awing with a menacing leer. "Do you want some too?"

Awing quailed and ran. He did not stop till he got back to the crew van.

The mob had moved on when he returned with police and a medic twenty minutes later. The scene of carnage made him feel weak again. As he peered through the blood, bruising, and facial distortion, he identified Seetoh and Goh. Both were battered but still breathing. The medic gave them a superficial check, and Awing's legs buckled as he stood up. A police officer caught him and asked if he was okay. Petrified, Awing said no, but that he would feel better when they found Ruby. He marshaled whatever composure he could and ventured further into the ransacked shop.

There she was. Clothed in fragments of material, dust, and blood. Awing felt his stomach convulse and bit his lip to distract himself.

"Why did you bring these Chinese here, you Javanese fool?" scolded an older police officer who'd recognized Awing's accent. "Foreigners too," he noted after pulling an identity card from Ruby's wallet. "This is going to be problematic."

Awing ignored the older man and squatted next to the medic as he checked Ruby's broken body. Assured that her neck and backbone were in one piece, unlike the skin on her back, he checked that her airway was clear and moved her carefully into the recovery position. The movement induced a weak groan, and Awing whispered, "Ruby, you're safe now. I will get you home."

Ruby opened one reddened eye. The other was sealed shut with heavy bruising and swelling. She stared at Awing for a few seconds before the lid closed once more. A younger police officer wrapped her body in material from a roll of green baize, the kind you see in jewelry shop cases. He assured Awing that an ambulance was on its way.

[ ]

Returning from Singapore some twenty-four hours later, Cain, Charlie, and Andy disembarked from an almost empty 'Emirates Shuttle' as the Temple-Speer advisors used to call it. They breezed through the empty Arrivals Hall at Soekarno-Hatta airport, but there was nothing 'breezy' about their mood.

© Steven Clark 2023
Lynnburn, Amisfield, Dumfries & Galloway, UK

Lena found it impossible to book flights to Singapore, so Charlie asked a favor from one of his former clients. All they had to do was get one-way tickets back to Jakarta, and there was little in the way of competitive demand for that journey.

The company bank account was established with all the ease and efficiency for which the 'Lion City' is renowned, but the trip hadn't been without its concerns. And even though they were driving back to central Jakarta in the safety of one of Andy's father's cars, the constant, gnawing tension that underpinned life in the city these days seemed to stream through the aircon vents.

Cain began to feel the return of a hollow ache in the pit of his stomach. He turned off the vent that was blowing directly onto him in a futile attempt to stifle thoughts of Ernest's murder, Ruby's angry departure, and his argument with Charlie about coming back here. He'd suggested staying in Singapore a little longer, but Charlie wanted to return for the sake of the business and reminded Cain that he needed to be in Jakarta to make up with Ruby when she returned from her assignment. He eventually agreed, but with deep reservations.

About halfway back to the city, their car driver slowed down. The driver pointed across to the other side of the highway. A western woman was standing by the side of the road, carrying a small child while her vehicle was being ransacked. They drove by the pitiless scene in a few seconds, but the expression of anguished desolation torn into the crying mother's face would stay with them for much longer. She watched through tear-filled eyes as her clothes and prized possessions were unceremoniously plundered. Her husband disturbingly unseen.

[ ]

Lena was working when they arrived at the office.

They'd all been deeply disturbed by what they'd witnessed on the toll road, but Charlie tried to muster all the cheer he could. "I thought you were supposed to be at home, young lady."

"You're back!" Lena shouted, ignoring his mock scolding. "Good job, too, because the contractor is basically done with the office."

None of the travelers felt good, but seeing Lena so happy, they tried to pick themselves up and look cheerful as she commandeered their attention and dragged them to see the store room. She knocked the walls; "Breezeblock, not plasterboard." She took her key and opened the 8-bolt security door; "So heavy, you see." Then she showed them the safe the landlord had procured.

Charlie grabbed the safe and tried to budge it. Finding it impossible, he turned and said: "This room's perfect for all our ill-gotten gains, client files, stationary, and, as discussed, our food stores."

Lena declared, "I know. They did a great job. Now, you lot need to tell me all about Singapore."

Returning to their central working area, the boys quickly glossed over their trip. Lena's expression changed.

"I was actually quite jealous that I could not go with you to Singapore, but from your expressions, I have to ask what on earth happened over there?"

Cain looked at the others and replied, "Well, we got treated to dinner with Sir James, the Major, and Feronika at the Ritz Carlton. They said it was a six-star hotel, whatever that means."

Lena couldn't understand the lack of excitement in Cain's voice and tried to be excited for him; "Wow, I've seen that place in magazines. Very Fancy!"

"Not according to Sir James," Charlie countered without energy. "It was Feronika's idea to go there, and she really took him to task when he claimed, 'The Ritz was nothing more than gauche opulence to attract the nouveau riche.' He'd clearly had a few too many drinks but he called it," Charlie coughed and began impersonating Sir James, "little more than a bloody concrete block that obstructs the splendid view from the Benjamin Sheers bridge as one approaches the city."

"And he did have a point," Andy added, "Looking out the cab's back window on the way to Changi airport, the hotel's position really did block the city skyline."

Lena voiced her frustration with them; "You tell me about bank accounts. You tell me about architecture. How about the Major and his…" she took time to settle on the right word, and when she said it, she was careful to convey her disappointment in him, "His girlfriend."

"Well, that's what we're all rather worried about," Cain explained, knowing that such a statement would help prepare Lena for what she was about to hear. "Andy got to the Ritz Carlton before us and overheard a conversation that made us question their relationship." He was about to continue but looked at Andy. "Sorry, you should actually be telling this story."

"Okay then," Andy began. "I got to the hotel early because I'd met a friend who is working in Singapore, and she dropped me off. Waiting for these two," he indicated Cain and Charlie, "I sat in an armchair, playing with my mobile, and became aware of a conversation in Bahasa Indonesia. Now, remember, I'd never seen Feronika, so when I looked, I only saw an attractive woman talking to two men. But growing up with my father, I could tell the men were military."

Everyone agreed with that, and then Andy was allowed to continue.

"The relationship between the woman and the men made me wonder who she was. Because the way she spoke to them suggested she was in charge, not them. She mentioned something about partners and questioned why they hadn't found the American's documents. She spoke quietly, but her tone really was quite rude. They repeated that their partners had not found the documents, only for her to repeat that they must be at the American's house. And then she really was very rude. She called their partners 'unreliable fucking amateurs' and told the two men to recheck everything themselves."

"Charlie couldn't keep quiet any longer. "And if that wasn't weird enough, what happened next will blow your mind. Go on Andy, tell her."

"The men stood up and left the hotel, but she went through the lobby and further into the building. That's when these two arrived, followed almost immediately by the Major and Sir James. I joined them, and we all went through to the restaurant."

He paused for effect, but Lena was impatient; "And?"

"And," Andy parroted, "That same woman greeted us from a table! It was Feronika!"

"Oh no," Lena said with a sense of dread in her voice. "What happened then?"

Andy continued, "Well, I couldn't say anything to these two, but I really was quite scared. Thankfully, from the way Feronika behaved, she didn't recognize me from the lobby."

Cain could tell that Andy was nervously pondering the probability of his luck and took the opportunity to reassure him with praise. "He was so cool during dinner that neither myself nor Charlie had any idea that something might be wrong."

Andy looked at Cain and asked him to continue; "After all, you were the one who first noticed the documents that Feronika might have been talking about."

Cain took another opportunity to fire up Andy's confidence. "It was a long dinner. I don't know how this man managed to hold it together, but he did."

Charlie voiced his agreement with Cain's sentiment, adding, "He even held it together throughout the cab journey back to the Hilton where we were staying."

"But as soon as we were alone," said Cain, "he told us about the lobby, and we realized that Feronika must have been talking about Pyle because we both knew that Cunningham passed a file to him that seemed to be important. One time Charlie even managed to sneak a peek inside."

Charlie had to cut in; "Yeah, it was in Pyle's office, and it had naff all to do with Temple-Speer. It was full of old Glenrovia stuff dating right back to the 1970s. Notes were written all over the pages, but it was all codes and technical jargon. We reckon Feronika was talking about that file."

"But we can't be sure, of course," Cain qualified. "We tried to call Pyle, but the way he travels, he might not even be in Jakarta because we couldn't get hold of him."

Andy looked at Lena and explained, "We only had Pyle's mobile number but wondered if you had his home telephone in your records."

"I know he was still waiting for the décor to be finished in the fancy Penthouse he bought, so the number I've got should work."

They called, but there was no answer. Charlie tried his mobile and got the same result.

© Steven Clark 2023
Lynnburn, Amisfield, Dumfries & Galloway, UK

284

Finally, they were all on the same page. Cain felt it necessary to apologize to Lena for ruining her mood, acknowledging that, "We had to tell you."

He thought he'd done the right thing and was therefore surprised when Lena got a little upset, saying, "You three need to stop treating me like a little girl. I guess I should be thankful that you are looking out for me, but please treat me as you would expect to be treated yourself. As a caring, committed, and able part of the team, ok?"

She waited. They all nodded a little sheepishly. "We need to call BG Kusnadi," she continued. "This is exactly the kind of thing he meant when he said we should call him if we think we might be in danger. We're not, but Pak Pyle might be."

Lena then called Kusnadi and explained everything. He thanked her for calling and said he'd send some officers to Pyle's address and check on him. He also told them to stay in the office as he was coming over right now. Quite pleased with herself at speaking so confidently to the BG, she hung up and turned to the others. "Hey, you guys never mentioned Pak Cunningham."

Charlie shared what Speer and Sir James had told them. "A private plane will be arranged by Sir James and his Presidential contacts to take Ernest's body to Singapore before it's flown to the UK. As for the investigation, Sir James said he was concerned by the lack of progress."

Cain interrupted because even though he'd questioned the closeness of the relationship between Sir James and Suharto in the past, Sir James seemed to know an awful lot about Kusnadi. "Sir James said something about a rivalry between two generals, which could render Kusnadi vulnerable because he has no military background."

"Which is true," Andy confirmed. "Suharto cultivates factions in his administration, and a lot of people's hopes are riding on the BG taking over the police force so that he can detach it from the military. But, of course, there are plenty of others who do not want him to succeed."

[ ]

Kusnadi was true to his word, and within an hour of Lena's phone call, he was listening carefully to their story. Hearing the description of Feronika, he said he'd heard of a woman like her who sometimes worked with the state security organization called BAKIN.

He'd ordered specific officers to go to Pyle's apartment. If he wasn't home, they were to gain access to the apartment with the assistance of building security. Inside they were to look for signs of anything that might be considered suspicious and to search for the JTH file.

Cain asked, what about Major Speer and Sir James? Do you think they are safe?"

Kusnadi responded, "What you have told me has given me cause for concern, but my immediate priorities are finding Mr. Cunningham's killers, establishing Mr. Pyle's whereabouts, and keeping you safe. As my investigation is taking place because Sir James appealed to my President, I sense he is not in any danger. Major Speer should therefore be safe in his company."

Kusnadi asked them to go about their business while he dealt with his other duties by phone. They did as they were told but found themselves incapable of anything except sharing their concerns about what was happening.

Thankfully Kusnadi's hand-picked officers worked with incredible speed. His mobile rang, and after taking the call, he revealed that Pyle's residence had already been visited. He wasn't there, so the building security manager let the officers in. Everything appeared to be normal in the apartment, but after a thorough search, they couldn't find the JTH file.

He concluded that, "For now, I think it is reasonable to treat Mr. Pyle as an adult with the capacity for making his own choices. I'll check immigration to see if he is still in the country. If that's the case, I will try to make contact every day until the weekend. On Monday, he'll be considered a missing person. As for you, I'd caution you all to remain extremely vigilant. I wish I could do more, but my officers are trying to manage the growing protests. However, if you are in danger, call me. You have seen how efficient my men can be." He stood up, but before leaving, he added, "And let me know if Mr. Pyle contacts you. I'd very much like to take a look at that JTH file."

09/05/98, Saturday

22)   Catchin on to Yerself

The gentle sound of waves lapping on Gili Trawangan's shoreline periodically broke through the din of worries clattering through Cain's mind, but it gave him no solace. A lot had happened since Trawangan, but right now, he didn't know if he was more concerned by the lack of communication with Ruby or the portentous approach of the time she said she might call him. He'd picked up his own phone several times, only to find himself staring at her name with his finger hovering over the call button. He made excuses; the new business, the crisis, and the threat of a violent death hanging over his head. But Ruby said she'd call him, didn't she? he argued feebly.

The team at Flint told themselves that Pyle could be somewhere like Bali lying low in the splendor of a friend's villa. But as time passed, their frail confidence in such hopes faded away. Afraid for his own life, Charlie was keenly aware of the other issues bearing down on Cain's misery; and with the arrival of Friday night, he insisted they put an end to their hermitage. It wasn't easy. Cain reprised his argument that they'd have been better off staying in Singapore. Charlie, who'd been in touch with the French guys, countered by saying nobody would try anything whilst they were surrounded by pals before reminding him that he was back in Jakarta because Ruby was scheduled to return any day now.

"The French lads are heading to CJs and JJs," Charlie continued. "Then if they've got any energy left, they're going to Stadium." Cain and Charlie had done what they called the 'Stadium Stamina Night' long ago. They both flinched at hearing its name, recalling the shock to the senses of leaving a dark, cavernous nightclub and walking into bright 9 am sunshine.

When they met the French guys in JJs, there was a strange feeling that the whole scene was totally out of sync with reality. The city was in turmoil, and yet everyone within the pleasure-seeking bubble of the club was behaving as if nothing was happening. The only glaring difference was the drop in expat numbers. The French guys joked that the working girls were way ahead of the government, as they'd been pegging their rates to the dollar for months already. The challenge, however, was operating in a market where supply had so outstripped demand.

The motivation for the evening was to let off steam, but Cain and Charlie drank bottled water as neither of them could totally let their guard down. They just danced all night with their new friends, some of them fueled by 'E' and others just high on life, albeit enhanced with old-fashioned, but far from vintage, alcohol. The night wore on and got a little crazy. Girls crowded around them and peeled off their shirts, laughing and joking that the boys were too sweaty.

Egos primed by an unexpectedly good night, Cain and Charlie left the club. The worthlessness of the Rupiah made wallets useless, so they peeled off notes from recently acquired money clips and paid their Silver Bird driver. Striding out, the shirtless revelers knew that Jakarta was becoming a popular landing spot for excitable reporters who were parachuting in, tempted by the bait of unrest. Cain and Charlie used that knowledge to reason that a walk from JJs to Jalan Thamrin, with its heavy security presence, might actually counterbalance any threat from the killers that might still be abroad in the city. Their lack of belief in that shoddy logic was, however, patently obvious in their nervous laughter as they hailed a taxi shortly after reaching Thamrin.

[ ]

With late morning sunshine streaming through the bedroom curtains, Cain tried to recall the previous night's merriment, but shrapnel from his ongoing torment kept tearing into those happier thoughts. It was only when his mobile phone rang that his mind stood still.

"That has to be Ruby," he told himself, feeling almost smug. He let it ring, coaxing his voice into action by saying 'hello' a few times before he answered.

His attempt to be cool was betrayed by the earnestness of his tone. "Ruby is that you?"

A moment of silence was followed by a man's voice. It startled Cain into sitting bolt upright and being suddenly very awake.

"Hello. Is that Cain Shaw? This is Daniel Miller. Ruby's father."

Cain's telling earnestness was displaced by worried bewilderment. He had to repeat what Mr. Miller had said to make some sense of what he'd heard. "Miller? Ruby's dad? Err, hello, sir."

Mr. Miller began to explain, but not in the order that Cain wanted. "I'm in Hong Kong with Ruby's mum. Ruby asked me to call you." His voice cracked. He sounded upset.

Cain was perplexed. He'd never met this man. Surely this can't be anything to do with that bloody fight? "Mr. Miller. Hi. You're in Hong Kong? But Ruby's on assignment in Bali, sir."

It seemed like an interminably long time while Mr. Miller composed himself, and Cain tried to hold his nerve. "Ruby's been hurt..." The desolate father only managed those three words before he stammered, "Sorry, Cain. Give me a moment."

Cain was beside himself. What the hell had happened?

"Ruby was attacked by a mob when she was reporting from somewhere called Medan." Ruby's father's voice wavered with sorrow before he could add, "They beat my little girl. They beat her within an inch of her life. They... the bastards raped and beat my daughter...."

He had to stop, inhaling deeply as if trying to stem a torrent of anguish.

Cain wanted to say something but knew there was nothing he could really say to this man he'd never met. He had to speak to Ruby.

Her father had begun to answer the questions burning in Cain's head, but feelings of guilt, regret, sadness, and anger all jostled for attention too.

Mr. Miller snatched at a moment of self-control. "Ruby's employers got her medevacked to a place called Pekanbaru, where she was patched up before an air ambulance flight to Hong Kong. Ruby's mum and I were here to meet her when she arrived, and I have to say, her treatment's been remarkable."

"She deserves the very best, Mr. Miller," Cain managed to say. "What's next? Do you … have a plan?" He stuttered over the awkward articulation of the question.

Another deep breath was followed by a staccato exhalation caused by the juddering chest of a heartbroken father. "The plan? I guess a period of convalescence here in Hong Kong until Ruby is strong enough to fly home to London."

"I'll get on a plane to Hong Kong as soon as I can book a ticket," Cain declared, only partially convinced that Ruby wouldn't have divulged what had happened between them.

Ruby's father coughed. Still friendly, the timbre of his voice became more assured. "Listen to me, Cain. Ruby told me that you two had parted on a sour note. But she also explained that she'd promised to get in touch when her assignment was over. That's why she told me you'd had an argument. She wanted me to explain why she hadn't called you."

Cain could feel the pace of his heart quickening, his cheeks flush, and his brow perspiring. He spoke freely, not constrained by self-protective prudence. "I'm sorry, Mr. Miller. I'm sorry about so many things. But please tell Ruby that I'll be on the first flight I can get up to Hong Kong and…."

Mr. Miller interrupted, "Look, son, Ruby expressly told me she doesn't want to see anyone right now. And if I know my little girl, then I know it's not about you or the argument. She's better than that. Think about what she's been through. She doesn't want anyone to see her in this condition."

He paused to catch his emotions, and with a lower voice, he acknowledged, "You'll have to take heart in the fact that Ruby insisted I call you. She obviously thinks a lot of you. But she's going through hell, physically and emotionally. Her doctor said she's suffering from something called Post Traumatic Stress, and it's really taking its toll. Her employers have been very supportive, and we're taking her home with us to London. Better that we see you when Ruby thinks the time is right. Okay…" He sniffed, and his voice cracked again; "I'll need to ring off. Be careful down there, Cain. Goodbye."

Cain strove to prolong the conversation; "But Mr. Miller, if I could only…."

Ruby's father hung up. Cain continued to hold the phone to his ear, listening to the flat tone of the ended call. It was a tone he'd never paid any attention to, but in that moment, it felt like a long, exasperated sigh that was slowly emptying out of him.

He'd never really had a proper adult relationship with a woman, and it looked like he'd totally screwed up any chance of establishing one with Ruby. Instead of trying to call her, he'd behaved like an asshole and gone out with the lads. Guilt started to invoke a trembling throughout his body, which quickly became enveloped in another cold sweat. A cramped desolation churned the pit of his bile-filling stomach. He found himself gulping back saliva as if he were about to vomit and kicked away the bedsheet that was still covering his legs.

Hugging his abdomen, anger bled into the guilt. He tried to believe it was directed at Ruby's attackers but couldn't escape the truth that he was the primary target. He recollected his father's words about being little more than a salesman. The taunt echoed all the louder this time.

"What bloody good am I to anyone?" he implored as if expecting an answer to emerge from the walls of the room.

Cain's fledgling adult life flashed before him. His professors had high hopes for him, but he hadn't wanted to remain in academia one moment longer than he needed to. He didn't want routine. He wanted travel and excitement. More than anything, he didn't want the humdrum, family guy life his father had struggled with. The role at Temple-Speer had offered him decent money and a chance to differentiate himself from his more static peers who'd soon be weighed down by the trappings of their narrower life-paths. But as time passed, he never truly thwarted his fear of mediocrity because whenever he told anyone about where he'd been or what he did, nobody really gave a fuck.

It was unstoppable. Chin quivering, he started to cry.

Like discovering a cave behind a waterfall, through his tears, he found himself back in the kitchen with Ruby. He remembered how his anger grew out of grief for Cunningham and fear for himself. That was it. He'd been frightened for himself, not for Ruby, never for her. He thought she'd be okay, that somehow the strength of her career ambitions would keep her safe. She said she'd come to Indonesia for him and not just for the story. But that was right in the middle of telling him she was taking off again.

Why Ruby? It had been so easy for her to push his buttons, but he recalled that even on the brink of losing control, he'd questioned the wisdom of losing a night's sleep after a fight. Had he been drawn into it, or had he actually picked the fight? The first option was regrettable, but the latter was unforgivable, especially with someone he professed to care about. Was this how he was with women? Was he the needy wee boy throwing his toys out of the cot? A number of his clients had been quite abusive when the crisis started to eat into their portfolio gains, but he didn't allow them to bother him too much. Just like Cunningham, he maintained a posture of indifference that cloaked him with an air of cool professionalism.

Jaysis, I admired old Cunningham, but I never wanted to be him. Then he took that thought one alarming step further, and I don't want to end up like him either.

His mind was racing inside his throbbing head. It was exhausting. He tried to rein in his runaway thoughts. He knew he'd been cruising, doing a job that barely engaged his brain. But it wasn't just work. He'd started to believe he was above the fray in most aspects of life when in fact, he was just clinging to a vantage point from where he could criticize without having to risk failure by actually getting involved.

He didn't need to look far to see others who were wringing out every drop of opportunity their lives presented. Ruby was given a break by the Harrier collapse and leveraged it to become a regular on-camera talent. Then there was Charlie. Given the growing anti-Chinese violence, he should have been the first to quit Temple-Speer and head home. He'd narrowly escaped being caught up in the torture of that Chinese couple in the supermarket, but the dogged wee bastard was still hanging on, giving his all to become a successful business owner. Life in Indonesia wasn't particularly easy for anyone at the moment, but at least he didn't have to worry about the color of his fucking skin.

"Jaysis, I'm pathetic!" he spat, cursing his self-indulgence. He had no right to be feeling like this. Ruby had nearly been killed, and his reaction was self-pity. Or was it self-loathing? Whatever it was, he knew it was wrong because he couldn't silence the voice saying, 'Catch on tae yerself. You see where yer big man act got ye? That lassie had the shite beaten out of her.'

He started to feel wretchedly ill again. A memory from deep in his childhood hemorrhaged and played out against this latest failure. His long-haired father shouting, "Where were you when your wee pal Colin was hit by those bullies? Did ye run and save yerself? There's a name for that."

The childhood memory vanished, but the berating continued. "Where were ye when that lassie was being raped? Oh, aye, playing Jack-the-lad in a nightclub. Well, doesn't that just about sum you up, boy."

Tears now fell like rain as he considered his worth to the world.

He'd actually been instructed to 'fuck the meek' by the very man he worked for. Andreas had told him of the region's lingering resentment of its colonial past, and now he could see why. The days of Empire had long since passed, but its callous and casual bigotry continued. At Temple-Speer, his job had barely touched the lives of Indonesians, but he'd used their country as a base to profit from the sale of nothing more than diaphanous promises of wealth appreciation to vulnerably naïve expats. He was no colonialist but exploitation for economic gain whilst contributing nothing of consequence to Indonesia started to sound like the very essence of neo-colonialism. With tears still streaming down his face, he turned to his mirror and saw the watery reflection of a wretched instrument of neo-colonial oppression. He needed to make real changes but couldn't convince himself that selling ethical funds would provide that change.

Beyond the white noise of his harried mind, the only sound was the whir of the ceiling fan motor and the clicking of the blades as they chased one another round and round. His eyes closed.

[ ]

He had no idea how much time had passed when the phone rang.

It was Charlie. "What a night that was?" he declared before babbling on.

Cain didn't want to listen. It wasn't difficult to affect a pained voice. "Charlie. I'm not feeling well."

"You didn't drink, so it's probably the Jakarta two-step," Charlie kidded, referring to the distance one gets from a toilet seat before having to return when suffering a bout of the shits.

Cain didn't laugh. He needed to sort himself out and thought he'd pre-empt any offer of help by saying, "I just need to rest, Charlie."

"Yeah, you probably do," Charlie agreed, "But as you pointed out yesterday, we shouldn't be alone too much. I could come over."

"That's okay, Charlie. There are always people at the apartment pool on the weekend. As soon as I feel up to it, I'll head down there and relax with a book. Then if all's well, I'll see you in the office on Monday. Have a nice weekend."

He hung up, painfully aware that the manner in which he'd swept Charlie aside was indicative of the self-centered behavior that was responsible for his present state of mind. Charlie needed the safety of friendly company just as much as he did, but Cain also believed that he needed time to let this perdition manifest. Maybe then, he could try to cope with the horrible news about Ruby.

He pictured her pretty face and searched his feelings. Of course, he cared for her. And, of course, people who care for each other sometimes argue. He needed to grow up and appreciate that, as Charlie said, the universe owed him nothing. If he wanted any kind of relationship with Ruby, then he'd better stop wallowing and do something about it.

Buoyed by that thought, he found her number on his mobile and pressed the call button. I just need to say hello. Nothing clever. Just apologize, ask how she is, and be supportive.

Building himself up so quickly sharpened the sting of the subsequent fall. Ruby's mobile was, of course, dead.

[ ]

By Sunday evening Cain had only used his voice once more, and that was to say thanks to the cashier who bagged his groceries in a nearby minimart. He'd lied to Charlie about feeling ill, but his weekend of tormented isolation had resulted in fever-soaked bedsheets all the same. Listening to the washing machine agitate and launder his bed linen, he thought about his parents.

He hadn't spoken to his father for quite a while, but his mother had called him a few weeks ago after watching a troubling report about Indonesia. She sounded anxious. "Wouldn't you prefer to come home for a wee while until the situation's improved?"

She was worried, and she knew nothing about the murder of his former boss. Cain had decided to keep it that way as such news would drive her from anxiety to terror. Instead, he promised to hop on a flight to Singapore if things got too hairy. But as she observed, from her point of view, he didn't have any pressing reason to stay on, and during that call, he hadn't felt confident enough to offer any. This time, however, he was ready to share the big news about starting his own business. The voice that told him to catch on to himself had been his father's when he was a boy, but Charlie had been correct when he diagnosed that Cain's only real detractor was himself. When his father heard that he wasn't at Temple-Speer anymore, he was bound to be pleased. And if that was indeed the case, Cain also wanted to ask about that curious memory he had. How on earth a soldier like his dad could have had long hair, even if it was the fashion back then?

His mother answered the phone, her soft Scottish lilt bringing a smile to his face. After the initial greetings, however, she quickly repeated her litany of concerns about Jakarta. "We don't get much news from Asia over here unless it's serious, but we're hearing more about Indonesia these days, and it really makes me worried about you."

"I know, ma, but I'm actually doing fine," Cain tried to reassure her before changing the topic in an attempt to distract. "I only called to see how everyone's doing back there."

It had been a while, so he knew she'd have a lot to tell. Pausing for breath in her bulletin, she suddenly exclaimed, "I can see your father. He's watering the vegetables. The Spring weather's been glorious over here. Hold on, son."

Cain heard her bang on a window and shout, "Andrew! It's Cain, calling from Indonesia. Hurry!" Then a few seconds later, "I'm just putting your father on, son."

Cain took a deep breath. Boy or man? What was he?

"How about ye, son?" his father panted after rushing to the phone. "Jaysis, but that Jakarta's starting to look like Belfast in the bad old days. You okay?"

"Doing fine, thanks. But as I was telling ma, I'm sure things look worse on the telly. You always used you to say that."

"Aye, telly cameras always focus on the worst of it. You never see ordinary people just trying to get on."

Cain had understood Northern Ireland's 'troubles' through his father, but it was only now that he could see it as living through history because that's exactly what he was doing in Jakarta. For the first time in his life, he felt he was the equal of his father. Feeling confident, he kept on topic; after all, history had once more rounded on Northern Ireland too. "Da, what do you make of the peace agreement in your old stomping grounds?"

"Don't listen to them, son. I never stomped on anyone."

That was unusual. He never joked about his service. It caught Cain off-guard, and his consequent guffaw sounded like a snort. Soon after, they were chatting about all the Americans visiting Belfast ever since the Good Friday Agreement was signed. "Jaysis, son, they need to build some decent hotels. It's no good putting Yanks up in Bed and Breakfast joints because that's when they all realize that maybe they're not as Irish as they'd thought. God knows where they put Clinton when he was glad-handing."

Cain took advantage of the mention of the American peacemaker. "Aye da, Clinton wants the world to see his role over there, but he's making damn sure his backhand meddling over here goes unnoticed. One of my former bosses told me that in return for China buying American debt, Clinton was making sure Asia's financial crisis goes on long enough to suit China."

Mr. Shaw sighed. "I guess I should be shocked, son, but I'm not. Politicians never bloody change. They'll shit on anyone for their own gain." But ever the astute interrogator, he added: "You said 'former boss,' are ye sure yer alright?"

Cain saw a perfect opportunity to talk about Flint. "Politicians don't change, but changes are coming for Charlie and me. We're starting our own business."

There was a moment of silence. Cain bit his lip till his father responded. "Given the situation over there, is that really a wise thing to be doing right now, son? Do you have any backers?"

Cain confidently slapped the arm of his chair. "We made sure of it. A well-placed, respected family is backing us. Their son helped us with the process of getting the business up and running."

There was another ponderable moment of silence. Then a huge grin spread over Cain's face as he heard, "Elizabeth, do you hear this? We've got a well-connected businessman for a son."

Cain knew that, to a certain extent, his father's positivity was making it clear to his mother that something good was happening and that she needed not to worry. He also wanted to convey a sense of happiness to lighten the mood still further. "Thanks, but hold on da. The reason I'm telling you is the company name. See if you get it. It's called Flint Independent Financial Advisory."

Within seconds, his football-loving father shouted, "You work at FIFA! Jaysis, that'll give the fellas down the pub a good laugh."

His father's interest continued and even seemed to grow as Cain outlined the business, perhaps over-emphasizing the ethical nature of the investment products he was hoping to sell. "At Temple-Speer, our futures were in the hands of our bosses. But now we're on our own, and we don't have to wait for the likes of Sir James Templar-Hawes or Major David Speer."

As Cain chuckled at his belittling of his former bosses, his father repeated one of the names. "Major David Speer? Was he in the Army Air Corps? And did he serve in Ulster at all?"

Cain was taken aback. "Do you know him?"

His father mulled over the name. "You mentioned working for an army officer, but you never said his name. Speer? I didn't know him, but our paths were supposed to cross. He was meant to drop supplies for my team. Claimed he'd been given the wrong coordinates, but we reckoned he bottled it because the drop was too hot. Not a man you can rely on."

Cain couldn't believe what he was hearing. "You actually knew David Speer?"

"I made my misgivings about Temple-Speer very clear, son, but believe me, if I'd known you were going to work for a shite like him, ye'd have never gotten on that plane to Asia. That bastard left my team FUBAR-ed, balls against the wall with nothing to defend ourselves."

Knowing what he did about the Major's broken promises and mid-life crisis philandering, Cain responded, "To be honest, da, that does sound kind of like him. But hey, you've reminded me to ask you something. In my memories of you when I was wee, how come you've got long hair? Surely the Paras wouldn't have allowed that."

There was silence. Then Cain realized his mother must have been close enough to listen in. She whispered, "Go on, Andrew, you can tell him. He's all the man he'll ever be,"

"Alright, son. I was in the Paras till I joined the Special Air Service. After that, the work I did in Ulster was less conventional, so no army haircuts. Britain needed men undercover. Being born in South Downe, I was a natural choice. Needless to say, that's probably why I sometimes gave you a wee bit of a hard time when you were young. The transition back from undercover work was never easy." He paused, and when he spoke again, his tone quietened. "Cain, you're calling long distance. I'll be able to tell you more when we're face to face."

Cain snapped to agreement. "Sure da, I totally understand."

"Thanks, son, much appreciated. Just know we're proud of ye. Like your mother said, yer a man now. So, it's good that you're carving out your own future and not waiting for the likes of Speer. I did, and it nearly got me killed."

For a long time after he set the phone down, Cain thought about what his father had said. His memories of their past, once a provocation, had become an odd sort of comfort, given what faced him in Jakarta. He was a son, but he was no longer a wee boy.

He remembered that Ruby had written her London phone number for him in the unread copy of Camus' 'The Stranger' he'd taken to the Gilis. He found it and vowed to call that number every day until someone picked up the phone.

Next to the book, he found the business card of a former client who'd made a rather intriguing observation, given the conversation he'd just had with his father. The son of landed gentry; he was a rich kid who worked at the British Embassy. According to him, "Father had been something in the secret service and, although in retirement, was still a considerable force for change." He'd remarked that Cain was just the type of guy they needed if that service was ever to progress.

He couldn't help but wonder if that would give him the direction he lacked.

23)   Engineering Chaos

For the second day in a row, Cain was the first to arrive at the office. Even though he'd beaten the worst of the rush hour, he still had to take an ojek motorcycle cab to zip through the long lines of police and army vehicles, checkpoints, and detours that had been deployed all over the place.

Monday had been a trial for him, and it was late morning before he summoned up the courage to tell his colleagues about Ruby. The cold sweat returned, at times enfeebling his voice as he struggled to relay Ruby's ordeal. He was so distraught that Lena made him some wedang jahe, or ginger tea. Afterward, his horrified colleagues quietly voiced their fears that such terrible things had become more commonplace in these uncommon times.

That evening Cain called Ruby's London home. No one picked up. Disheartened but not defeated, he'd call again tomorrow.

Tuesday had got off to a more normal start, but the arrival of a substantial food delivery, courtesy of Ginung from Hard Rock, reminded them all that these were not normal times. They'd just finished storing the food in the new strong room when Lena's telephone rang. Ashen-faced, she hung up, retrieved a business card from her purse, and dialed another number.

Cain and Charlie may not have fully understood the content of her conversation, but there was no doubt about who she was talking to. After an uncharacteristically heated outburst, Lena fell silent. Hardly drawing breath as she listened, her anger jettisoned within the aching sadness of a tear. She signed off, saying, "Thank you, BG. I will tell them."

Andy saw the tear and said: "Kenapa?" asking her why she was upset. They spoke quickly and animatedly in their own language before realizing they were being watched by Cain and Charlie.

Tears now streaming from her eyes, Lena met their stares and shrieked, "What is happening to my country?" She looked at Cain; "Yesterday, you told us Ruby was beaten and raped. And just now, Nisa told me the police shot student demonstrators at Trisakti. According to her, hundreds are injured, and they killed at least four!"

"Nisa from Hard Rock?" asked Cain, not understanding why she would call the office.

"Yes!" sobbed Lena; "She also said two of our friends had disappeared. So, I called the BG."

Cain, Charlie, and Andy all gathered closer. Charlie's face bore a supportive expression, "I'm sure the BG's a bit busy right now."

Lena rounded on him; "Two of my friends have disappeared, Charlie! Last time the BG was here, he told me to call him if I needed to."

Cain tried to speak in a calming tone; "Well, he seemed to have reassured you a bit."

"He said it could not be his officers. They were armed with rubber bullets. He blamed the shooting on BAKIN agents, and I know he is speaking the truth because I have seen them make such trouble before. And even though he knows he will be blamed for the shootings, he still promised to find out what happened to my friends. I am to stay here till I get another call from him."

As Andreas was the only one who'd fully understood Lena's side of the telephone call, he asked what she meant when she'd promised Kusnadi, 'I will tell them.'

Lena took a moment to recall, "Oh yes. Kusnadi said he had matched footage from several CCTV cameras in prominent areas of the city and believes Pak Cunningham's killers are most certainly still here, probably on faked business visas. Terence Pyle is now officially listed as missing. And the last thing BG said was that Pak Cunningham's body would be flown to Singapore from Halim on Thursday. He asked us to inform Major Speer and Sir James."

"Poor guy," said Andy. "The BG is so well-respected. But with Suharto's Golkar party becoming so factionalized, there are people who feel uncomfortable and maybe even threatened by a guy with no military background, and therefore allegiance, doing so well. He looked thoughtful for a moment and added, "They could use this to fire him."

"You really reckon he'd be hung out to dry over this?" Charlie queried.

Andreas nodded. "Even those who support him will now be trying to work out who will win and who will lose when my country recovers from the political side-effects of this economic crisis."

Lena pointed her thumb at Andreas; "If you go out on the streets, you'll quickly see that politics is no longer a side-effect." Then she looked around at her colleagues and admitted: "I've attended some of the demonstrations going on around the city. And I've been cooking with my mother to help make our money last a little bit longer. People are already going hungry, but they're hungry for change too."

They all nodded their agreement with Lena. Cain wanted to know more about the demos she'd been attending, but Charlie said they needed to call Speer about the arrangements to transport Ernest's body. He looked at Cain, "Maybe you should make the call. You were always a bit closer to the man than me."

Lena and Andy went back to work, but Charlie didn't move, and Cain was searching through his mobile for a text from Speer with the name of his hotel. Finding it, he heard Charlie quietly cautioning, "Lena, you have to be more careful. Think about what would happen to your family if anything happened to you. You're the only one bringing in any money."

Cain tried to look like he was still distracted with his phone when he saw another tear fall down Lena's face. Charlie reached out as if to wipe it away, but Lena did it herself before gently shaking Charlie's forearm. "Don't worry, Charlie. That tear was more to do with happiness than sadness. You always show such concern for my family and me. And just to assure you, I don't think I will be attending any more protests."

Acting as if he'd heard nothing, Cain exclaimed, "Got it. The Regent Hotel," and used his desk phone to call the Major.

Put through to his room, a female voice answered. "Hello darling, how did the meeting go?"

Cain was thrown for a second but recognized Feronika's voice which immediately set him on edge. "Hi, Feronika, it's Cain Shaw. May I speak with Major Speer?"

Having been so certain of the caller's identity, Feronika also sounded surprised; "Cain? Oh yes, of course. David is not here. He's signing a contract for his new job. But... maybe you'd like to talk to Sir James. He's just arrived to meet with David, who is running a little late."

There was something off in her tone and her over-explanation that Cain couldn't simply put down to the surprise. He took a deep breath and waited for Sir James, who took just a little too long to answer.

Cain thought he'd maybe been surprised when Feronika obliged him to take the call.

Cain told Sir James that Ernest's body would arrive in Singapore on Thursday. He seemed very relieved, saying he'd be in touch with Suharto's people. Sounding more assured, he went on to caution Cain about the situation developing in Jakarta, urging them all to take care. "Especially that fine young lady in the office."

[ ]

Hanging up, Sir James turned to Feronika. "Nika, you little minx. You and I alone in a hotel room without David? That would sound strange, and we can't let anything slip right now."

Feronika pouted, "You weren't always so old-fashioned, Om Jacob. You used to love being alone with me. Of course, I was much younger then. I was still your special girl. But you needn't worry about those little boys in Jakarta. I guarantee they wouldn't think twice about you and me. And as for Bapak Suharto, he will be very happy with you working in the defense business again. After he resigns, he knows Habibie will buy him plenty of time. But Bapak also knows that he still needs to be pulling the strings of Indonesia's defense even if he's very much in the background."

Sir James was amazed at how his clever little Nika had grown up, slipping through life with ease, assuming characters, and lying with a confidence he found hard to believe. He chuckled at the perplexing contradiction of finding a talent for deception so hard to believe. "Well, my girl, if he wants Indonesia to assume its true position as ASEAN's dominant power, he'll certainly benefit from having David in ADT. It should work perfectly with myself and Tsang pressing the flesh in markets that don't ask too many questions."

It was Feronika's turn to giggle. "And I'll keep pressing my flesh against David until he is settled into his new role. He told me his wife had paused the divorce proceedings. And knowing David the way I do, he needs a woman. Out here on his own, he clung to work because that was his only comfort. So when I disappear, I think he'll definitely go back to her." Feronika touched her index finger against Sir James' nose, adding, "We just need to make sure that he brings her out here. And if he doesn't understand the importance of staying in Asia, you can use those photos to persuade him. I just hope the cameras caught my body in a flattering light."

As she laughed, Sir James sniggered, "Right from the very beginning, I knew you were an absolute one-off."

Feronika cheekily kissed the seated Sir James on the top of his head; "Thank you, uncle. You always said I was gifted... and not just at my schoolwork." She sat on him, straddling his legs. "And for my part, I am happy that everything has worked out well for you."

Sir James' face darkened, and he jerked his legs to make her get off. "Let me assure you, I could never describe any part of this as working out well for me. For you and your so-called colleagues, this was a cold kill. I had to deal with the murder of a man I'd known for decades. He was so bloody clever! What was he thinking, stealing documents to pass on to the Yank? And on top of that, he'd all but said he wanted a big fat bonus whilst threatening to leave me. The blackmail and betrayal were totally reprehensible. I knew I had to do something to protect my reputation, but it was Bapak's state intelligence officials who suggested he should be killed."

Recovering from being unexpectedly spurned, Feronika flattered him; "Yes, but they also told me about how you prepared the way, cleverly using Tsang's desperation to get your money while promising that you'd help him reap his revenge." Then her voice turned a little harsher, "As it turned out, the only weak link was his idiot nephew."

Sir James wagged his finger at Feronika. "Your colleagues insisted we use Tsang's people. Then, if necessary, the whole thing could be blamed on Hong Kong Triads even though it happened on Indonesian soil. At least your chaps managed to push Hing to complete the task."

"Feronika shook her head; "Even though Hing was convinced he was doing it to restore his uncle's honor, his amateurish hesitation gave Pyle time to hide the documents."

Sir James looked at her and hissed, "Tsang doesn't give a shit about honor. I only asked that Ernest feel no pain, but even that request fell on deaf ears. His boy really is a fucking idiot."

In the ponderous silence that followed, Feronika observed quietly, "For all Pak Cunningham's faults, I think it was a very difficult thing for you to do."

"You see," he began to argue, in what was more of an attempt to convince himself than Feronika, "We'd been through a lot together. Rhodesia, Uganda, here in Indonesia, and dealing with Marcos in the Philippines." He grimaced; "There was some poorly timed work in Argentina for the French, and by Christ, we had a perilously close scrape in Iran. Such escapades typically forge bonds between men, but that was never possible with Ernest."

Feronika watched as the old man stood and looked out of the window at Singapore's wealthy Tanglin neighborhood. Without turning, he said, "Now that it's done, my blood pressure might improve. All this has taken a heavy toll on me."

Feronika stood behind him at the window and rubbed his shoulders. "There, there uncle. Today you can put this all behind you. Bakin officers switched the bullets in riot police guns, and some students were killed.

Sir James turned, "And Kusnadi's ruination will be a small but opportune by-product of that action. Bapak will condemn the shootings. Kusnadi will be removed, and the investigation into Pak Cunningham's death will come to nothing."

The phone rang. But before Feronika picked up, she advised, "You should leave. David and I will take a stroll over to the Four Seasons to see you later."

[ ]

The violence of his fall caused Denny to scream. His bound arms were useless to protect his already battered torso as it smashed into the dirt and the cable ties gouged deeper into the broken skin on his wrists. He struggled to stand, all the while running his tongue over the jagged edges of a newly cracked tooth.

He could hear cars, and peering through the hood that had been pulled over his head, he could just make out their fast-moving headlights. He could also smell food being cooked, and where there was food, there would be people, so he stood still and waited.

It didn't take long. A woman's voice asked if he was okay, and Denny pleaded with her to remove the hood and untie his hands, explaining that he'd been abducted.

Released from the hood, Denny's eyes adjusted to the scene. He was near the toll road in an area called Slipi, quite close to Trisakti University. The woman took his arm, and they walked a short distance to where a number of street vendors had gathered around the steps of a pedestrian bridge over the highway. A street cobbler cut Denny's hands free, after which he was obliged to share his story. He did so, most sparingly.

© Steven Clark 2023
Lynnburn, Amisfield, Dumfries & Galloway, UK

In return, he was told about the students being shot and how looting had started in several areas of the city. Denny was relieved that he hadn't mentioned being a student leader when he heard that their peaceful demonstration had metastasized into ethnic violence, targeting Chinese Indonesians and their businesses.

Another street vendor took pity on him and gave him money for an Ojek to Trisakti. Denny accepted and went straight to a friend's room at the dormitories, where he finally took out the piece of paper his interrogator had stuffed down his pants before squeezing his balls, snarling, "Goodbye, you disgusting little queer," and throwing him out of a van.

Denny stared at the phone in the empty dormitory corridor. He was scared, and his hands shook as he dialed the number on the piece of paper. After just two rings, the phone was answered. He swallowed and said, "I'm sorry to bother you. My name is Denny Darsono. I was given this number and ordered to call you."

"Pak Darsono. This is Brigadier General Kusnadi. I am very sorry for the trouble you experienced today. Your friend Lena Ngurawan informed me that you had possibly been detained. I, therefore, made some inquiries and had you freed."

Denny was stunned. The famous BG was talking to him like a friend. "Thank you, sir. I owe you my life."

Always disarming for a man of high rank, Kusnadi advised, "Don't thank me, Pak Darsono. You need to thank Ms. Ngurawan. Without her help, I don't know what might have become of you. I will call her now. Please wait ten minutes and then call her yourself."

[ ]

Thank you, BG! Thank you, thank you!

They all looked on during Lena's telephone call. The ominous atmosphere that had descended over the office was finally broken.

A shiver ran through Lena's body as a cold wave of relief swept away the dread that had consumed her. She was elated.

Charlie grinned, "Reading between the lines, I reckon that was Kusnadi."

She folded her arms, still beaming. "So clever guru Charlie. And thanks to God, he said Denny will be in touch soon."

And it wasn't long before her telephone rang again. This time her colleagues crowded around. As soon as Lena heard Denny's voice, she started to cry. "Rayi, where are you? she beseeched, using her 'little brother' term of endearment. Denny was also crying as he tried to tell his story. Lena felt her heart break as she listened to him. He was always so eloquent, but he struggled to find the words and then utter them between gasps of shallow breath. She tried to comfort him and then told her colleagues that he was back at Trisakti. "I will go there now."

Cain was unusually decisive. "No way Lena. We're all going to pick Denny up. He really shouldn't be alone. Andy, can you drive us to get Denny? Your father's license plate should get us through the checkpoints quickly. We'll go to Hard Rock. And dinner's on me."

Lena didn't need to tell Denny because he heard Cain's offer. Using English, he said, "Thank you for your kindness, Pak." Then he explained that in order to make the journey faster for everyone, he'd go to Plaza Senayan, where he'd wait for them by the Sogo entrance.

[ ]

Andreas' SUV hadn't even come to a complete stop when Lena slid the side door open and jumped out to greet Denny. Almost bursting with relief, she hugged him tightly till she felt him balk. "Sorry, sister. It hurts," he whimpered.

Lena took his face in her hands, inspecting the tell tales signs of the torture he'd briefly described over the phone. How could anyone treat such a sweet boy so cruelly, she thought as Cain shouted over, "Good to see you, Denny. Come on, you two, let's get going."

Lena took Denny's hand and couldn't help squeezing it tightly as they walked to the SUV, where Denny shared his story on the way to Hard Rock.

At midday, some six thousand students and even some university staff began a 'Long March' downtown to the People's Representative Council. They'd only walked a short distance when they were stopped by a phalanx of riot police.

Lena's emotions were tugging at her self-control. She focused on her pride that Denny was able to tell his story in English for her colleagues and marveled at his ability to do so after all that had happened to him.

"Ikraem is our leader," Denny explained. "We couldn't go on any further, so he told everyone to do what he called a 'sit-in,' and we blocked S. Parman Street. As we sat there, we noticed more and more police and security officers. After a couple of hours, the Law Faculty Dean arrived. He talked to the police and then pleaded with us to return to campus. Ikraem was against it, but I convinced him to go back to Trisakti. Most of the students were uncomfortable sitting in the sun, so they were easily persuaded. The trouble was, we'd led everyone out, so now we were bringing up the rear. I didn't see a thing. I thought I was surrounded by students. Some linked arms with me as we walked, and the last thing I remember was being jabbed in the neck."

He paused, and Lena saw Denny begin to shudder. Instinctively, she reached out and put her arm around him. He looked at her. "Take your time, Rayi," she advised and stroked his face softly with her free hand.

Cain asked, "Jabbed? You mean one of those students injected you with something?"

Denny nodded.

Lena added, "Those students were probably BAKIN agents."

Deny winced but was soothed by Lena's soft caresses. "The next thing I remember, a hood was being jerked off my head." His voice began to break as he forced himself to continue. Lena squeezed his shoulder.

"Oh, Lena, I was so scared. I was naked and tied to a small chair in a room that smelled like a clinic but felt like death. Two horrible big men stood in front of me, and another sat behind asking me about Ikraem and a Professor called Kamaruddin. I said Ikraem was my friend and that I had heard of the Professor but never met him. He said my answer was... how to say it? Yes, it was unsatisfactory. He told me Ikraem was being much more helpful. The two big men made fun of me and threatened to ram their batons up my bum. They called me a stupid little queer because I didn't know Ikraem was being financed by Professor Kamaruddin. They kept hitting me. The pain was horrible. They kept on hitting me until I passed out."

Lena remembered meeting Ikraem and why she'd never really liked him. He'd been so conceited when he refused to accept her contribution during that first protest at the roundabout. Now she knew that he'd been well-financed from the start. She turned Denny to look straight at her, wiped his tears away, and asked, "Did you see Ikraem?"

Denny nodded slowly. "I came around when I heard terrible screams. A short while later, the three men came back into my room, cut my ties, and told me I had some very important friends. They gave me my clothes and led me along a dark corridor. The leader stopped outside a cell just like the one I'd been in. A man was inside, slumped naked on a chair. Dirt and blood covered his body, and the floor around the chair was a pool of black blood. There was a hammer on the floor, and I noticed that I couldn't see the toes on his left foot."

The memory caused a violent shudder to run through his body. Lena stroked his face to calm him down and said, "I know it is difficult, Denny, but please try to tell us everything."

Denny nodded and gathered himself together. "The agent walked behind the man, lifted his head by the hair... it was Ikraem. He lifted Ikraem's arm, saying, 'Wave goodbye to your friend.'"

Denny started to sob. "Then they stuffed a piece of paper into my pants, telling me to call the number on it, and tied my hands again. We took an elevator, and now I come to think about it, it went upwards? I... I must have been underground?" He stopped, clearly trying to take in this new realization. It was as if saying it out loud that Denny was able to further stitch together everything that had happened to him.

"After a short journey, they threw me out of their van. I was blindfolded, and my hands were tied. I chipped a tooth when I landed." He paused for a moment running his tongue over the damaged back tooth. "A woman took off my blindfold, and I saw that I was quite near to Trisakti. People helped me. A cobbler cut my ties, and someone gave me money to get to college, where I called the number on the paper. That was when I knew the BG must have been the important friend the agents had spoken about." Denny looked at Lena and smiled weakly. "Just like you said, he was so nice. He told me to call you."

Concluding his story, Denny's chin began to quiver again. Wiping away another tear, he said, "I don't know what to say to Nisa."

Lena nodded; "I know what you mean. I think Ikraem was her first love." She looked at Cain and Charlie and then back to Denny. "But she will be very happy to see you again. Why ruin that? Just say you don't know anything about Ikraem."

Charlie added supportively, "Lena's been telling us about how close you and Nisa are. Seeing you again will definitely lift her spirits."

Cain and Andy added their agreement, and they all tried their best to quietly and sensitively overcome the intense mood created by Denny's story. Quietness slipped into a troubled silence which was eventually shattered by Charlie. "Woah, look at him!"

A completely naked man was walking like a zombie against the traffic on the busy six-lane road they were driving along.

Denny just stared out of the window, uttering a word that didn't need to be translated for Cain or Charlie. "Narkoba."

[ ]

Nisa ran from the Hard Rock kitchen and hugged Denny tightly, causing him to yelp at the pain in his ribs from the expertly delivered beating he'd suffered. Belatedly aware of his discomfort, she put her forehead against his, cupping his face tenderly with both hands. He did the same. "Thanks to God they didn't spoil your handsome face," she said as they sobbed together.

Nisa asked about Ikraem. He just shook his head; "I don't know."

Lena could see that he felt awful lying to Nisa, but Denny held his nerve and maintained a heartening eye contact with his village sister.

Ginung let Nisa sit with her friends and covered her tables. As Lena had expected, Denny got on well with her colleagues, and they even chatted about the possibility of him working at Flint.

It wasn't perfect, but she had to admit that it was a good end to a very dark day.

24) Mass Bloodletting and a Personal Absolution

Overnight pockets of looting and violence against Chinese-owned businesses had erupted in several parts of the city.

Lena called the office first thing, and Cain answered. "You've been in super early every day this week," she observed in her usual chirpy manner."

"I got here even earlier today because there was hardly any traffic on the roads this morning. Just long lines of military vehicles. By the way, how's everything out in Bekasi?"

"That's why I'm calling. I can't make it to work this morning Cain. Me and mum have been making food and coffee for my father and brothers all night. They joined our neighbors to guard against gangs of thieves."

Cain had seen the TV reports about the looting and mobs torching Chinese businesses. "Sounds a bit scary, Lena. But what about you? That's the important thing. Are you okay?"

"I guess so, but the radio says there are looters all over the place. Monday night, I brought Pak Lubis to the office before he drove me home and gave him some food for his family. Now I know I should have taken some for my family too."

Cain didn't hesitate; "If you can reach Pak Lubis, me and Charlie will load his car with bags of rice, tinned veggies, coffee, condensed milk, and sugar for you all."

"Thanks, Cain. We will definitely need some more food to get through this. And maybe Pak Lubis could also collect Denny from his house and bring him to stay with my family. Nisa is already on her way. They are both worried about their safety and too scared to take the long journey home to their village. My family can make room for them here."

From what Cain could hear down the phone, it sounded like Lena's house was already quite full.

"That'll be fine Lena. Tell Pak Lubis we'll pay him here at the office."

"Thanks, boss. Did you get through to Ruby yet?

"Not yet, but I'll keep on trying. That's all I can do."

Lena agreed and excused herself by saying she should go help her mum and page Pak Lubis. Cain promised not to leave the office till Lubis arrived.

The quiet office provided a moment of contemplation. He'd been tightly wrapped in his own problems for so long that he was actually feeling a sense of release. So much had happened since the trip to Singapore. Time itself seemed to have been bent out of shape to accommodate it all. He recalled Charlie's strangely lackluster Friday pep talk before the trip. His spirit had always seemed indefatigable, but if his friend was wavering, then he needed to step up and help hold Flint together. He looked around the office, happy at what they'd achieved. He and Charlie had started the whole 'platoon of two' thing as a bit of a joke, but he understood that now more than ever, they could use it to help them survive whatever Indonesia threw at them.

He was 20 stories above the city, but he could still sense the apprehensive tension running through the streets. It had been like that for some time, but the atmosphere had become very highly charged, and with all the predictability of lightning strikes, it was generating sporadic spasms of wanton violence. It seemed like the whole country was starting to convulse in the grip of a visceral fear of imminent

© Steven Clark 2023
Lynnburn, Amisfield, Dumfries & Galloway, UK

societal collapse. Cain looked out of the window. He and Charlie had been through so much already. He mouthed the word Fuck.

Charlie and Andreas barged through the door, causing Cain to spin around. The sight of them helped Cain discharge some of the tension that had so quickly taken hold of him. "Jaysis, it's the Blues Brothers," he wisecracked as they walked in wearing almost identical suits.

Giving Cain a dismissive 'V" sign – the one that doesn't mean 'peace' – Charlie declared, "We need to get cable TV in here. The city's on a hair trigger, and we need to know what's going on."

Andy reassured them by saying he'd tune into Sonora FM, which was broadcasting regular updates on the violence that was ripping into parts of the city. "The thing is," he added, "My Father says this is all very strange. The local TV and Radio and even some of the foreign press are calling it 'anti-Chinese' violence, but it has come out of nowhere. Father suspects that some of these mobs might be bought and paid for by someone in power. He worries that if these mobs can create any kind of anti-Chinese sentiment, anti-Christian sentiment, or wind up any old prejudice, then the whole pro-Democracy message will get lost in the mayhem and be forgotten."

Cain and Charlie looked at each other, quite flabbergasted by what they'd heard. Charlie spoke almost absent-mindedly, like he was just thinking out loud. "God and Bennet. Someone's paying for this mayhem? Well, I hope the arsehole will also put his hand in his pocket when his fucked-up plan bleeds our business dry."

No one had a response for Charlie. Cain looked at Andreas with an expression of incredulity and then at Charlie. "Mind you, if Andy's dad's correct, then for all its horror, that plan is a work of pure evil genius."

Andy replied sullenly, "Unfortunately, such genius is probably more common in Indonesian politics than anyone would ever believe. And thinking about the business Charlie, like you, I also believe that if we can just keep going, this situation will pass. If the violence is being created, then it isn't actually real. Just Wayang Kulit, as we say here. A shadow play."

Cain looked at Charlie, who was holding his chin up with both his hands and shaking his head. He placed his own hand on Charlie's hunched back and remembered Lena's call. Lowering his voice as if trying to protect the dignity of a team member, he explained, "She needs food, and she needs to have Denny picked up."

Looking at the contents of their store room, Andy observed, "Between this office and the kitchens at Hard Rock, I reckon we're doing alright."

Cain looked at him quizzically. "Did you just speak in a cockney accent? Oh, bloody hell, this place is going to the dogs."

Andy laughed, and Charlie affected the posh accent he'd used in Hong Kong. "On the contrary, dear boy. The effect will thankfully dilute the tartan-clad, Jockistani distemperature you bring to the company, all mixed up with an overpowering whiff of Paddy."

Cain lurched at Charlie and pretended to swing a punch.

"Hey, not the face!" Charlie cried. "You'd break the hearts of thousands of women."

Pak Lubis greeted them, "Selamat pagi semuanya" or 'Good morning, everyone.'

Charlie offered to travel with him, explaining that he could use the trip to pick up some important paperwork from a client in Chinatown. Cain and Lubis tried to talk him out of it, but Charlie argued that he'd be fine. "Cain, you explained that you and your dad agreed things always look worse on the telly. My client is leaving town tomorrow, so I need to do this."

Cain remembered his journey into work and how quiet it had been. Maybe things will calm down in daylight, he thought. "Just make sure you take your Surefire torch, you stubborn wee bastard."

Lena called with Denny's address and was happy to learn that Charlie was coming to her house again, as it might help erase any lingering bad memories from his first visit.

They all carried food down to the basement carpark.

[ ]

It was quite a disjointed journey: West to pick up Denny, then East to Lena's house. And during the rainy mid-morning, the streets were eerily deserted. The operator on Pak Lubis' radio was advising that South Jakarta was the current place to avoid. Pak Lubis declared that, in his opinion, the sooner Suharto returned to Indonesia, the better. He'd left for Cairo on May 9th to attend a Group of 15 meetings but was now expected to cut that trip short.

[ ]

Denny was peering through the grill that covered a hole where a window might more commonly be found. His lodgings were simple but immaculate. He'd added tasteful notes of decoration to make them more bearable, but after his terrifying ordeal, he couldn't stand being alone. He'd lain awake all night, hoping Ikraem might be freed so that Nisa could be happy again.

A Silver Bird drove slowly down his street. It had to be Pak Lubis. Turning to his duffle bag, he prepared himself for the agony he knew would shoot through his torso when he lifted it. Descending gingerly down the narrow flight of stairs, every step reverberated through his body. He made it to the roadside just as Pak Lubis was drawing to a halt, and to his surprise, the back door opened. Charlie greeted him and told him to make himself comfortable for the long ride East to Bekasi.

Pak Lubis pulled the front passenger seat forward and Denny carefully placed his duffle bag in the floor well because the boot was full of food. The movement made Denny wince and Charlie saw the pain it caused him. Denny turned and once again braced himself to move his body and sit in the car, but as he did so, his attention was captured by a tough looking Chinese guy staring menacingly at him while riding a moped slowly past the taxi. With anti-Chinese sentiment flaring up again, he figured that was why the Chinese guy seemed so angry. His passenger was also Chinese and his eyes had a wild intensity.

"You okay, Denny?" asked Charlie.

Watching a police car pass in the opposite direction, Denny fibbed; "Yes, thank you Charlie. But my body is still painful after yesterday."

Denny was introduced to Pak Lubis and the cab resumed its journey to Lena's house. Lubis avoided the main roads as the radio operator had warned of vigilante gangs blocking several of the city's main arteries. As they drove, they passed through several violence-scarred neighborhoods where shops and small businesses had been torched.

Pak Lubis wore his usual blouson jacket to buffer him against the vehicle's air-con, but even he was feeling cold as he kept the aircon high despite the cool weather. Charlie asked him to turn it down but Lubis said it made good camouflage for them. Denny helped Lubis explain that having the car colder than the air temperature outside meant foggy condensation clung to the outside of the windows. The rain accentuated this effect and would help prevent anyone on the streets from seeing inside. The DIY invisibility cloak created by the juxtaposing elements of the cold aircon and warm rain was comforting, but the rationale for creating it was unsettling. Protected by nothing more than a thin mist of condensation, Charlie sunk a little lower in his seat.

He'd always appreciated the cleansing aspect of rain, but on this day, Charlie suspected that it would take a lot more than rain to clear the air in Jakarta. Falling lightly, it persisted till they reached Lena's neighborhood. Pak Lubis turned into the estate of small bungalows and had to slam on the brakes. He'd been here several times before and hadn't expected to be confronted by a makeshift barrier. Behind it were a dozen men carrying sticks, clubs and machetes known locally as 'parangs'. They were all straining to see the passengers in the Silver Bird. One pointed his parang and Charlie heard the phrase "Orang Cina." He gulped back the saliva that flowed into his mouth. Thankfully Lena appeared, explaining that was it only Pak Lubis and her friends. The barrier was cleared and Lena cheerfully climbed in with Charlie and Denny.

As the cab drew up, Lena called to her mum who came out to greet Charlie, Denny and Pak Lubis. Nisa had arrived an hour earlier and appeared quite anxious when she also came out to greet them. In the absence of public transport, Ginung had given his favorite waitress a ride to Bekasi despite having barely slept, after closing up Hard Rock at 4 am. When Nisa saw Denny, she began to cry again and they hugged each other carefully.

The car boot was opened and everyone carried food into the kitchen where Ibu Indah took Charlie's hand and looked at him warmly. "Thanks to God for your kindness Charlie. My family is forever grateful. You and Pak Lubis must stay for noodles and coffee."

Both men were hungry and happily accepted her offer, whilst noting the irony of eating food at the household where they'd just delivered emergency supplies. As they wolfed down their food, Lena's father and brothers took a break from guarding the barrier to express their own gratitude to Charlie who was really quite overwhelmed.

Charlie and Lubis were aware of time passing. The rain had stopped and steam was rising from the sodden streets when Lena's family and neighbors saw them off, doing their best to cheer their spirits as they headed toward a district whose very existence was born out of bloodshed. Glodok had been Jakarta's Chinatown for some 250 years because that was where the remaining Chinese population was moved after a massacre of 5,000 souls.

Out of respect for Pak Lubis, Charlie was about to sit up front rather than behave like a passenger. But recalling the look he'd received at the entrance to Lena's estate, he took his fingers off the front door handle and let them drag along the car to the rear door.

Driving cautiously, Lubis engaged his encyclopedic knowledge of greater Jakarta's quieter backstreets to travel North and West from Bekasi, over to Kelapa Gading, and on to the port area of Tanjung Priok where Charlie got a call from the office. The connection was clear, and given the importance of the call, that was a blessing. Andy told Charlie about reports of trouble in North Jakarta but as yet, neither local or international media were looking for motives behind the curious reignition of violence against the Chinese. As he listened to what was happening, Charlie became increasingly worried. The box containing the hatred suppressed throughout most of Suharto's rule, was once again being prised open.

Andy passed the phone to Cain who had troubling news. "Kusnadi called to say he's been removed from the investigation into Cunningham's death and Pyle's disappearance. He wanted to let us know so that we weren't shocked when another officer got in touch with us."

Charlie asked if the Brigadier General was okay.

"He must be really pissed off but for the most part, he hid it well," Cain replied. "He admitted it was still too early to tell what happened when the student protestors were shot, but insists that his officers were only armed with rubber bullets." Cain paused before letting the tone of his speech become more excited. "You'll remember what Andy told us this morning about the Generals. Well, possibly because he's very angry, Kusnadi allowed himself to be uncharacteristically indiscreet, even if for just a moment. He also mentioned a growing power struggle between two generals. And now I recall, that's kind of what Sir James blurted out when he was hitting the bottle at the Ritz Carlton that night in Singapore. The BG described it better though. 'When two elephants fight, the grass around them gets flattened'. Any of this sound familiar?"

"Very familiar," Charlie intoned.

Cain continued; "Well after the Trisakti shootings, and with Suharto out of the country and beyond blame, the BG claimed, one of those Generals was now stirring up the old anti-Chinese sentiment to create the kind of trouble that only the army could resolve. A military-linked presidential heir-apparent seems to be making his move for the throne, methinks."

"Shit! Andy was right," Charlie gasped. "This place is nuts."

"Couldn't agree with you more," Cain affirmed. "Meantime the BG did admit that his career might be over unless there's a significant change in the political landscape soon."

"So bloody typical!" Charlie exclaimed. "Kusnadi's a good bloke and just because two army wallahs are having a biggest dick competition, the decent guy gets screwed."

A warmth in Cain's voice suggested he was smiling. "As ever, your use of our hallowed language paints a most lucid and lurid picture. Hey Charlie, one more thing. Kusnadi told me that he's pretty much kicking his heels and reminded us to call him if we're in trouble."

"He's a diamond that bloke," said Charlie as Pak Lubis slammed on the brakes causing the phone to fly out of his hand, hit the dashboard and land on the floor.

He clamored forward but the phone was beyond his reach. Lubis reached down into the passenger seat well and passed it to him.

Charlie shouted; "Hello Cain, are you there?" But the line was dead and Charlie finally saw the reason why Lubis had braked so hard.

Not wanting to jinx the journey, neither man had voiced any belief that they'd been very lucky traveling across the city without incident. Spoken or not, any such verdict was now invalid. Petrified, Charlie put his phone in his breast pocket. About 300 meters away, a group of men were stopping vehicles and had hauled a family out of their car. The children were screaming in terror as their parents were slapped around, and their vehicle was ransacked.

Pak Lubis was the first to react. He started to take off his jacket and told Charlie to do the same. The old Batak stared anxiously at the small crucifix hanging around the rear-view mirror of his cab. He reached out and touched it whilst murmuring a line from a prayer. Then he took the cross down and hid it under his floor mat.

Watching the inhumanity unfolding down the street, Charlie recalled the time when the Chinese couple were beaten in the supermarket and was immediately transfixed by the same stupefying fusion of anger, impotence, and shame.

Pak Lubis hit Charlie hard on the shoulder to knock him out of his miasma and gestured for him to put on his blouson jacket.

Charlie shook himself and did as he was told. Pak Lubis threw Charlie's jacket on the floor behind the passenger seat and told him to get down low. He then opened his driver's door and got out. Blocking the view of the vigilantes, he opened a back door and told Charlie to crawl to the back of the car. With Charlie crouching behind the taxi, Pak Lubis nonchalantly walked around to join him. He lit a kretek, opened the boot slightly and told him to get in.

Charlie peered into the Nissan Cedric's cavernous boot and felt a wave of nauseous fear run through his body. He shook his head but a dreadful squeal from down the street prompted him to lurch clumsily inside. His right thigh dragged across the edge of the boot and a jabbing sensation reminded him that his strike bezel torch was in his trouser pocket. He took it out and held it tightly as Pak Lubis shut him in.

Pak Lubis and Charlie may have successfully prevented the vigilantes from seeing what they'd done, but the whole act had been performed in clear view of three men on two mopeds about 100 meters behind them. They all wore helmets with mirrored visors. A pillion rider was standing next to the mopeds. He gave a command and straddled the rear portion of the moped seat nearest to him as the two riders put blood-stained clubs, like small baseball bats, into their jackets.

Pak Lubis was scrutinizing the vigilantes ahead of him, waiting for the right moment to maneuver out of the line of traffic and do a U-turn. As he stared ahead, there was an almighty crash next to his head. Shattered glass flew from the window next to him and became embedded in the side of his head. He fell sideways onto an elbow that allowed him to right himself and sit up. The sole of a booted foot however, made sure that he did finally collapse sideways onto the passenger seat, embedding yet more glass into the other side of his head.

Charlie had heard the moped engines as he cowered in the darkness. He also heard the glass shatter and felt the car roll on its soft suspension. He gripped his torch tightly as adrenaline coursed through his body, tensing it like a coiled spring. In the perplexing way that time can concurrently fly and drag, he waited for something else to happen.

The car boot sprang open, momentarily blinding Charlie while four arms reached forward and pulled him out onto the street. He was flanked by two men holding him tightly by his arms. A third, stood in front and removed his helmet. "Hello Charlie Cheung or is it Lam today?"

Charlie was totally confused. He'd expected to be the next victim of the vigilantes but Jared Hing was standing in front of him. Still terrified, he was somehow emboldened to see the young banker he and Cain had deceived last August. In this scenario he could at least communicate. "Hing, what the hell are you doing here? And why the fuck did you kill Ernest Cunningham?"

Hing mocked him with a sad face and teased, "Aw, you don't know? Cunningham's old news. By the time we'd finished with Pyle, we needed half a dozen garbage bags for him."

A million questions should have been bouncing around in Charlie's mind, but adrenaline was now tightening every sinew of his body. It focused his mind on one single question, that most primal of choices – fight or flight?

All of a sudden, the high-pitched whine of a very nearby moped engine distracted everyone. Both of the men flanking Charlie loosened their grip and peered over the side of the open boot door. It had prevented any of them from seeing Pak Lubis crawl from the cab and steal one of their mopeds. One man threw a knife but it bounced off the moped as Lubis sped toward the vigilantes.

Seized by terror; Charlie rounded on the knife thrower, ramming the torch's bezel into his visor which smashed and pierced his eyes. As he howled and gripped his face, Charlie held the torch like a dagger and struck Hing with a ferocious backhand that knocked him to the ground.

Charlie ran.

He ran in the direction that took him away from the vigilante group and saw a small alleyway on his right. Glancing back as he ducked into it, he saw Pak Lubis further down the street, talking to the vigilantes. Hing was back on his feet, holding his throbbing jaw arguing with the associate who was still standing. Charlie had only run a couple of hundred meters and was already breathless, but the adrenaline was pushing him onwards at a speed he hadn't thought he was capable of achieving.

Hing and his accomplice left the bleeding man behind and gave chase.

Still running, Charlie reached for his phone and, feeling the material of Pak Lubis' jacket, he shouted, "God help me!" as he remembered that his phone was lying in the back of the cab, inside his own jacket.

His heart was pounding as he reached the end of the alleyway. A main street with four traffic lanes ran perpendicular to it. Beyond that, there was a big longkang, as his father would have called it, edged on the far side with what looked like another four lanes. Longkang is a Malay word for drain, and this was one of the many storm drains that crisscrossed the flood-prone areas of Jakarta. About ten meters across, its concrete walls dropped about ten to twelve feet into some very dirty-looking water.

With only a vague idea of where he was, Charlie wished he'd paid more attention whilst being chauffeured around Jakarta. Barely hesitating, and blind to any traffic, he ran across the road to the zebra-striped wall that edged the longkang. He climbed over and hung by his hands for a moment, scarcely believing what he was about to do. He, scrunched up his face, loosened his grip on the wall, and dropped. It was a horrible feeling, but thankfully, despite the earlier rain, the water level only came up to his waist. He couldn't stop, and grimaced knowing his prized, flat-front brogues and clothes had probably been ruined forever by the fetid soup of rainwater and sewage, garnished with a crust of garbage.

He remembered that he'd run away from the vigilante checkpoint, then turned right down the alley. He, therefore, turned left again and started to wade through the foul water, hoping the longkang would obscure him from view at street level.

He couldn't move very quickly as his shoes would likely get sucked from his feet, and taking a single step in such water, without the protection of shoes, would be very risky. There was a road bridge ahead, but before that, he thought he could see a step ladder attached to the far side of the longkang. Determined to get out of the water as fast as possible, he quickened his pace. As he got closer, he was relieved to see that his eyes hadn't deceived him. A series of iron-rod steps led up the wall to the other side of the road with four more lanes.

He heard Hing singing a taunt like a schoolyard bully; "You're going to die today, Charlie Lam."

Charlie turned and saw his pursuers gazing down the longkang from near the spot where he'd dropped into it. He tried to bolster his confidence, muttering to himself, "There's no way that ponce is gonna get into this shit. They'll need to take the long way via the bridge."

Making his way across the longkang, Charlie was keeping an eye on Hing when he suddenly began to fall forward. It seemed to happen in slow motion as he remembered that longkang in less flood-prone areas tended to dry out, revealing a smaller channel in the middle of the larger drain. Assured by that memory, he made a face and tried to dive forward. Pushing against the weight of the water and stretching out a foot, he only managed to avoid complete immersion by reaching beyond the other edge of that smaller channel. He heard a wild cackle and saw Hing and the other man running down the street toward the bridge. Charlie should have been shattered, but fear and the anger he felt for his sodden clothes forced him to get back on his feet. He climbed up the ladder to the other side of the road and was confronted by the sight of a large shop on fire, flames licking through the ground floor. Resisting the temptation to be awed, he climbed out and squelched across the road into a smaller street that ran along the right side of the burning building. This side was further away from the bridge, and he reckoned that at the very least, he had a minute's lead over Hing. He started to run again.

[ ]

A bloodied hand opened the rear door of Pak Lubis' cab, retrieved Charlie's jacket from the floor, and took out his ringing mobile phone. It was one of the checkpoint vigilantes. The old man on the moped had explained that his cab was broken into by Chinese gangsters, but he'd escaped by stealing one of their mopeds. Holding the ringing phone in his hand, the vigilante didn't know what to do with it. He was one of three men dispatched to check out the frightened taxi driver's story and help him. The old man hadn't said anything about beating one of his attackers, but they found a Chinese man with blood streaming down his face. Not only was he Chinese, but from their understanding, he'd beaten up the poor old Indonesian taxi driver. The man was killed for his crime. Stabbed with a knife that had been found a few meters away.

The phone stopped ringing, and the three vigilantes returned to the checkpoint. They handed it to the Silver Bird driver, who, having watched the whole thing, was relieved to learn that Charlie had escaped. Expressing his profound gratitude, he left the moped with them and jogged back to his cab, where he opened Charlie's Startac clamshell phone to see that Lena had just called.

He returned her call and explained what had happened in the district of Kota and where Charlie was likely heading. Lena's fondness for Charlie augmented the shock she felt listening to Pak Lubis' news. She quickly told Lubis about Hing and why he'd be chasing Charlie. Then she called the office and spoke to Cain and Andreas, recounting what Lubis had told her and telling them to contact Kusnadi. After that, she called Charlie's phone again, telling Pak Lubis that Cain and Andreas would be coming up to Kota to find Charlie. He told her he'd clean the broken glass from his cab and use it to search for Charlie.

[ ]

"What did Lena say? Is Charlie okay?" Andreas asked, even though he'd heard most of the conversation with Lena.

He and Cain had tried to call Charlie back after the line went dead but couldn't get through. The ensuing minutes had been a tortuous wait, and both had dived for the office phone when it rang.

Ruby's attack had awakened Cain to the reality that his template job and cushioned lifestyle had slowly blinded him to the needs of people he cared about. "Jaysis! We told Charlie not to go out. I should have gone to Glodok instead." Cain smacked his hand down on his desk, "I knew it! I fucking knew it!"

Andreas raised his voice, clearly trying to break through Cain's internally directed reprimand. "So, Charlie's missing?"

"Yes! The stubborn wee bastard ran off after Lubis' cab was smashed up. He's on the run near bloody Chinatown with mobs jumping at the bit to kill Chinese people!" He stabbed his finger in Andreas' direction; "And if your dad's right, they're basically mobster mercenaries paid to stir up trouble for a fucking political takeover!"

"What did Lena say we should do?" Andreas implored, clearly frustrated with Cain.

Surprised by Andreas' tone, Cain snapped, "Well, we can't fucking stay here, can we."

Andreas started to take off his jacket, preparing to head outside. "I should go to Kota. I know the city, and as I'm Indonesian, I'm less likely to get into trouble."

Cain reached out to stop him, pulling off his jacket. "Hey not so fast. Lena was right. She said Charlie might call the office as this is likely to be the only number he'd remember. One of us needs to stay here."

Andreas retorted, "And for the reasons I've already mentioned, plus he was a brilliant mentor to me, I should go."

"Andy!" Look, if anything happened to you, your father would close down FIFA and have Charlie and me thrown out of the country. Stay here, man the phones, and please keep me updated. Charlie's my best friend, and I owe him big time."

From the look on Andreas' face, he needed more convincing. Taking off his own jacket, Cain declared, "I have to do this. I've become a real arsehole during my time here in Indonesia. I criticize expats for all their bullshit whilst I'm no bloody better. There was Ruby being gang raped while I was at JJs on a lad's night out. What a fucking prick! Well, I'm not letting any harm come to Charlie or you. This is *my* responsibility."

With that, Cain ran out of the office and headed down to the streets far below.

After the morning's rain, the air was heavy with humidity, and by the time Cain hailed an Ojek, he was already glistening with sweat. He told Dede, the Ojek driver, to head to Kota and pulled on the spare helmet.

Giving a lift to his first ever Bulé passenger, Dede rode his motorcycle very carefully through the traffic and cordons of police and military vehicles on the city center streets. Riding past the 500-foot national monument called Monas, Cain noticed that his almost constant stomach aches had gone and that his senses seemed to be operating with extra clarity. The heightened focus also allowed him to forget that he'd eaten nothing since breakfast, and his hunger abated.

Passing through areas of destruction, he was, however, grateful for his identity concealing helmet. Sitting behind Dede, he remembered conversations with expats who'd never been near an Ojek, whining with ablutionary pretensions about donning a helmet that hundreds of people had worn. 'If only they knew how well Indonesians took care of themselves, they'd have no problem at all,' thought Cain. He saw a fire-blackened building and whispered to himself, "Jaysis, if sharing a helmet is such a big issue, you really need to have your friggin head examined."

His mobile phone rang. It was Pak Lubis who tried to tell him where to meet, but Cain didn't know where it was. He held the phone over Dede's ear. After a brief chat, Dede shouted his thanks into the phone, turned his head to the side, and shouted, "Okay, Mister, I know how to go."

Cain felt for his Surefire torch, reassuring himself that whatever this day threw at him, he'd be ready to batter his way through it and save his friend.

[ ]

The small road Charlie was running along would normally be crowded with street vendors selling everything from exotic birds to vitality medicine to keep men 'strong.' Charlie surmised that he was close to Chinatown. The area was full of small shops and massage parlors, the latter providing ready custom for patrons armed with the vitality tonics sold on the street. All the shops were boarded up with steel shutters. If they weren't, they'd already been looted; their shutters smashed and lying in the street. Blackened concrete walls distinguished the businesses that had been torched overnight with no regard for the presence of any unfortunate souls cowering inside.

Charlie spotted two Chinese men having a very animated conversation in an alleyway. He ducked inside and ran toward them. They were panicked by his approach until they saw that he was also Chinese. Charlie gambled with bits of the Hokkien dialect he'd picked up in Singapore and Jakarta, asking if they had a mobile phone he could use.

There was very little air movement in the alley that bisected the block of residences, shops, and small businesses. One of the men made a face and, speaking in Hokkien, told Charlie he smelled like shit. Bonding over the dialect was a real stroke of luck, and Charlie explained his aroma and his predicament, changing a fundamental element of his story to increase the chances of winning the support of the two men. He claimed he'd been chased by an angry mob manning a checkpoint a few blocks away and lost his mobile phone as he had to wade across the big longkang. Recognizing the mob and longkang factors, the men clearly understood why he smelled so bad. One of them handed his phone to Charlie, who called the office.

"Andy! Thank God you're there! Listen, I don't have much time. I'm being chased by Hing, who's threatening to kill me."

Andreas was overjoyed to hear Charlie's voice. "Charlie, where exactly are you?"

From the corner of his eye, Charlie saw Hing and the other man running past the alley. He froze. Eventually, he heard Andreas repeating his question. Charlie exhaled heavily, relieved not to have been seen. He asked the men for the name of the nearest main road, and they promptly told him.

Andy also heard what the men said. "Okay, Charlie. Listen, Cain is on his way to meet with Pak Lubis. They will be looking for you. Look out for Pak Lubis' cab. Can I give the guys this number?"

There was a shout at the end of the alley; "You slippery bastard Lam."

Charlie saw a partially silhouetted Hing and what looked like a club in the hand of the other man. "Shit, they found me!" Then into the phone, he said, "Don't call this number, Andy. Not my phone!" He handed it back to the stunned businessman mixing Mandarin and Hokkien to thank them; "Xianshengmen, kamsiā kamsiā."

He had wanted to ask them for the location of the road with the longkang but missed the chance. Instead, Charlie toppled several piles of alleyway clutter to slow down his pursuers.

[ ]

Andy called Cain and then Lena to tell them where Charlie was. As her colleagues had forgotten to call Kusnadi, she said she would. The BG rose even higher in her estimation when he said he'd be happy to help and would head to Kota on a police motorbike, which would be faster. This boosted Lena's confidence, and she insisted on helping the BG find Charlie as she owed him so much. Kusnadi mounted a nominal opposition before agreeing to get a motorbike to fetch her from Bekasi to the national police headquarters.

Very proud of herself, Lena telephoned Andy again; "The BG is going to help find Charlie. He will be on a motorbike. Please pass that message on to Cain or even Charlie if he calls again." Excited as she was, Lena didn't want to hear any more 'big brother advice' from men and resisted telling Andy that she'd be accompanying Kusnadi.

[ ]

Charlie turned left when he reached the far end of the alley, as it meant there was a shorter run to the end of the block and another possible turn. His breathing was labored, and his legs were beginning to tire, so he took a risk. He knew his pursuers had seen him turn left and that they'd follow and likely keep going to the end of the block, where they'd need to turn again. Charlie laid down on the ground and wormed his way under a parked Toyota Kijang MPV. He held his breath as Hing and his partner ran past.

Exhaling, he then took another deep breath and nearly retched as he inhaled his own stench. Underneath the Kijang, he could see across the street to a shop with its aluminum shutter hanging precariously from one remaining rivet. He thought that if he could hide behind it, he could wait till his friends drove by. He crawled out from under the Kijang, ran toward the shop, and hid behind the shutter. All the while, he gripped the torch that had provided his initial escape. He prayed that he wouldn't need to use it again.

[ ]

Lena called Andy, and he called Cain and Pak Lubis about where to meet the BG. He surprised them by being out of uniform, but that surprise paled in comparison to the sight of Lena riding pillion. She shut them down before they could say anything; "Don't even think about it. I'm staying. Charlie's my friend too."

Taking off his helmet, Kusnadi explained that the police were expecting more trouble in Kota because of its ethnic mix. "We need to be careful, but as we can communicate with one another, we should split up to cover more ground.

Pak Lubis and Cain were amazed and appalled at the amount of destruction that had already taken place in the Kota. Along some streets, it seemed like every window had been smashed. The contents of buildings had been turned out onto the streets, and on several occasions, they had to clear the debris strewn across the road so they could pass. They saw gangs roaming the streets trying to find shops to loot, but the number of unscathed businesses was rapidly dwindling.

In an ominous tone that begged Cain's full attention, Pak Lubis predicted, "Things are going to get very bad for Chinese people here. I told you about the gang that was stopping the traffic. They said that some gangs are already painting the kerbs red outside Chinese houses."

[ ]

The light was beginning to fade, and the early evening turns swiftly into dusk in a city that lies just six degrees south of the equator.

Hing cleared litter from a small wooden table, leaving a piece of cardboard on it. He emptied the small zip-lock bag of the remaining cocaine he'd been periodically snorting and cut a couple of lines.

"We need a pick-me-up," he said and snorted a line. He then offered the other to his tired and increasingly unwilling partner, who, nonetheless, took a hit.

"Okay," said Wang; "Let's find this fucker for what he did to Mok. I want to go home and eat Cha Siu that's not made from fucking chicken meat."

Nodding in agreement, Hing patted him on the shoulder. "Right, let's go. Charlie fuckin Lam needs to die."

[ ]

Sitting behind the shutter, Charlie had found it hard to believe how the Hong Kong trip had turned his world upside down. He remembered laughing when Ruby called the Harrier team wanky bankers. They'd been so naïve. Not one of them comprehended how deadly their little attempt at corporate espionage might become. We were fucking idiots to get involved, he concluded.

Charlie was starting to believe that Hing had given up. He nurtured that confidence with his recollection of how he'd handled himself and escaped, except, of course, when he'd fallen into that stinking water. He'd become almost oblivious to the stench, but every now and again, he caught a whiff and was shamefully reminded.

"Bugger this, it's been ages," he muttered whilst dragging his stiffened body back to a standing position and rubbing his aching backside. He stared up and down the street and decided to walk back to the main road with the longkang. Watching the sun sink in the west, he'd reasoned that the longkang road ran North-South, and if so, he'd turn right and head South toward the Central Business District. He caught a glimpse of himself in a large piece of glass dangling within its frame. He was incredibly dirty. Sitting on the ground for so long, his pale skin was buried beneath a layer of breeze-blown dust that had caked onto his sweat-soaked face and soggy clothes. Instinctively, he brought his hand up to wipe his face with his sleeve but then recalled how he'd been forced to hide for most of the day. Putting the hood up on Lubis' jacket, he saw that his features were almost unrecognizable, and his dirty clothes made him look like a down and out. Just what I need, he thought.

Reaching the road with the longkang, he ascertained that it did indeed run North-South. He pulled at the hood of Pak Lubis' jacket to make sure it was covering his head and was determined to cross a bridge this time rather than wade through that stinking storm drain. Shortly after achieving that small goal, he saw a small mob walking toward him and was forced off the main street again. With his mind becoming more attuned to such challenges, he reasoned that he could just walk around the extensive block to the east and rejoin the longkang road a little further South.

[ ]

Kusnadi called Cain and suggested that with the onset of nightfall, they'd be safer if they all searched together. They agreed to meet at a petrol station on Jalan Gajah Mada because the BG suggested he could use his police credentials to get fuel for his motorbike and Pak Lubis' taxi.

[ ]

"Charlie! Why don't you just give up?"

As Charlie still had his hood up, Hing must have been simply trying his luck. But too late, he'd reacted to hearing his name. He glanced over his shoulder to see his pursuers running toward him. Hing's cheek and jaw were now bruised and misshapen from the strike with the torch a few hours ago. Charlie's entire body was aching, but at least his feet were basically dry, and that made running easier. He was heading back to the longkang road just as Cain and Pak Lubis were driving south on that same road to meet Kusnadi. Charlie didn't see them pass, and they were equally unaware of him.

Pak Lubis looked into his rear-view mirror at the almost empty street and saw someone wearing a jacket like the one he'd given Charlie, climbing over the wall of the storm drain on Jalan Gajah Mada. Then he saw two other men do the same extraordinary thing.

He shouted, "Charlie!" and slammed on his brakes. He guessed Charlie would likely cross to the other side of the drain. The nearest bridge was behind the cab. Cain helped stir Lubis into action shouting, "Potor Balik." Lubis was thinking the same. He spun the cab into a U-turn and drove the wrong way up the road, hoping to quickly cross the bridge and meet Charlie on the other side.

Thankfully the water level in the drain only came up to his mid-thigh. The sky wasn't yet totally dark, but this time Charlie was ready. He slowed down a little and managed to feel the edge of the channel. He took a big step forward and jumped, clearing the ditch in the middle. Thankful that he'd avoided being almost completely soaked this time, he made for the nearest set of iron steps he could see. Behind him, he heard a cry and stole a look. In the dim light, Hing hadn't really seen what Charlie had done. He started to fall into the small channel and cracked his shin against its far side, trying to avoid total immersion. His associate grabbed for him, causing them both to fall.

Hing was incensed and clearly in pain, but pumped up on cocaine; he kept running, albeit with a slight limp. Back at street level, Charlie headed in the direction he'd initially been trying to follow, believing it would take him toward central Jakarta.

Pak Lubis and Cain rounded the bridge and, once again driving the wrong way on the debris-strewn but traffic-free road, headed to a point where Charlie would likely have emerged from the drain.

Cain had called Lena and shouted their location with help from Lubis.

Charlie's pursuers came into view ahead of the cab. A little further away, Charlie was clearly flagging. At that very moment, a large group of men rounded a corner just in front of their friend. The streetlights were out, and some of them carried torches of fire, whilst others carried clubs and parangs. Pak Lubis had intended to halt the car for just a moment to consider what to do next, but seeing Charlie being chased, Cain jumped out. Desperate to redeem himself, his intention was to catch Hing or the gangster and do whatever it took to save his friend.

Charlie knew he was between a rock and a very hard place. Pulling at his hood to make sure it was still up, he ran toward the mob and then veered over to a line of trees in big plant pots that edged the longkang at this location. He stank, and he knew how dirty he was. He prayed his features were as unidentifiable as they'd been in the broken shop window.

On fresh legs, Cain was catching the club-wielding gangster. He knew this guy was a cold-blooded murderer, and any rational thought should have sent him running in the other direction. But there was nothing rational about Cain's world in that instant. He only wanted to save Charlie.

Cain leaped at the man, and the pair of them were sent crashing to the ground. Hing whirled around at the hollow sound of Wang's club hitting the road. A knife flashed in his hand as he walked toward the fight. Charlie may have been his intended target, but his Gweilo sidekick had appeared and looked like easy prey.

Seeing the knife in Hing's hand, Charlie gasped. He called out to the mob and pointed manically to the fight. "Dua Orang Cina! Tionghoa! Chindo!" he screamed, telling them that the two assailants ahead of them were Chinese and hoping against hope that his filthy face was still unrecognizable.

Cain was frantically trying to resist the strength of the gangster when a searing pain shot through his shoulder. Wang took advantage of Cain's sudden weakness and pinned him securely to the ground.

Cain's shoulder felt like it was on fire when he saw Hing raise his blooded knife for another strike and realized he'd been stabbed. He'd been writhing with desperate ferocity against the man pinning him down, but it was useless.

Holding the knife high for a dramatic execution, Hing glared at Cain with cold-blooded hatred in his eyes.

Cain stopped writhing and stared back at the banker kneeling over him. The knife flashed again as Hing tensed his arm to plunge it downwards. Terrified, Cain bent his legs, lifting up his knees, and wrenched the gangster toward him. The combination of moves pulled the man down over Cain's body.

Eyes transfixed and face horribly contorted, the gangster gasped in mortal agony. His body became momentarily rigid before he arced away from his victim. Cain took advantage of that sudden movement to push, punch and kick the man till he could throw himself sideways and frantically crawl away.

Hing knelt motionless, his knife buried deep into the back of his accomplice. Losing strength, Cain was still dragging himself away when he heard an almighty, primeval noise. His eyesight was becoming blurred, but he saw the bodies of his attackers disappear just before he lost consciousness.

The mob had already worked itself into an altered state of pack madness. They'd ransacked and torched the Chinese-owned department store Charlie had seen burning earlier that day. Drunk on the delirium of that attack, they'd looted and torched several smaller businesses whilst remaining totally ignorant of the large number of fellow indigenous Indonesians they'd trapped in the supermarket basement of that department store. Eyes flashing wildly, their rage-contorted faces tugged at their lips to expose bared teeth.

Curled up and squatting against one of the big plant pots with his arms wrapped around his legs, Charlie watched the horror unfold right in front of him with a blank expression. He was too exhausted to look away. The mob undulated like the wild waves of a stormy sea, battering the lifeblood from Hing and Wang.

BG Kusnadi and Lena arrived behind the mob, with Lena jumping from Kusnadi's motorbike and looking desperately for Charlie. Trying not to draw anyone's attention but Lena's, he gave her a weak smile and an awkward, furtive wave. She noticed the wave and immediately saw through Charlie's camouflage of filth. Clearly still trying to process her shock at his appearance, she ran toward her dear colleague. He used the rim of the nearest big plant pot to help him stand up on his tired and aching legs, and Lena made sure her Indonesian features masked Charlie's ethnicity beyond suspicion with unbridled acts of affection. As he hugged Lena, Charlie watched Lubis and Kusnadi drag Cain's unconscious body away from the pulsating crowd before putting him on the back seat of the Silver Bird.

The mob moved on, but a few stragglers lingered at Pak Lubis' taxi, watching the two men with curiosity as they cared for the Bulé. Then they simply ran off to catch up with the pack.

Charlie's shout was all that was needed to unleash the same kind of frenzy that had almost killed Ruby and her crew in Northern Sumatra. The same kind of frenzy that would repeat itself many times over in the next few days. The violence may have been targeted, but when leavened in execution by such a berserk fury, the consequences proved to be lethally indiscriminate, snuffing out the lives of around a thousand victims in Jakarta alone.

Pak Lubis' face was covered in blackened, dried blood, and Kusnadi told Charlie to drive the cab behind his motorcycle to Jakarta General Hospital, where his friends could be treated for their injuries.

Propped up against Lena's shoulder, Cain regained consciousness. Charlie noticed his friend's eyes open in the rear-view mirror and said, "Thanks for saving me from those bastards, Cain."

"We saved each other," Cain slurred, straining against the pain.

Looking at Lena in his rear-view mirror, Charlie was full of admiration. "You are an absolutely amazing woman. By hugging me, I reckon you managed to hide my Chinese-ness from the attentions of that gang."

Cain smiled as he listened to Charlie flirt with Lena. He was weak, but somewhere in his hazy consciousness, he started to believe that he'd finally liberated himself from his haunting bouts of self-recrimination. Between labored breaths, he whispered, "Jaysis Charlie, you stink. You've forever ruined one of my favorite smells." He pointed with his good arm, "That air freshener."

The cab went quiet for a while. With his head resting on Lena's shoulder and trying to stay awake, Cain noticed a curious sight when they stopped at a traffic light. He pointed and murmured, "Hey, Charlie, what do you think that means?"

Charlie read the graffiti. "*Santiago '73 sends its regards to Jakarta.* After the day we've had, that's a bit too cryptic for me, mate."

25) Rebirth

The older beliefs stored deep in the long memory of Indonesia's sons and daughters of the soil are, perchance, correct after all: Good and bad spirits, fate and curse, birth and rebirth. The agonizing post-colonial birth pangs of Sukarno's Republic were restaged with different actors in a horrific anti-communist purge during the 1960s. Three decades later, the country was dragging itself through the same grim rabbit hole to induce yet another tortuous rebirth. This latest incarnation would be given the name of 'Reformasi,' a title that needs no translation. It wouldn't happen quickly, and it would not be perfect, but the course was set, and Suharto recognized the change accorded with the time, just as China's Book of Changes had described the solstice.

The words frenzied, havoc, chaos, and savagery were readily employed by the international press in its coverage of the violence that erupted in Jakarta and many other cities and towns. But as the stories emerged of more than one hundred ethnic Chinese victims of sexual violence, words like 'organized' and 'targeted' became more commonplace.

There were attempts to muzzle the local media from reporting the rapes, but rumors spread quickly from the lucky few with access to Indonesia's fledgling internet connectivity. The world wide web was bringing to an end the era when the ruling party could simply black out the pages in Time or Newsweek that it disagreed with. The country's next President seemed to understand this, and he publicly stated that the suffering of the Chinese community was regrettable and against Indonesian cultural values. One General even apologized for the violence, admitting that elements of the armed forces had been involved. Other high-ranking officers unequivocally denied any such involvement.

In Singapore, Sir James Templar-Hawes had watched with delight when his old friend Suharto followed his advice. In a televised address on May 21st, the President relinquished the reins of power to Vice President Bacharuddin Jusuf Habibie. And while factions of the nation's governing elite bickered over the causes of the violence that foreshadowed 'Bapak's' resignation, the people and their uncertain new President were challenged to find a new path toward healing and renewal.

[ ]

Cain and Pak Lubis were already very much on the mend as they stood on the tarmac at Jakarta's old Halim airport with Charlie, Lena, Andy, and Brigadier General Kusnadi. They were gathered to pay their respects to Ernest Cunningham as his body was finally being transported to Singapore.

A metal box was wheeled across the tarmac to be loaded onto the waiting aircraft causing Charlie to quip; "Old Cunningham would have been outraged. He was more your First-Class kind of traveler."

Kusnadi responded with the gloomy observation that; "We are all equal when we travel in Jim Wilson class."

The bemused looks he received begged an explanation. "Airline crews refer to corpses they are transporting as Jim Wilson."

They all looked back at the metal box as it was maneuvered into the hold. Cain was sad and frustrated. So much had happened that he couldn't remember the last time he'd seen Ernest, but he smirked, recalling how the old man had so desperately tried to draw his attention to the JTH file. Desperation was not a word he'd ever associated with Ernest Cunningham, who he now remembered fondly. As the box containing the body of his late boss disappeared, he got the sense that Temple-Speer was finally a thing of the past and that he could move on.

[ ]

With the exception of Pak Lubis, who was back on the streets collecting fares, everyone returned to the Flint office, where they swapped stories about recent events and opinions about the future. Charlie, Andy, Lena, and even Cain were more determined than ever to make a success of Flint.

Andy passed on his father's good wishes; "He's very impressed by our commitment to Indonesia at this difficult time and promised that he'd help us in any way he can."

Kusnadi agreed, "I must say that I am also very impressed by the way you all supported one another." He turned to Andy, "And the blessing of Andreas' father will certainly help you win the trust of other investors because we Indonesians remember those who stand by us."

"That's very reassuring, BG," Charlie responded; "And I don't want to rain on the parade of impressing future clients, but I'm off to London soon to placate my parents. My old mum's been going spare about what's happening over here."

Cain was the first to respond: "No problem. Myself, Andy, and Lena can hold the fort in your absence." Then he turned to Lena, "And it'll be your happy job to inform Denny that we can take him on for a bit of paid work experience till his university course starts again."

Lena jumped for joy and gave everyone a kiss on the cheek, including a startled BG.

He tilted his head, absorbing Lena's surprise gesture of affection, very aware that they were all staring at him. In a possible attempt to conceal his embarrassment, he cleared his throat and shared some information he'd received. "Harry Tsang was contacted about his former employee and nephew Jared Hing, as well as a man called Danny Cheung Pak Hei who used the alias, Wang. Tsang denied any knowledge of Wang and claimed he had no idea why his nephew was in Jakarta. He signed off abruptly after stating that he had great confidence in Indonesia's justice system and hoped the people responsible for Jared's murder would be found."

Confirming their expressions of incredulity, Kusnadi added, "Yes, I thought the same thing as you."

Lena picked up on the theme of missing people; "Since Nisa's boyfriend disappeared, she has become quite unstable. She says the city has beaten her confidence from her, and as soon as it is safe, she wants to return to her village."

Kusnadi responded with intelligence and care. "You know, Lena, I used to believe this was a city of absolutes; but with a spate of qualified phrases, contradictions, half-truths, and proposed half-measures, I am starting to believe that compromise is seeping into the fabric of Jakarta. It's horrible to countenance, but some things and some people are just going to be forgotten as we struggle to recover from this episode. I am not sure Ikraem will ever resurface."

That prompted Cain to ask, "What about Terence Pyle?" Has there been any progress in finding him?" He paused and then asked the darker question; "Or did Hing's claim to have killed him turn out to be true?"

Kusnadi appeared downhearted. "Nothing yet. At first, it seemed like the Americans were planning to make a big deal of Pyle's disappearance. A US Under-Secretary of State even flew here to manage his case, but something happened in Washington, and he was recalled. Since then, there has been no more news."

Kusnadi then sighed heavily; "That lack of news, however, may simply reflect the fact that I have been kept out of the loop on many things since the shootings."

Lena was the first to say, "Sorry, Pak." But they all felt the same pang of guilt, realizing they'd been talking about their own concerns when Kusnadi was under so much strain.

He held up his hands as if trying to repel their sympathetic expressions. "Look, there's very little I can do to affect the investigation into the student shootings. But I do get the sense that real change is coming, and a couple of my supporters have said that with our new civilian President, I might hold on to my position." He looked at Andreas, "And the continuing debate about the Police becoming separated from the military as early as next year gives me grounds for hope."

He smiled wistfully. "But who knows? I may have to take you guys up on your job offer. After all, I know lots of people, and many of them trusted me with their security. So they might trust me with their money too."

It was just the right note on which to part. The Brigadier General said his goodbyes, and Andy said he'd take Lena home, as he'd also like to meet her family.

Alone in the office, Charlie told Cain about a club and restaurant the French guys had been raving about. "Japanese fusion food! And the club is supposed to be brilliant. It's called Jalan Jalan, and it's up the top of the Menara Imperium building." He saw Cain trying to roll his injured shoulder and added, "We could check it out after a steam room session to ease that shoulder?"

Cain couldn't believe what he was hearing. "Man, they've only been here five minutes, and they know the city better than us. But if the place is open, I'm up for it. Somewhere different to go."

He pondered what he was saying for a moment. "I really get what my dad said about events of civil unrest. No matter how troubling, things do always look worse on TV or in the press."

Charlie was about to start locking up but was clearly intrigued by Cain's statement and asked; What do you mean?"

Cain collected his thoughts. "This city... well, the entire country has gone through so much torment, and yet things like the club scene have pretty much stumbled through it all."

Heading over to the central light switch, Charlie said in his typically offhand manner, "Jakarta's just too big, mate. Like Lena once said to me, the world's just full of people trying to get on as best they can."

Cain shouted, "Leave the lights a moment, Charlie. Give me a minute to check my email."

After listening impatiently to the sound of the dial-up connection, he opened his email and saw that he'd received a new email from JTHsir@yahoo.co.uk just fifteen minutes ago. He clicked on the message and read.

Thank you for making sure our dear Ernest got a good send-off from Jakarta. That was very good of you all. Best regards to you and your team. Don't wait too long to establish your own Fund because Asia is a young man's game. I rode the wrong wave, but the Asian Century is coming, and the next wave of growth will be world-changing. Be prepared to reap the rewards of hard work, but follow what I call my Noah Principle and always be ready to act before any long-lasting season of rain. I wish you every success.

Best Wishes

Sir JTHawes

Cain stared at the initials and muttered; Where the hell did Pyle hide those JTH files?" He read the message again, pondering the significance of the biblically-inspired business lesson, and remembered the pirate ship at the deserted tourist resort on Gili Trawangan. Noah? What do you know, old man? He scoffed silently. The only ark I ever saw was nothing more than a folly that sucked the life out of someone's dream.

He forwarded the email to Charlie, logged out, and shut down his PC.

"Okay, Charlie. Let's go see this Jalan Jalan place."

Cain switched off the lights, letting darkness fall on the space that promised such a bright future.

[ ]

Ruby and her parents had only returned to their Maidenhead home the previous evening. She was still rather fragile and very jet-lagged. For those reasons, her father didn't immediately disturb her with the courier-delivered package. But after 14 hours of sleep, his precious daughter was now fully awake, and he thought it might be a good distraction for her ever-active mind.

Ruby scrutinized the large and heavy package with its Washington DC postmark. Very few people knew of her whereabouts, so, more than a little suspicious, she slowly opened the box. It contained an attaché case in which she found a thick pile of files and papers. Taped to the front of the first file was an envelope containing a handwritten letter from Terence Pyle.

Dearest Ruby,

Firstly, apologies for not meeting you when you were in town. I hope to get another chance to see you soon. Maybe then we can both follow up on the project I'm proposing. So proud of you Ruby. Your career is taking off, and just like in the old days, I'm here for you whenever you have questions.

<u>Please read the following carefully</u>: Before he was killed, Ernest Cunningham entrusted these photocopied documents to me from Sir James' offices in London. He was concerned for his safety. If I haven't conveyed it strenuously enough in the following notes, then I need to say it here - Ernest Cunningham was a fine man who just wanted to retire peacefully. He realized that would not be possible after you, Charlie, and Cain were discovered in Hong Kong. He actually paid your bonus, not me. He asked me to say I paid it because he needed to appear to be doing Sir James' bidding. To distract everyone, we even pretended to fight bitterly over the whole sad episode. Ernest gave me all these documents. They paint a dark picture of the life and times of Sir James Templar-Hawes. I've done my best to collate and make sense of them as well as detail the demise of Temple-Speer. I haven't made further copies as the risk of them being found is too great. I am instead passing the entire dossier to a contact at the US Embassy. He'll get it out of Indonesia and has been instructed to send it to you. This may all sound a little dramatic, but I'm convinced Templar-Hawes was complicit in Ernest's murder, so much so that I'm now worried for my own safety. Aiming to fly up to Singapore or Hong Kong in the next few days just to get out of Jakarta for a while.

Ok, here's the melodramatic bit, haha - If you don't hear from me soon, use the draft I've written to cross-check and verify all the accompanying documents I worked through, admittedly in quite a hurried manner. Almost all the evidence is here, but Ernest told me to investigate Sir James' Cambodian orphanage if I really wanted to finish him. His Establishment pals will try to protect him, but I know you'll do a great job, and I'll hopefully see you soon so we can work on nailing the bastard together.

Much love
Terence

She scanned the long and detailed draft Pyle had written, astonished at the nature of the contents. She recalled Cain's confusion learning about the very friendly photograph of Sir James and Tsang after their meeting. A meeting that, according to Cain, must have ended acrimoniously because Tsang failed to return Sir James' money.

She reached for her mobile and called Terence Pyle's number. The line was dead.

She felt her heart beat a little faster. Scrolling quickly down her contacts to 'S,' she tried to calm her nerves and made another call.

"Hello, Cain. It's Ruby... Yes, I'm doing better now, thanks... What? You've been calling here every day? That's so sweet of you, but I just arrived from Hong Kong last night… Cain, please listen because I've got some massive news for you and Charlie. I've just opened a jiffy bag, and inside, there's a note from Ernest Cunningham and two tightly wrapped bundles of cash. Cunningham said it's your money for the Hong Kong assignment.

Cain started to laugh. "Jaysis, the old boy, came through for us. He said he'd see us right."

Ruby listened and chuckled before adding, "There's also a note from Terence Pyle. It seems he and Cunningham were working together and have compiled decades worth of information casting Sir James in a very bad light. He even thinks Sir James was responsible for Cunningham's murder."

She listened for a response, but there wasn't any. "Cain, are you there?"

After a pause, she heard Cain exclaim, "Oh my God! Pyle wrote to you? Ruby, do you have a folder there labeled JTH 77-81?"

She looked at the folders scattered across her bed. "Yes, I've got that one and a whole lot more besides. Pyle's note says there's enough here to finish Sir James."

Cain started to chuckle. "With that file and your photo of Sir James and Tsang… Yeah, I think Pyle is probably right."

Ruby cut in. "By the way, Cain. In his letter, Pyle seemed to be worried about his safety. I just tried to call him, but the line was dead. He always kept in touch with me, and I'm sure he would have given me a new number if he had one. I'm really worried about him. Have you spoken to him lately?"

2001, Springtime

Epilogue: A Malevolent Phoenix

He'd aged, but even though he walked with a stick, he breezed down the stairs outside the courtroom building and approached the assembled media pack with the sure-footed confidence that triumph bestows. His legal team was well-versed in delivering post-verdict press briefings, but this was their client's moment, and Sir James was determined to deliver his own message.

"Ladies and Gentlemen. Ladies and Gentlemen," he repeated, preparing his stage and silencing the questions being shouted by competing reporters.

"Thank you for your patience. A virtue with which recent events have forced me into a debilitating reacquaintance because this day has been far too long in coming. I never doubted this verdict and my rightful freedom from the spurious claims of a callously mal-informed journalist. That poor young woman who looked up to him as her mentor had already suffered terribly whilst covering ethnic violence in faraway Indonesia. My heart goes out to her. As the court has shown, she mistakenly believed the egregious claims of a drug-addled drunkard and whore-monger. A man too ashamed to emerge from the shadows where he currently resides and pay for the fantastical, drug-maligned falsehoods that have caused such harm."

Pausing to let his accusations sink in and be noted, he continued. "I want to thank the jury for seeing through the lies leveled against me. I will also be forever grateful to my legal team and to the Indonesian authorities for their assistance in compiling the supporting evidence so crucial to my defense. Ernest Cunningham was very dear to me, and I still mourn his passing. I trust that one day, the Indonesian justice system will uncover the truth and let the full weight of their justice bear down on Ernest's killers. We live at the dawn of a new millennium, a new and exciting age. And on this beautiful Spring day, the season of renewal, I'm committed to starting afresh. Now if you'll excuse me, I'm going to pay a long overdue visit to the grave where the ashes of my old friend are buried. My legal team will answer your further questions. Thank you."

Milton Keynes UK
Ingram Content Group UK Ltd.
UKHW051002120124
435908UK00011B/61